Oh My Goddess!

ああっ女神さまっ

40

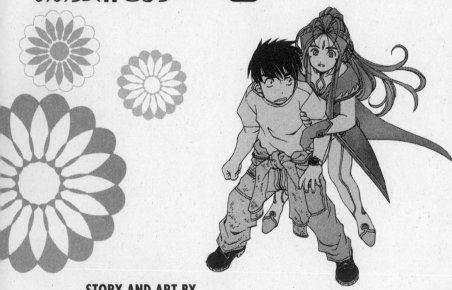

STORY AND ART BY
Kosuke Fujishima

TRANSLATION BY
Dana Lewis AND Christopher Lewis

LETTERING AND TOUCHUP BY
Susie Lee AND Betty Dong
WITH Tom2K

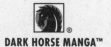

DARK HORSE MANGA™

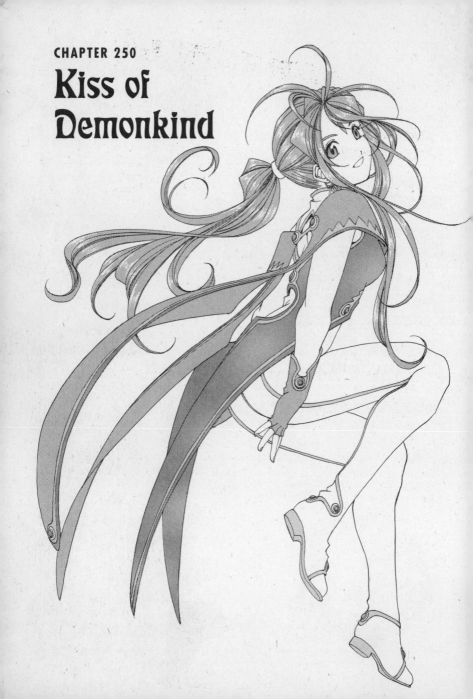

CHAPTER 250
Kiss of Demonkind

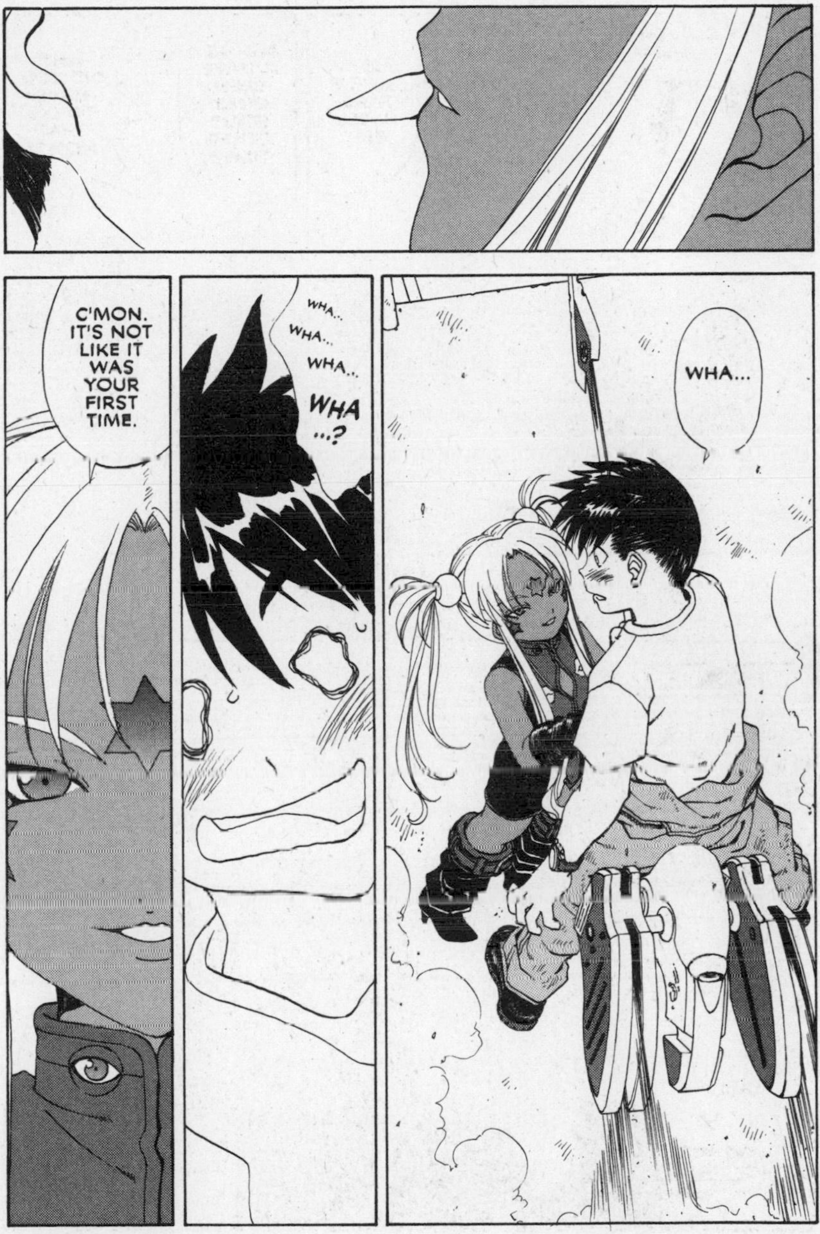
WHA...
WHA... WHA... WHA... WHA...?
C'MON. IT'S NOT LIKE IT WAS YOUR FIRST TIME.

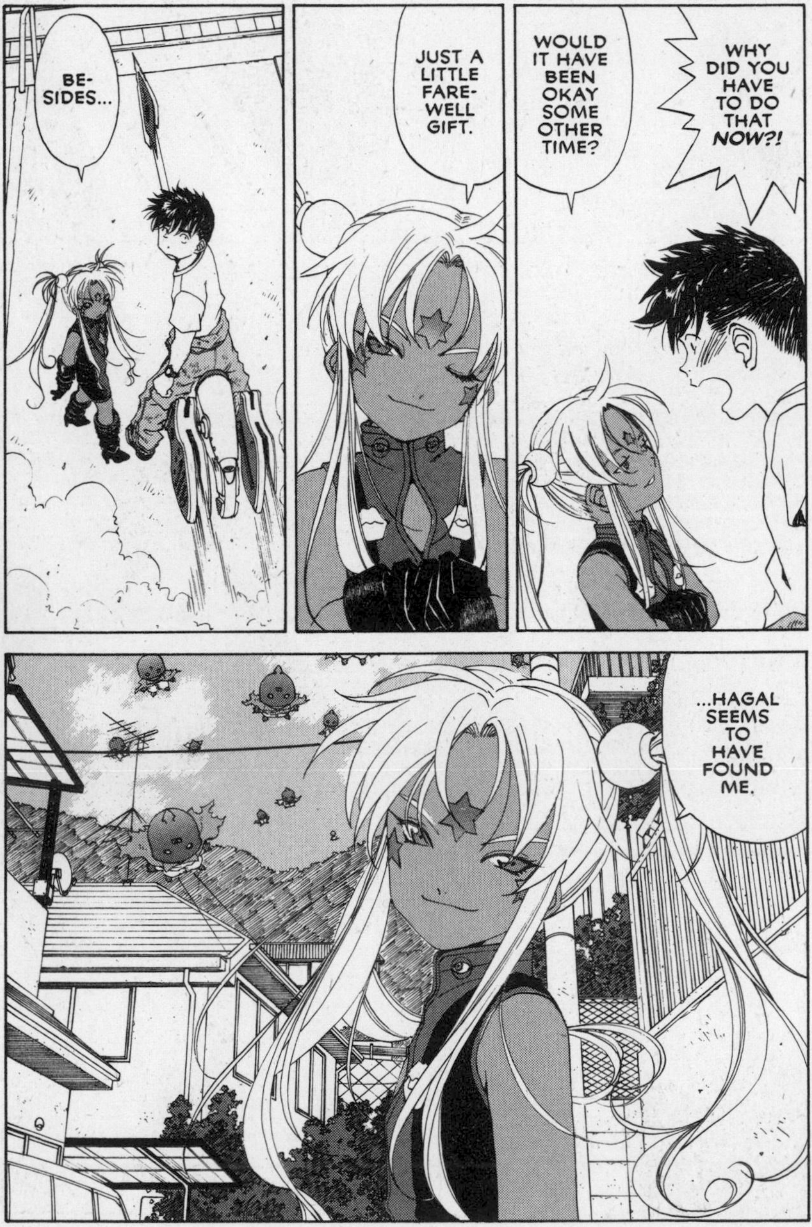
WHY DID YOU HAVE TO DO THAT *NOW?!*
WOULD IT HAVE BEEN OKAY SOME OTHER TIME?
JUST A LITTLE FARE-WELL GIFT.
BE-SIDES...
...HAGAL SEEMS TO HAVE FOUND ME.

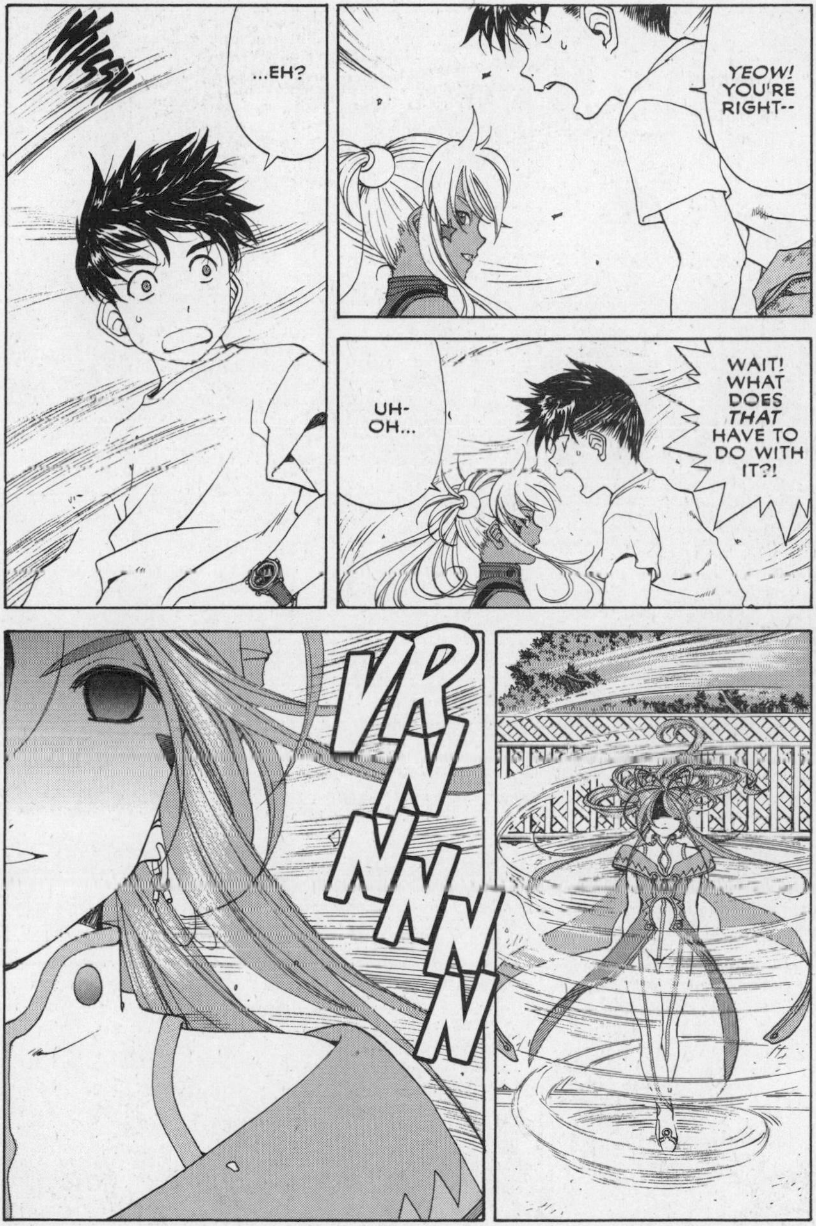
YEOW! YOU'RE RIGHT--
WAIT! WHAT DOES *THAT* HAVE TO DO WITH IT?!
UH-OH...
WHSSH
...EH?
VRINNNNNN

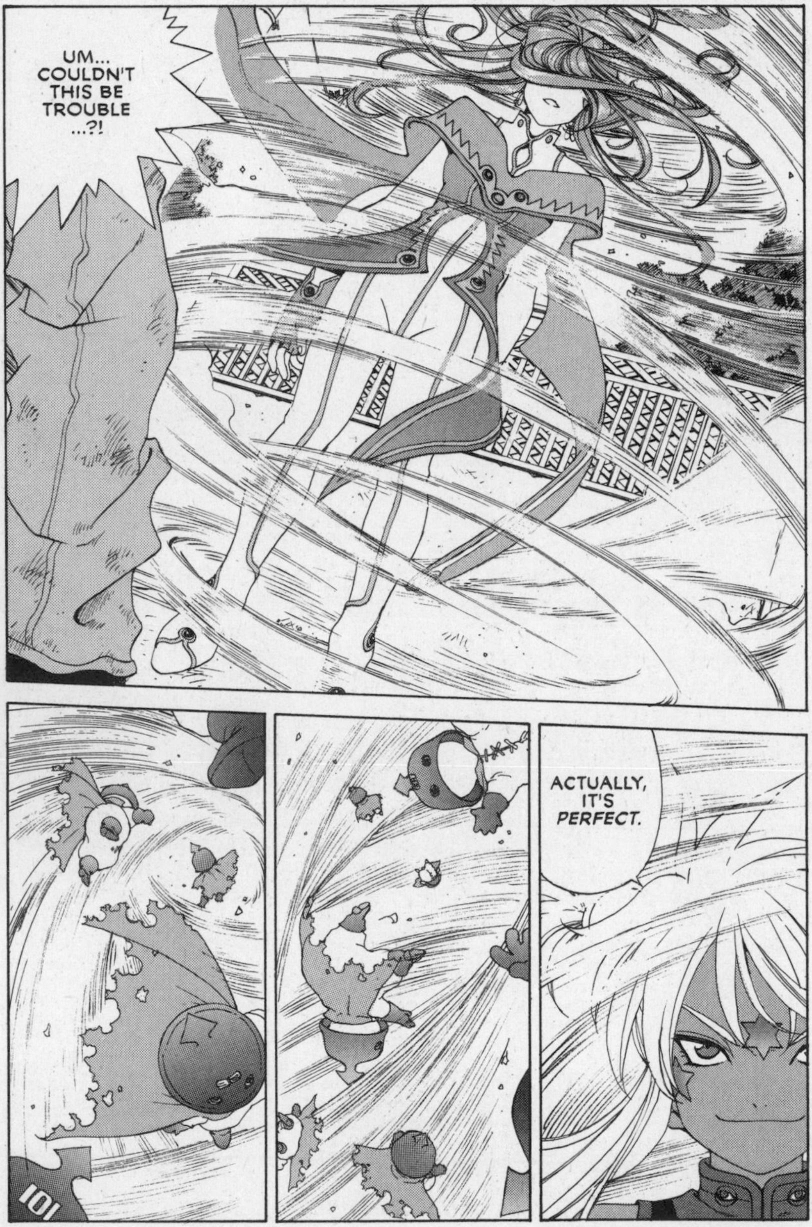
UM... COULDN'T THIS BE TROUBLE ...?!
ACTUALLY, IT'S *PERFECT.*

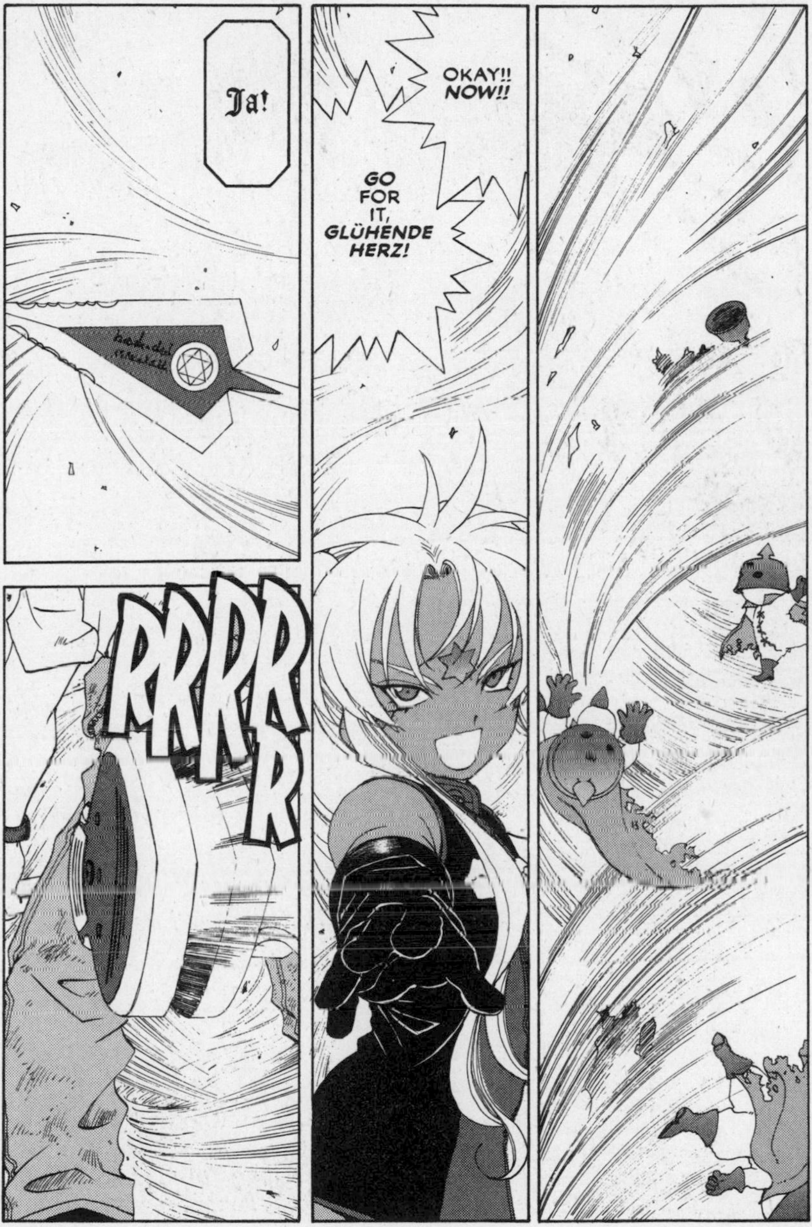
OKAY!! NOW!!
GO FOR IT, GLÜHENDE HERZ!
Ja!
RRRRR

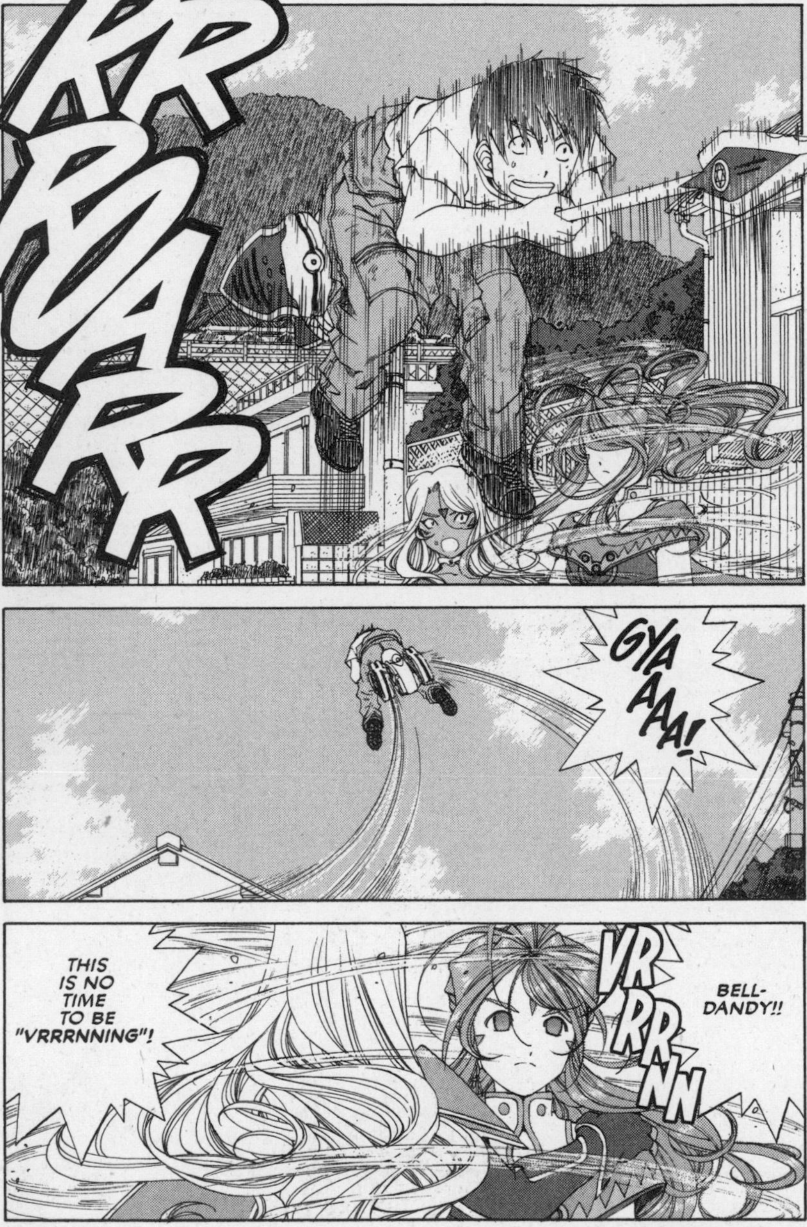
RRRAARRR
GYAAAA!
BELL-DANDY!!
VRRRNN
THIS IS NO TIME TO BE "VRRRNNING"!

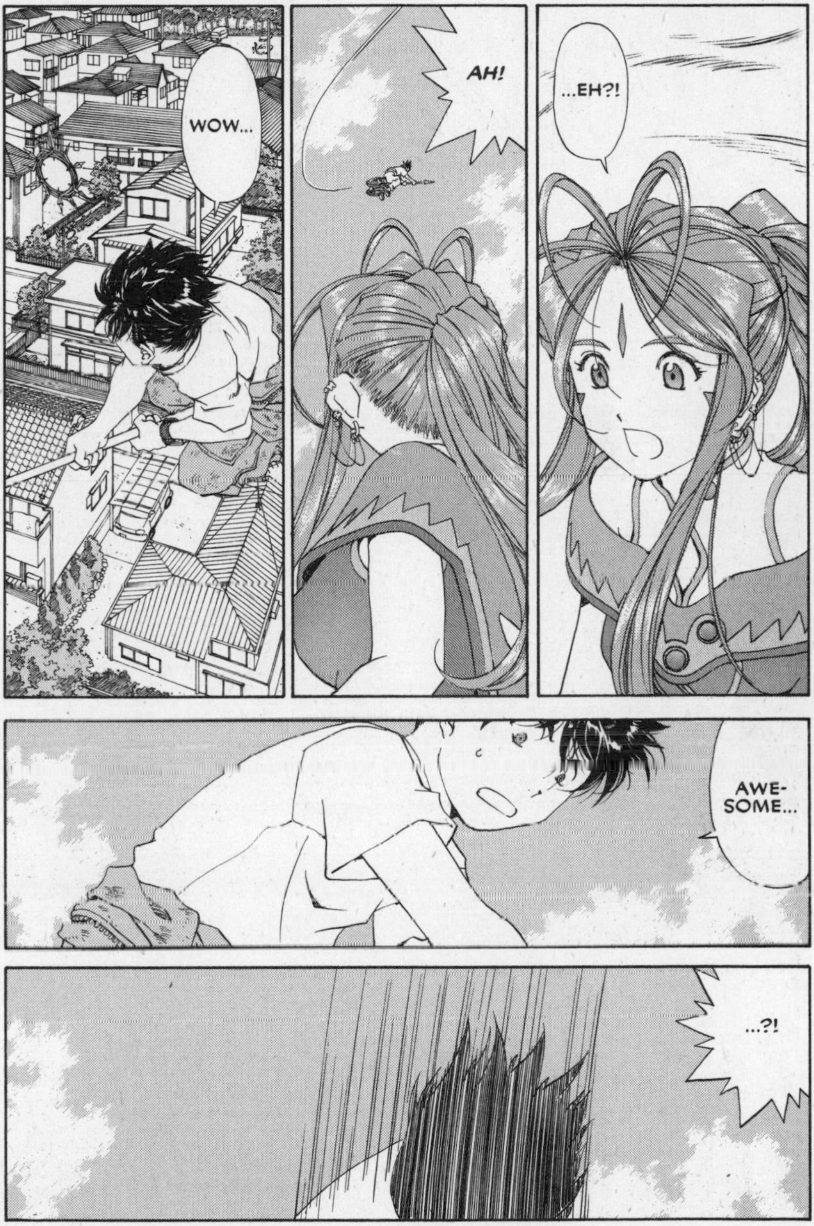
...EH?!
AH!
WOW...
AWE-
SOME...
...?!

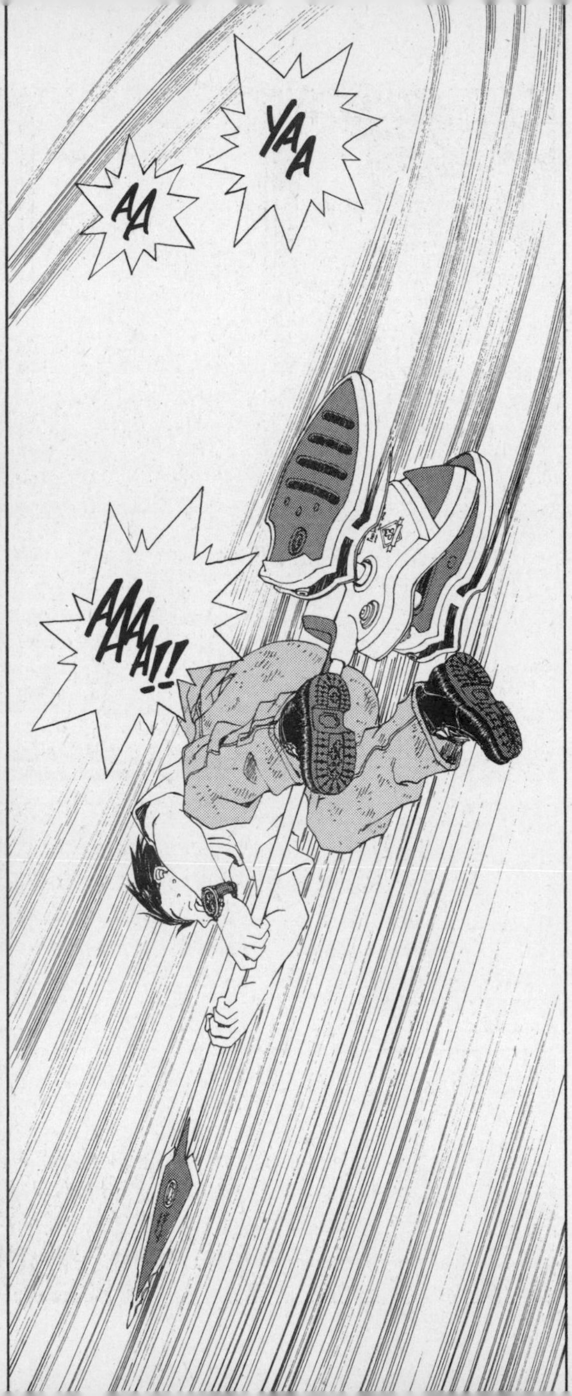
YAAA
AA
AAAAA!!

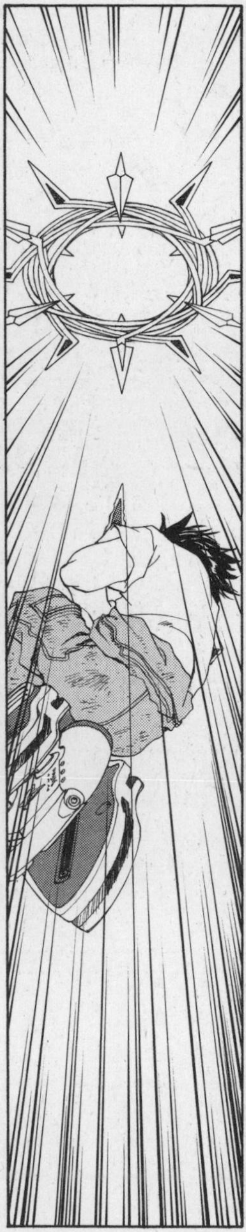

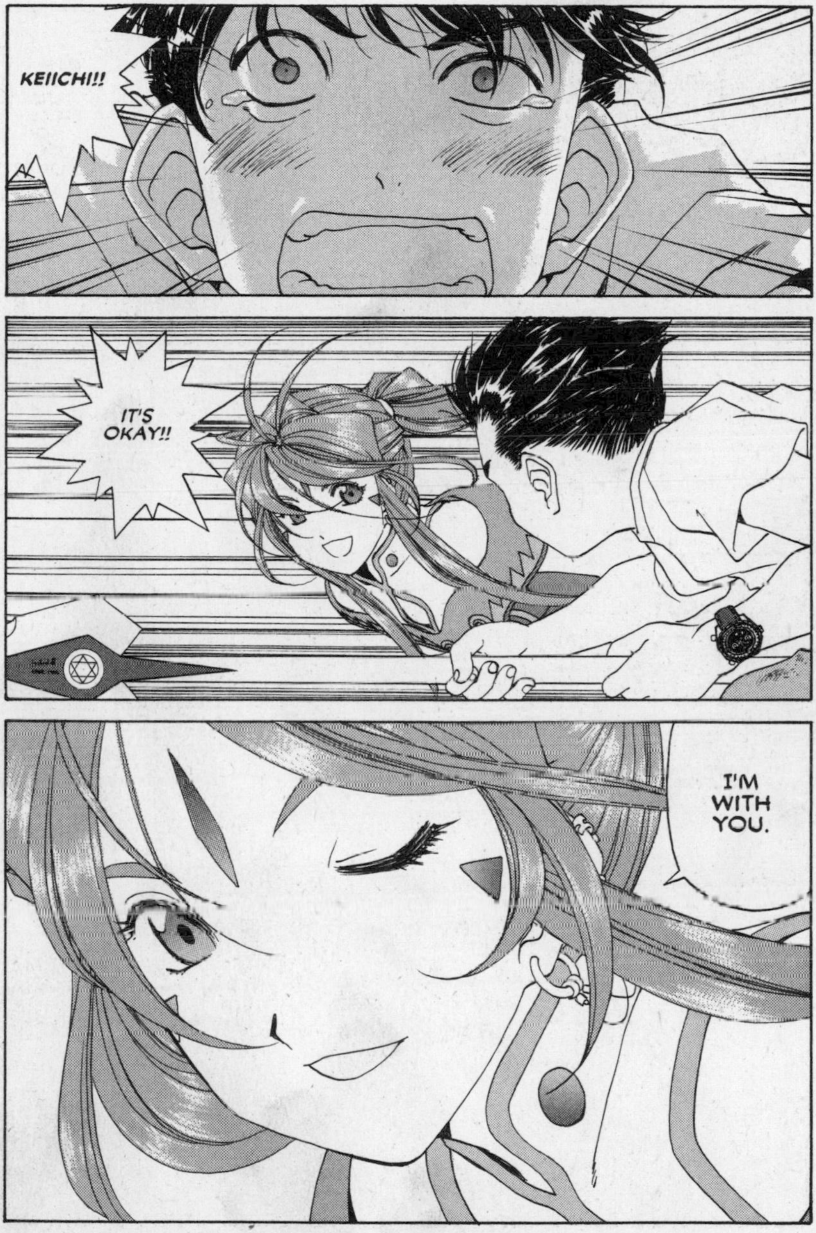
KEIICHI!!
IT'S OKAY!!
I'M WITH YOU.

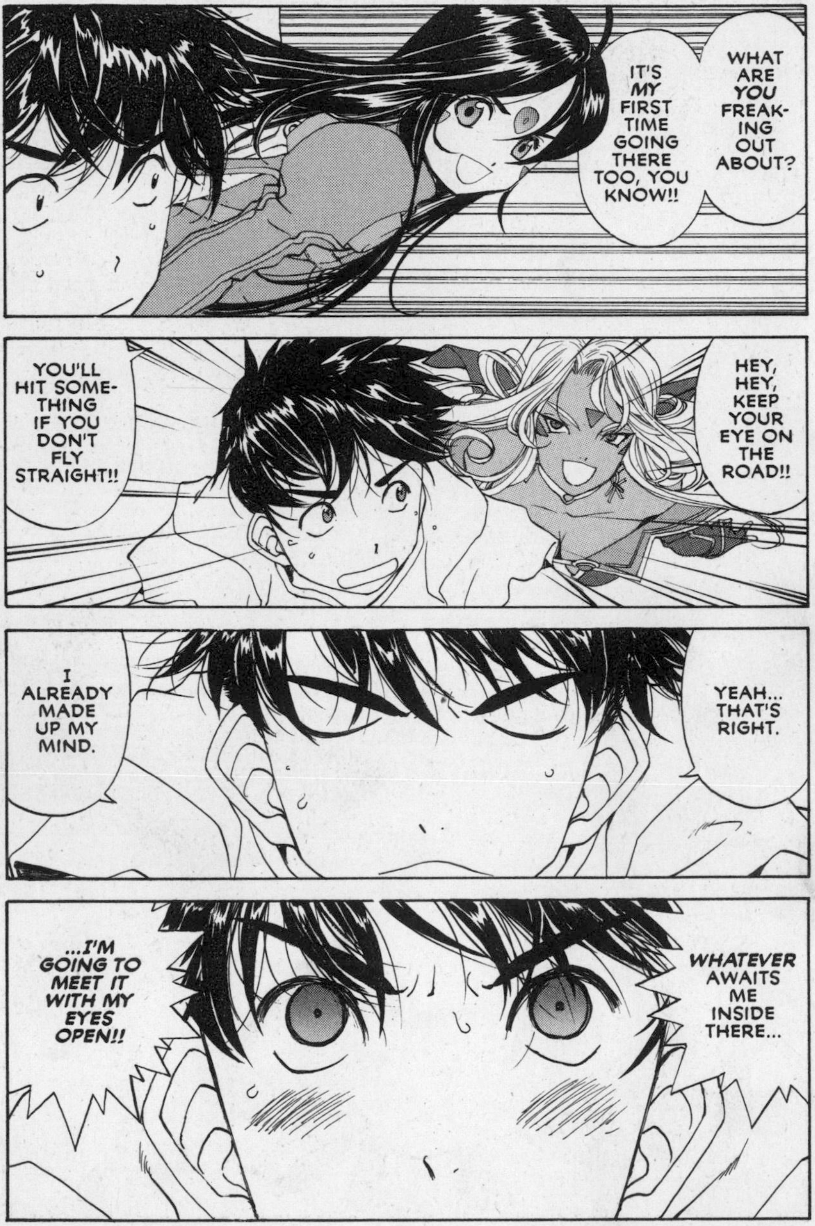
WHAT ARE YOU FREAKING OUT ABOUT?
IT'S MY FIRST TIME GOING THERE TOO, YOU KNOW!!
HEY, HEY, KEEP YOUR EYE ON THE ROAD!!
YOU'LL HIT SOMETHING IF YOU DON'T FLY STRAIGHT!!
YEAH... THAT'S RIGHT.
I ALREADY MADE UP MY MIND.
WHATEVER AWAITS ME INSIDE THERE...
...I'M GOING TO MEET IT WITH MY EYES OPEN!!

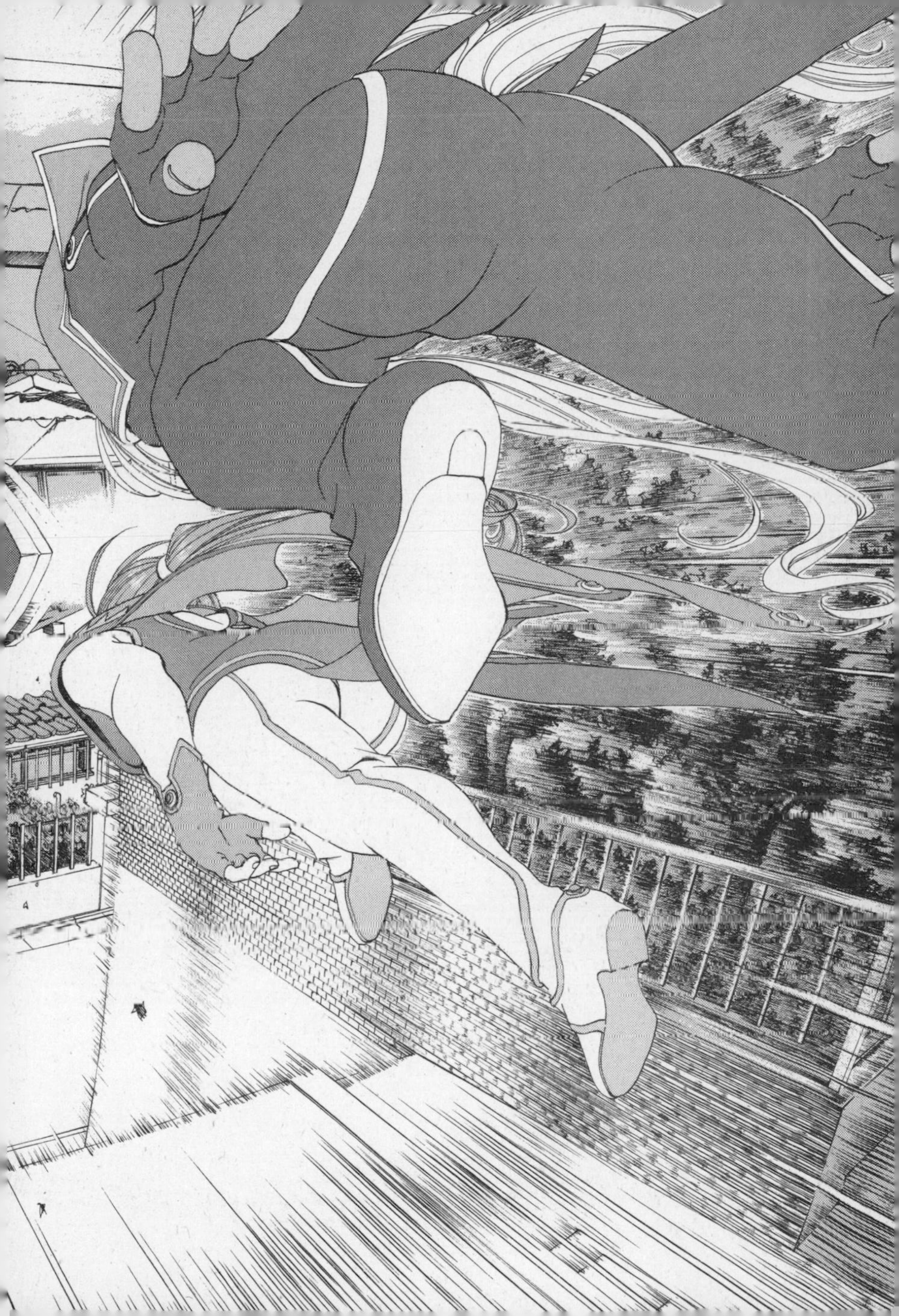

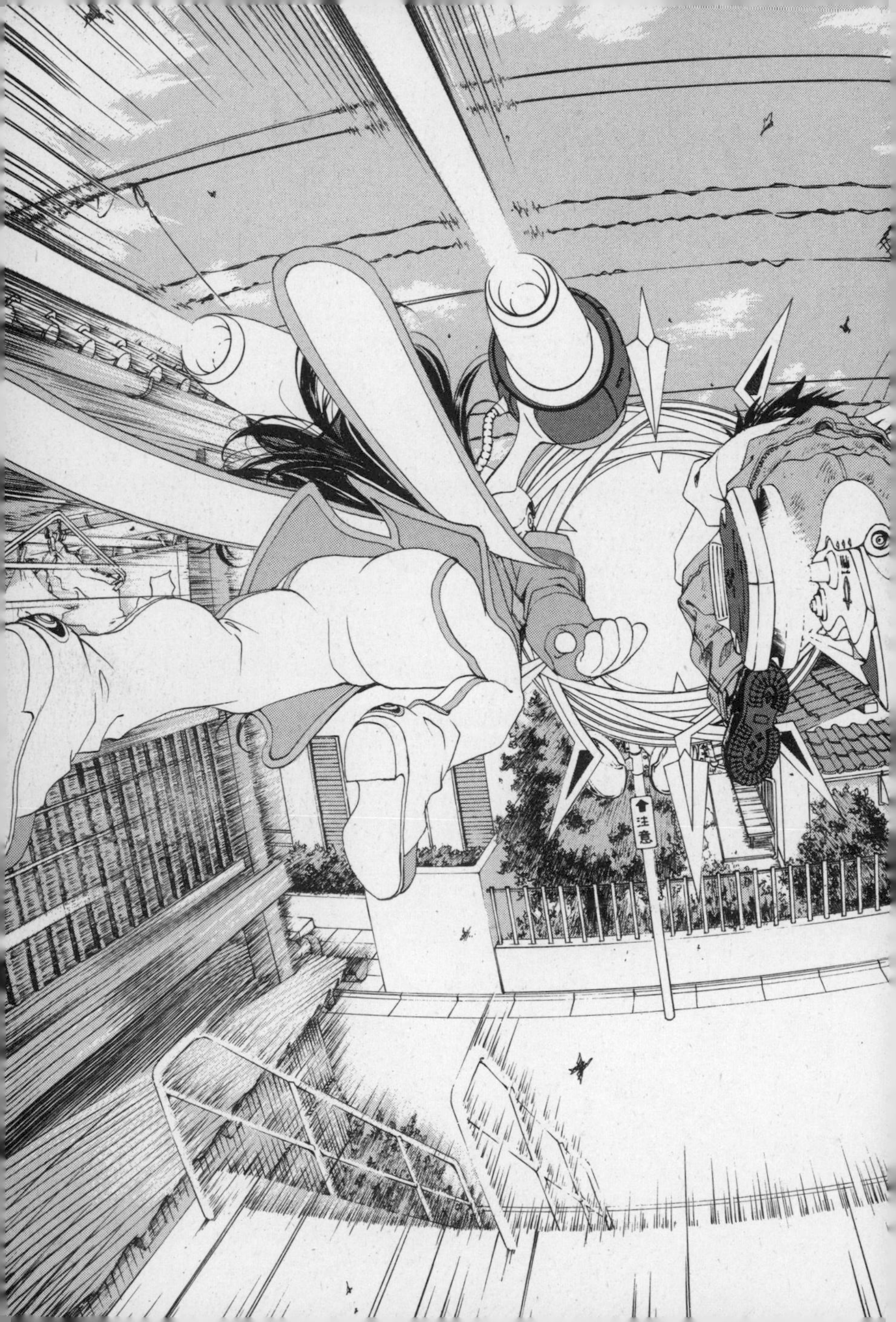
注意

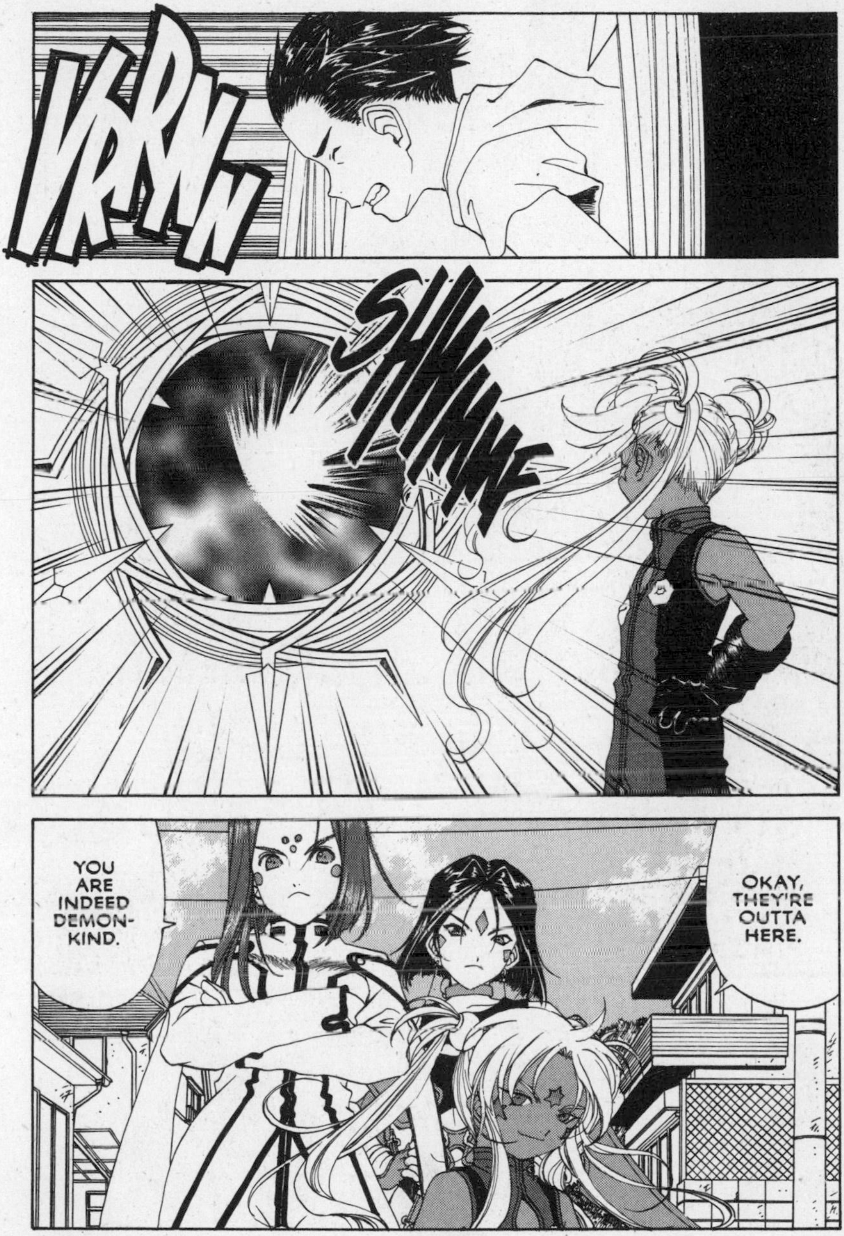
OKAY, THEY'RE OUTTA HERE.
YOU ARE INDEED DEMON-KIND.

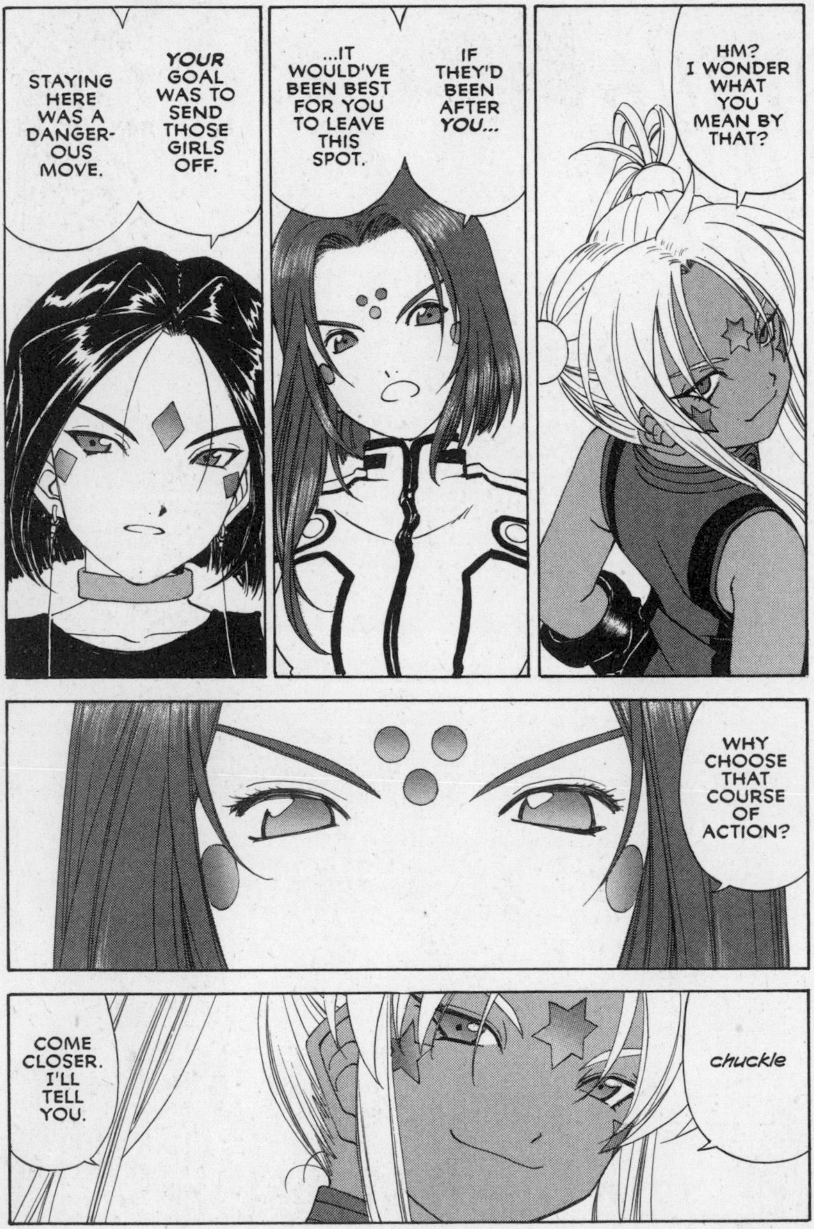
HM? I WONDER WHAT YOU MEAN BY THAT?
IF THEY'D BEEN AFTER *YOU*...
...IT WOULD'VE BEEN BEST FOR YOU TO LEAVE THIS SPOT.
YOUR GOAL WAS TO SEND THOSE GIRLS OFF.
STAYING HERE WAS A DANGER-OUS MOVE.
WHY CHOOSE THAT COURSE OF ACTION?
chuckle
COME CLOSER. I'LL TELL YOU.

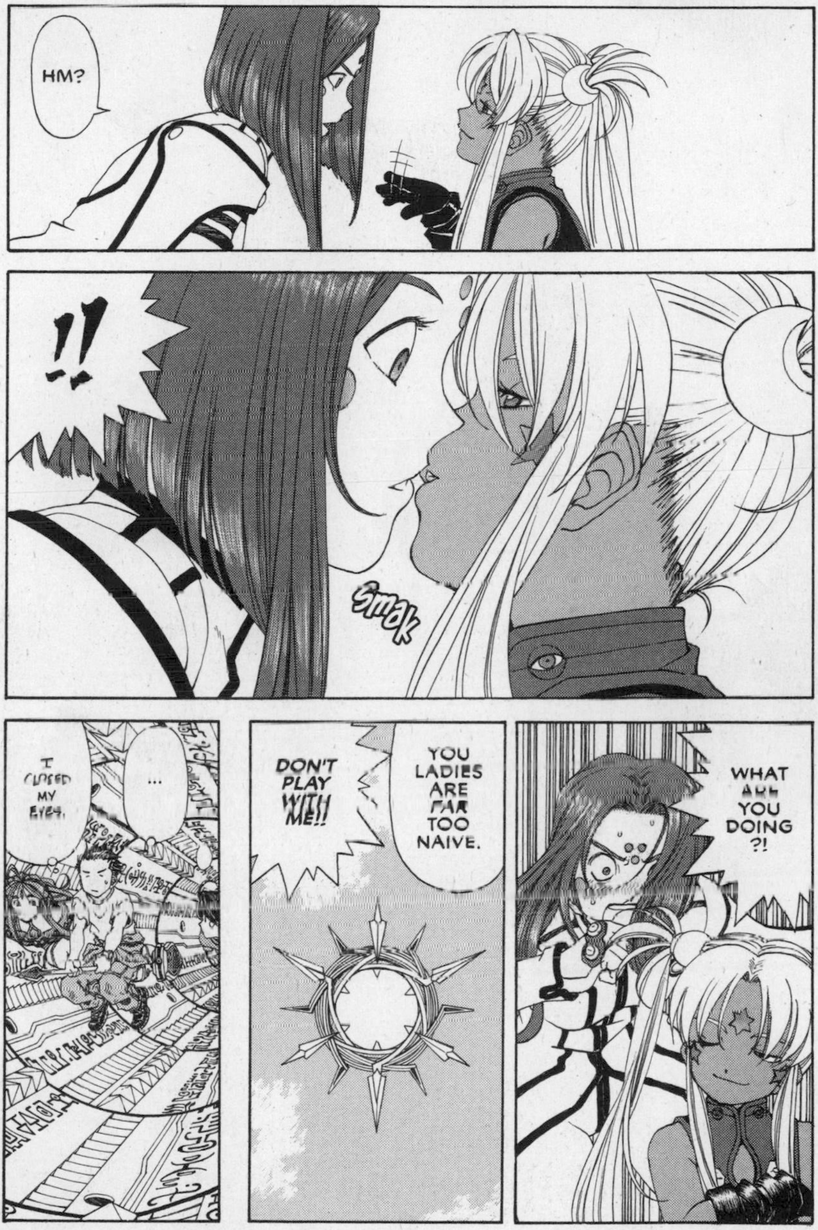
HM?
!!
SMAK
WHAT ARE YOU DOING?!
YOU LADIES ARE FAR TOO NAIVE.
DON'T PLAY WITH ME!!
...
I CLOSED MY EYES.

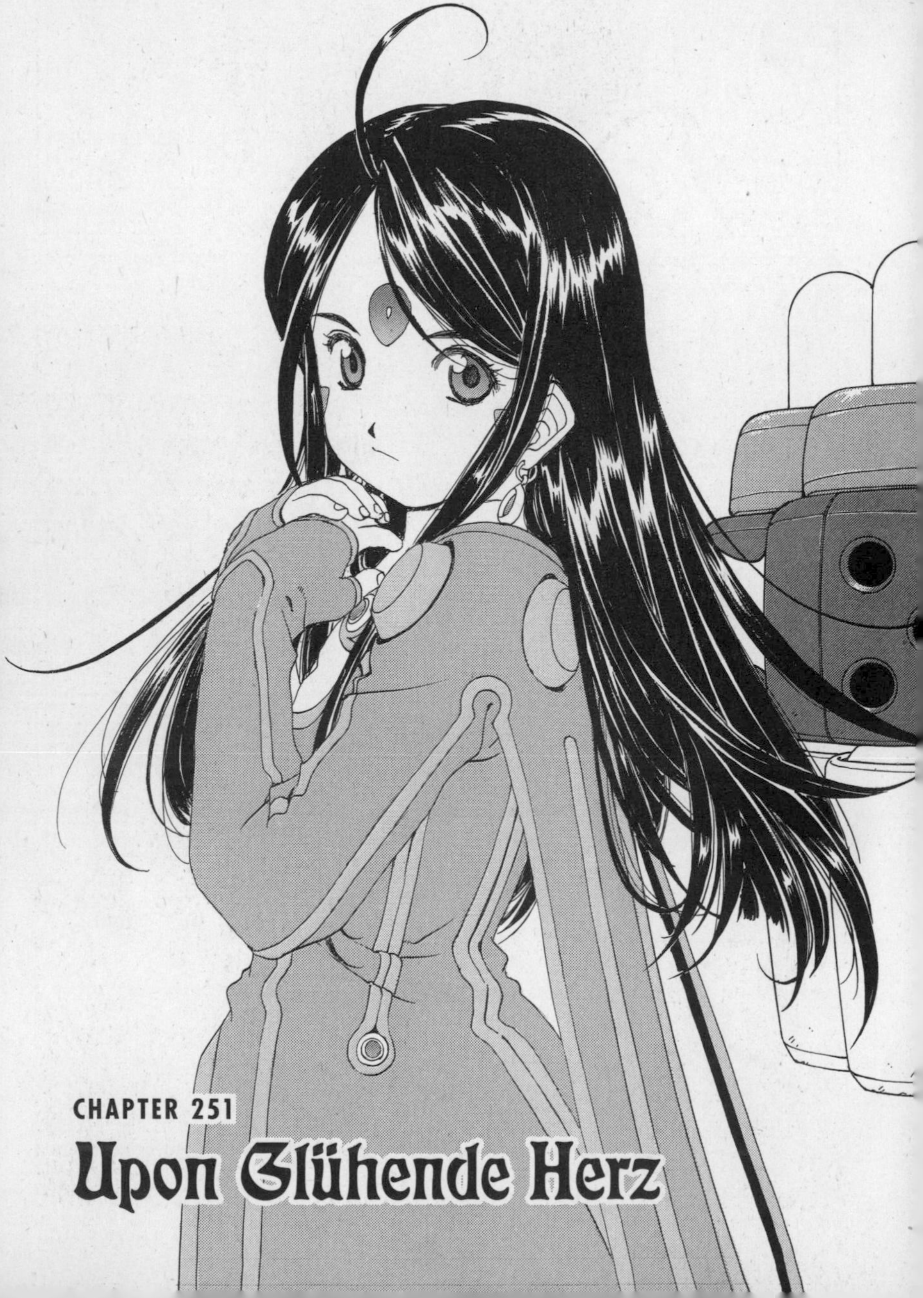

CHAPTER 251

Upon Glühende Herz

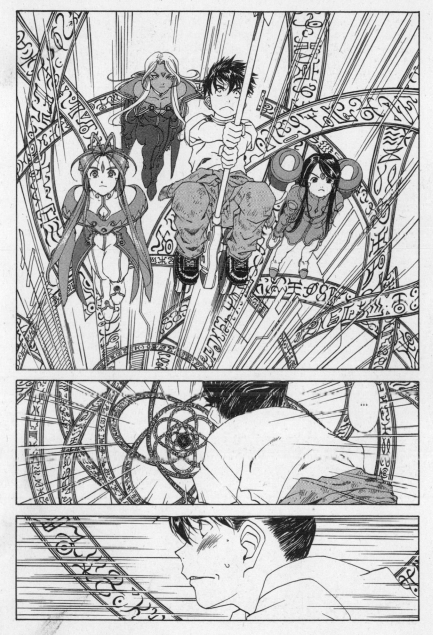

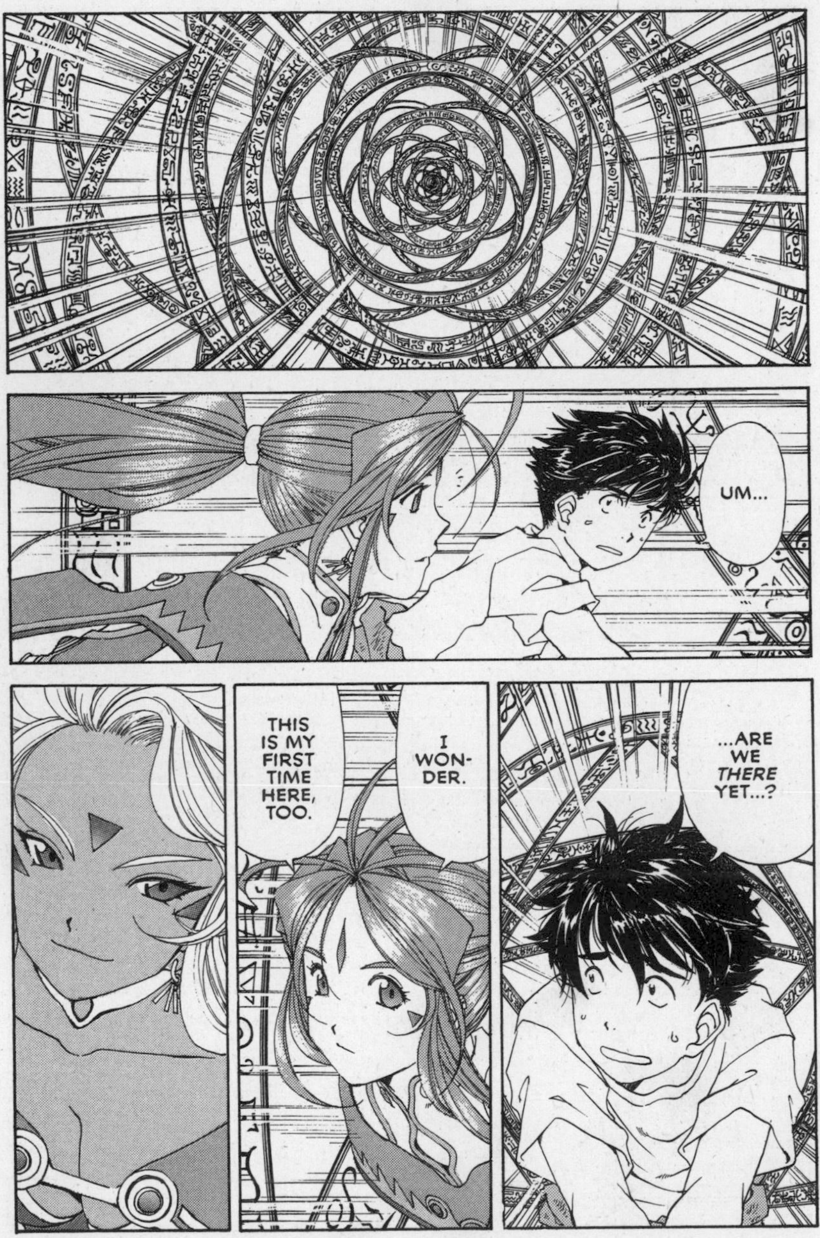
UM...
...ARE WE *THERE* YET...?
I WONDER.
THIS IS MY FIRST TIME HERE, TOO.

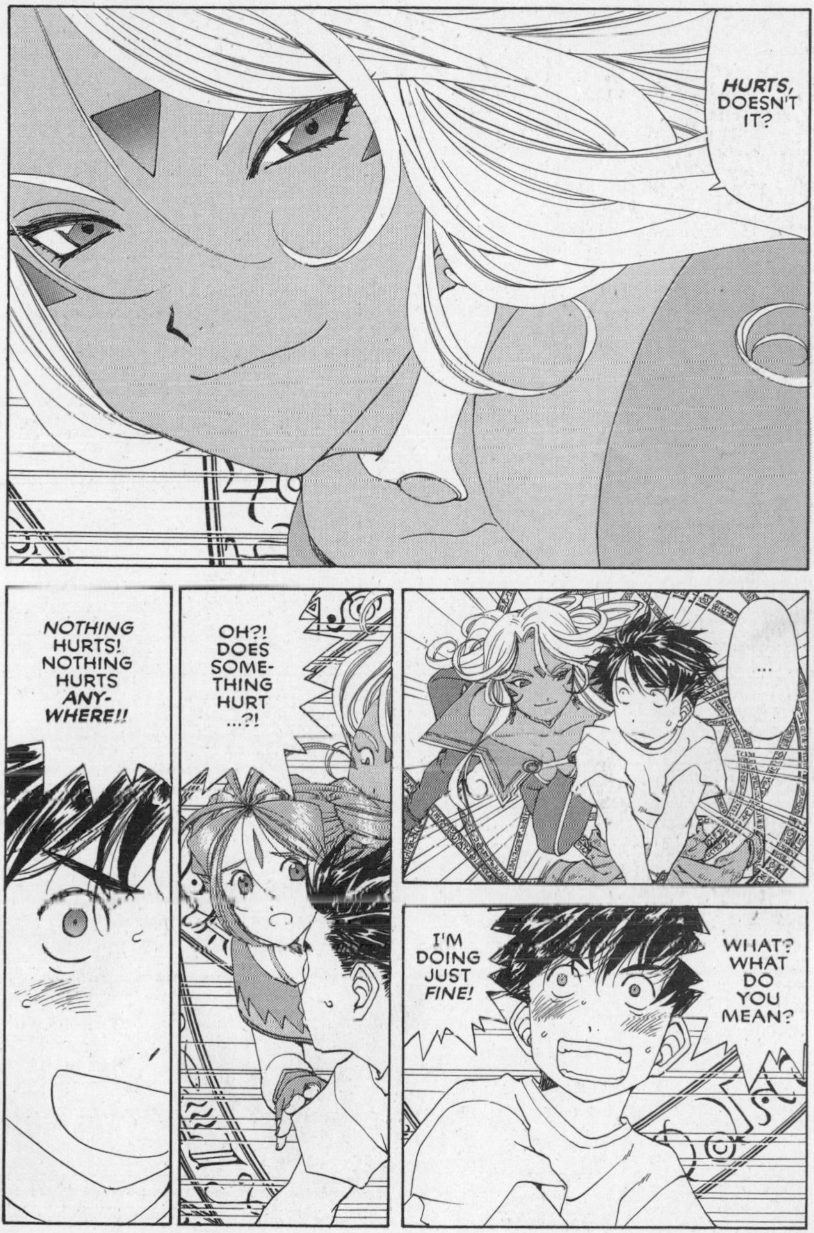
HURTS, DOESN'T IT?
...
WHAT? WHAT DO YOU MEAN?
I'M DOING JUST FINE!
OH?! DOES SOME-THING HURT ...?!
NOTHING HURTS! NOTHING HURTS ANY-WHERE!!

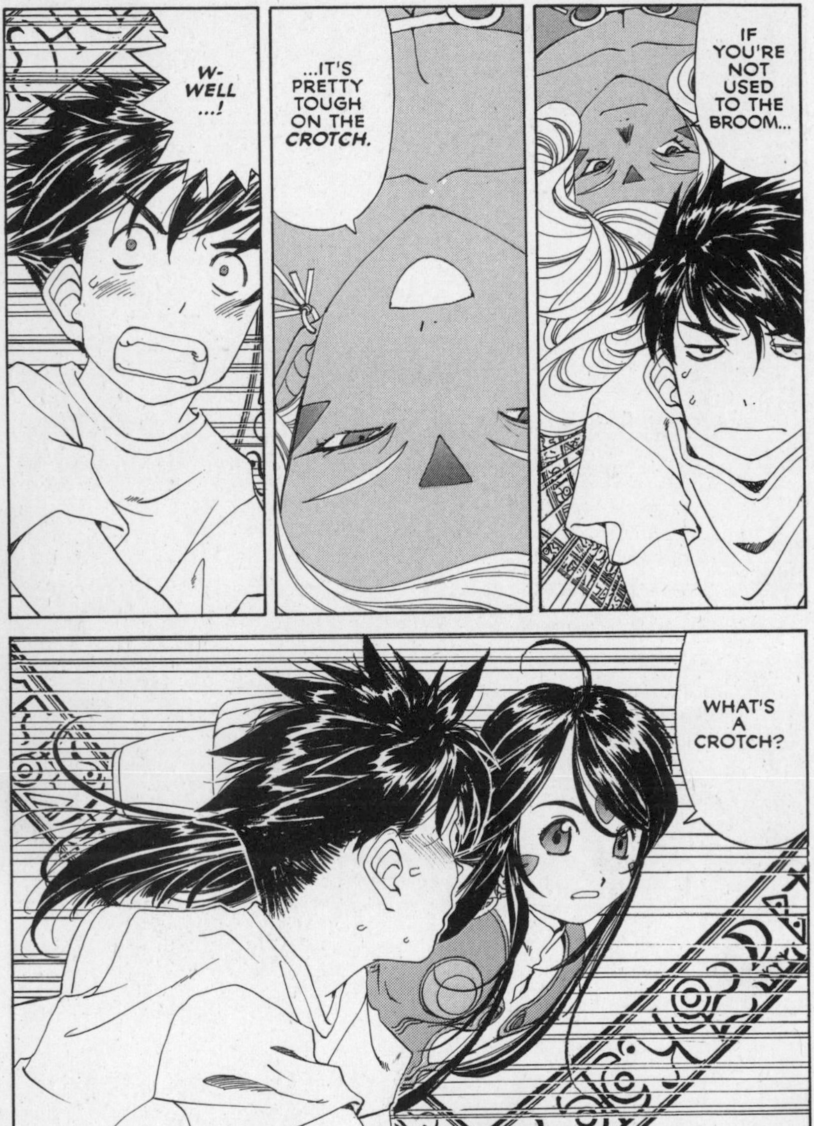
IF YOU'RE NOT USED TO THE BROOM...
...IT'S PRETTY TOUGH ON THE *CROTCH.*
W-WELL ...!
WHAT'S A CROTCH?

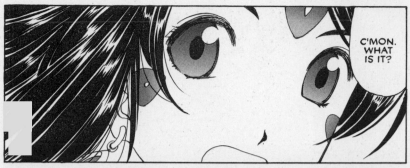

C'MON, WHAT IS IT?

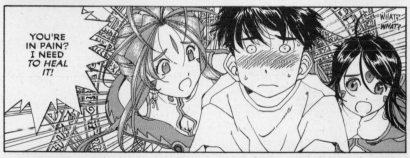

YOU'RE IN PAIN? I NEED *TO HEAL IT!*

WHAT? WHAT?

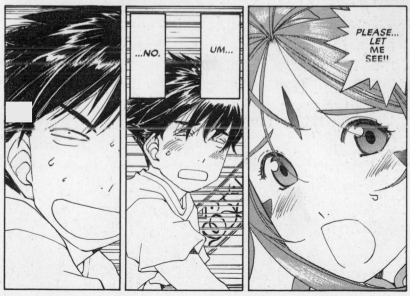

...NO.

UM...

PLEASE... LET ME SEE!!

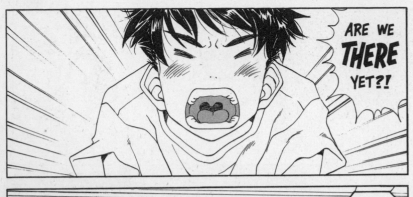

ARE WE **THERE** YET?!

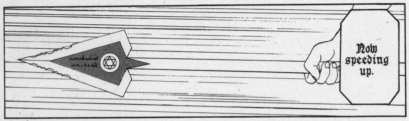

Now speeding up.

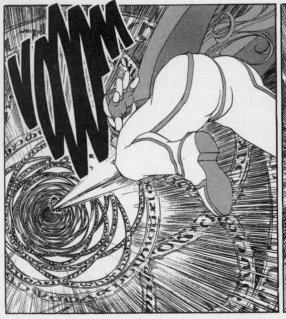

VMMMM

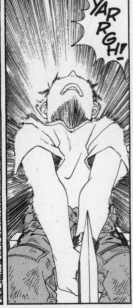

YAR RGH!

25

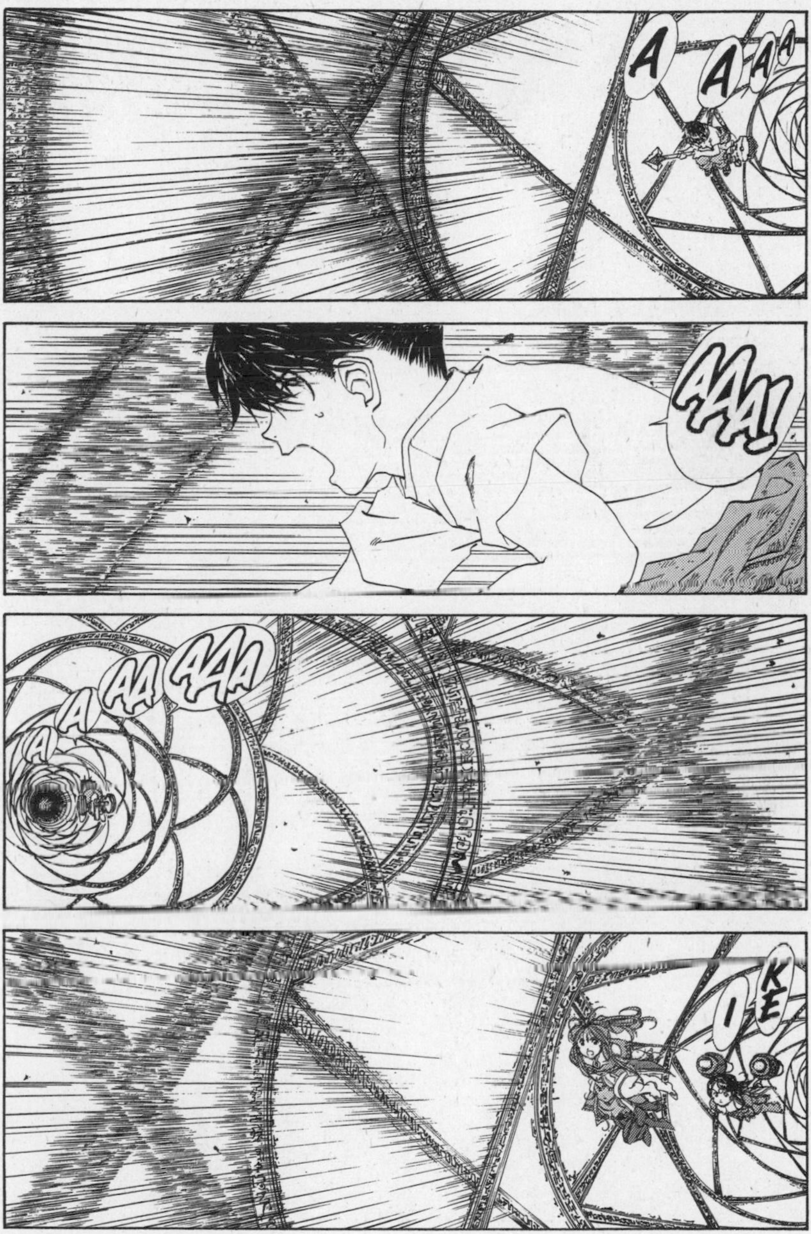
A
A
A
A
AAAA!
AAA
AA
A
A
KE
I

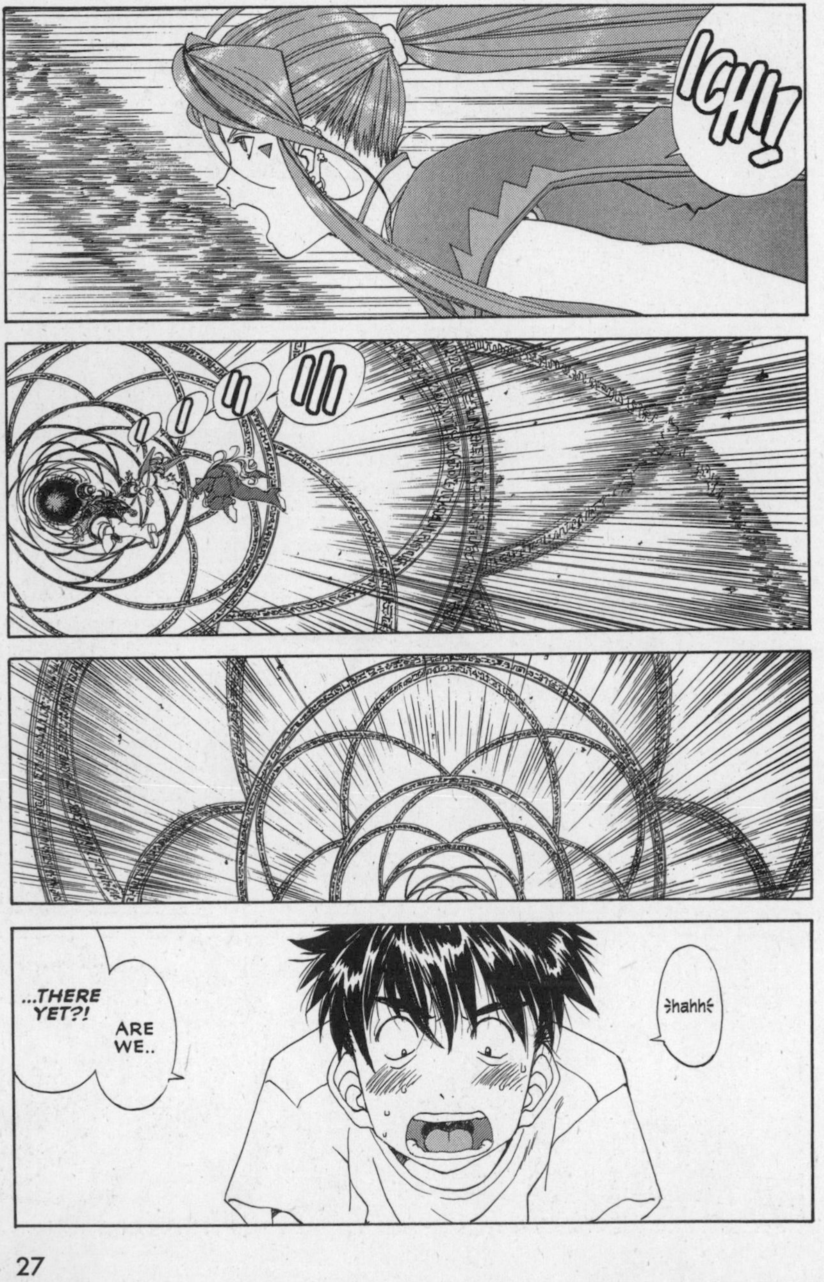
ICHI!
≠hahh≠
ARE WE.. ...THERE YET?!

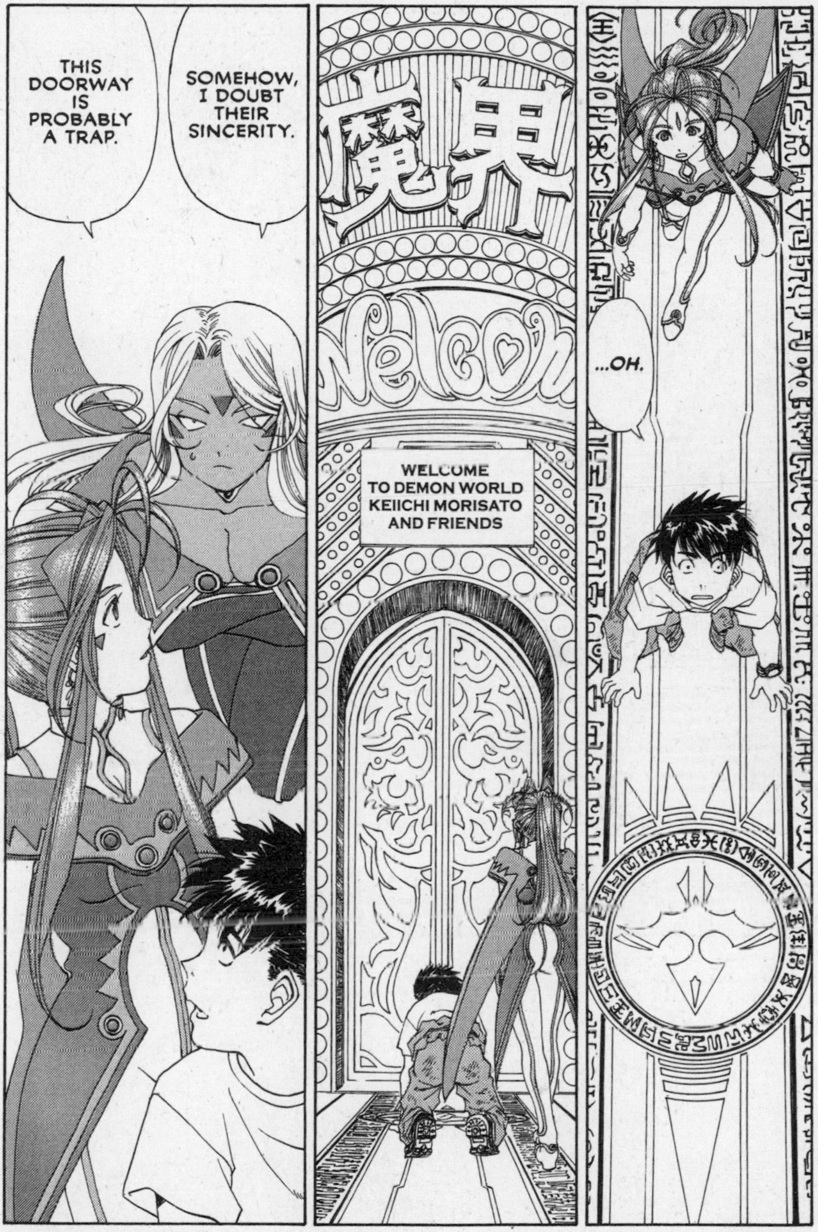
...OH.
魔界
WELCOME TO DEMON WORLD KEIICHI MORISATO AND FRIENDS
SOMEHOW, I DOUBT THEIR SINCERITY.
THIS DOORWAY IS PROBABLY A TRAP.

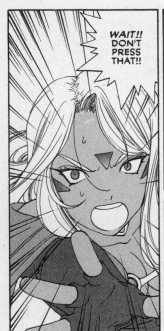

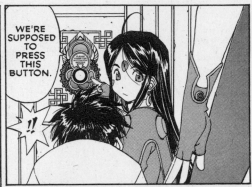

WE'RE SUPPOSED TO PRESS THIS BUTTON.
!!
PLEASE PRESS THIS BUTTON FOR SERVICE
WAIT!! DON'T PRESS THAT!!
DON'T PRESS *THIS?!*

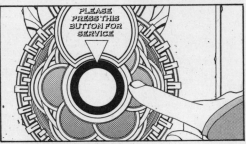

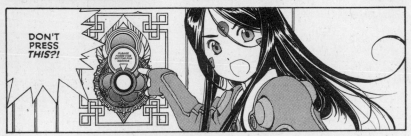

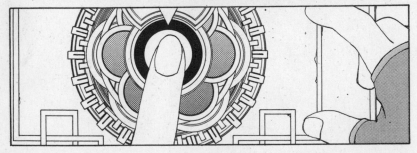

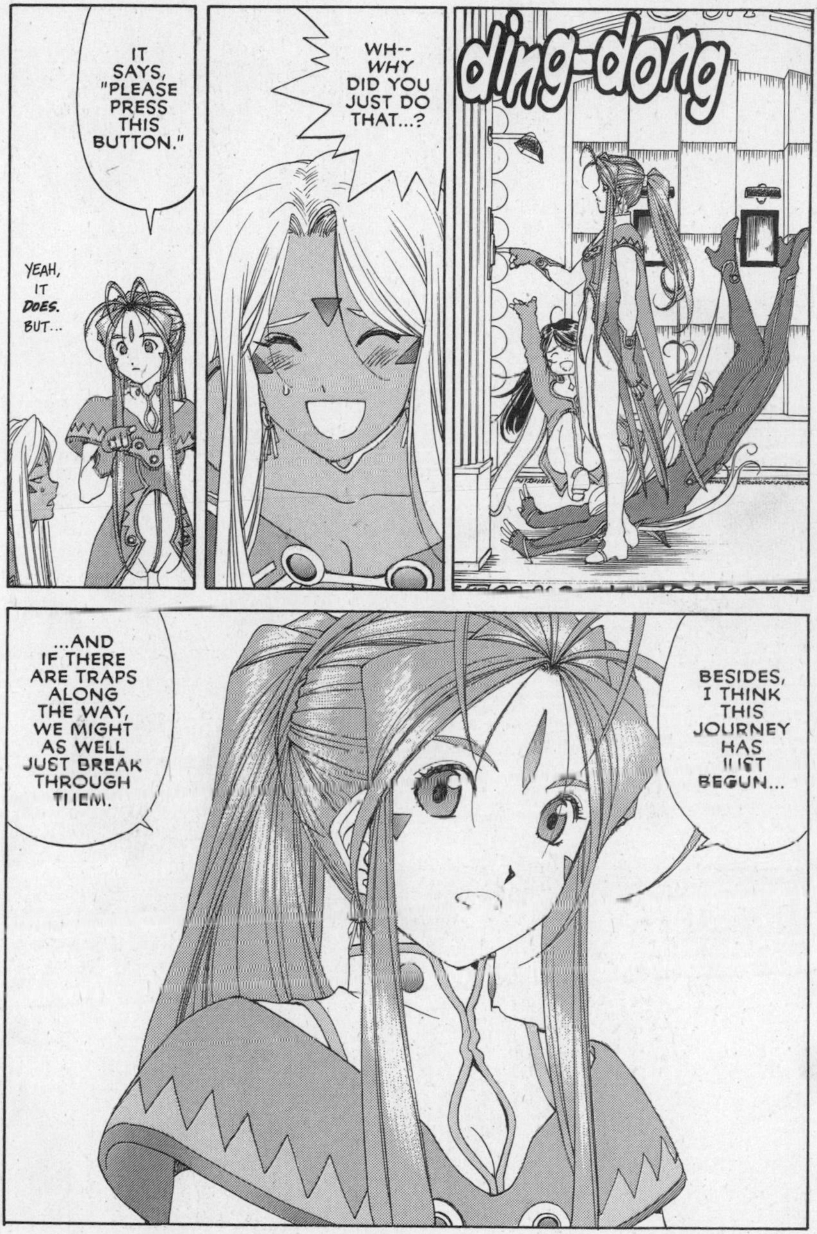
ding-dong
WH-- WHY DID YOU JUST DO THAT...?
IT SAYS, "PLEASE PRESS THIS BUTTON."
YEAH, IT DOES. BUT...
BESIDES, I THINK THIS JOURNEY HAS JUST BEGUN...
...AND IF THERE ARE TRAPS ALONG THE WAY, WE MIGHT AS WELL JUST BREAK THROUGH THEM.

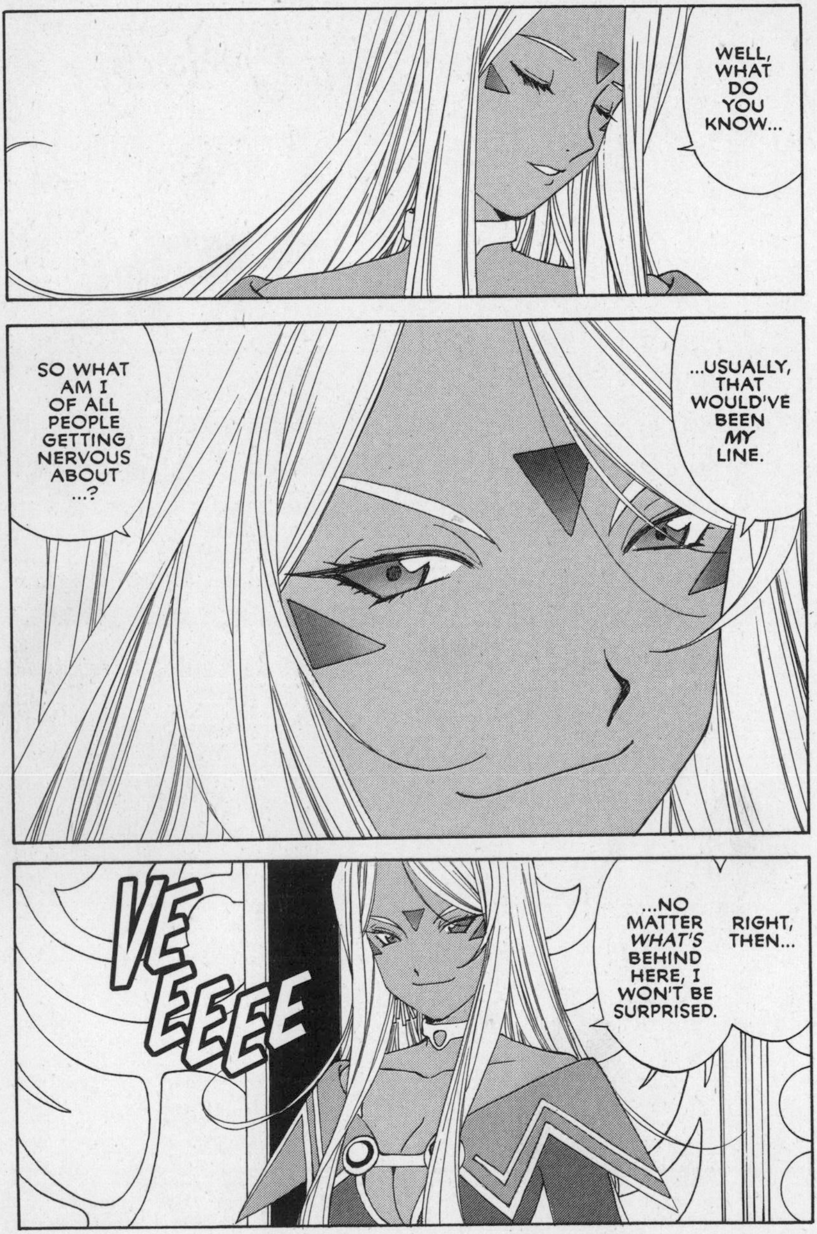
WELL, WHAT DO YOU KNOW...
...USUALLY, THAT WOULD'VE BEEN *MY* LINE.
SO WHAT AM I OF ALL PEOPLE GETTING NERVOUS ABOUT ...?
RIGHT, THEN...
...NO MATTER *WHAT'S* BEHIND HERE, I WON'T BE SURPRISED.
VEEEEE

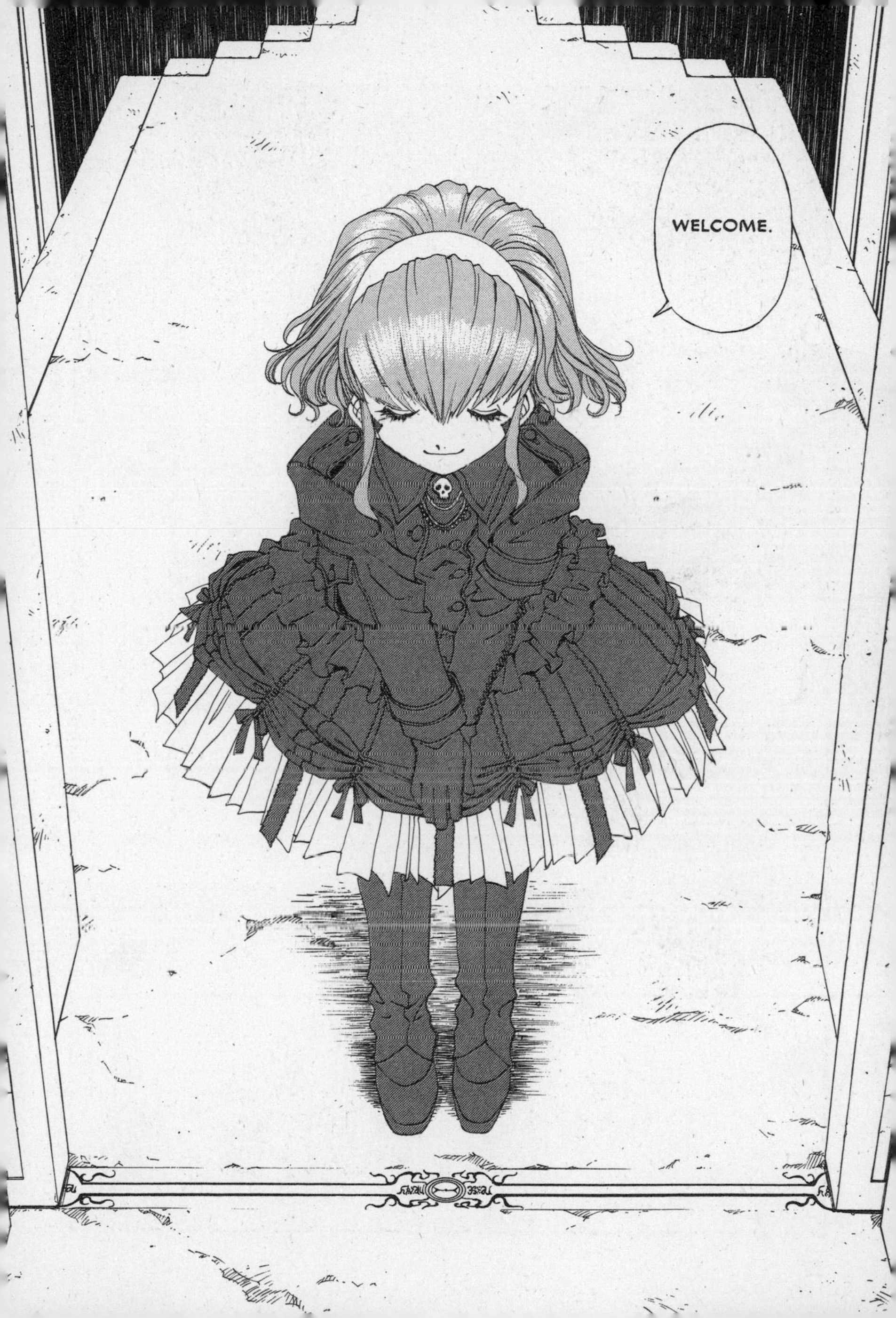
WELCOME.

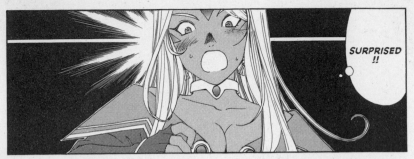

SURPRISED!!

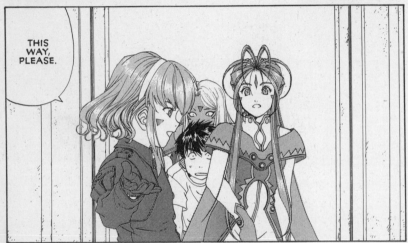

THIS WAY, PLEASE.

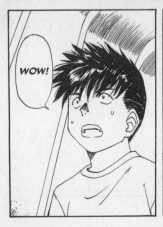

WOW!

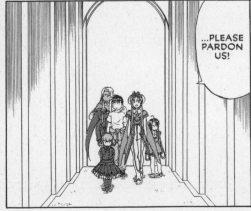

...PLEASE PARDON US!

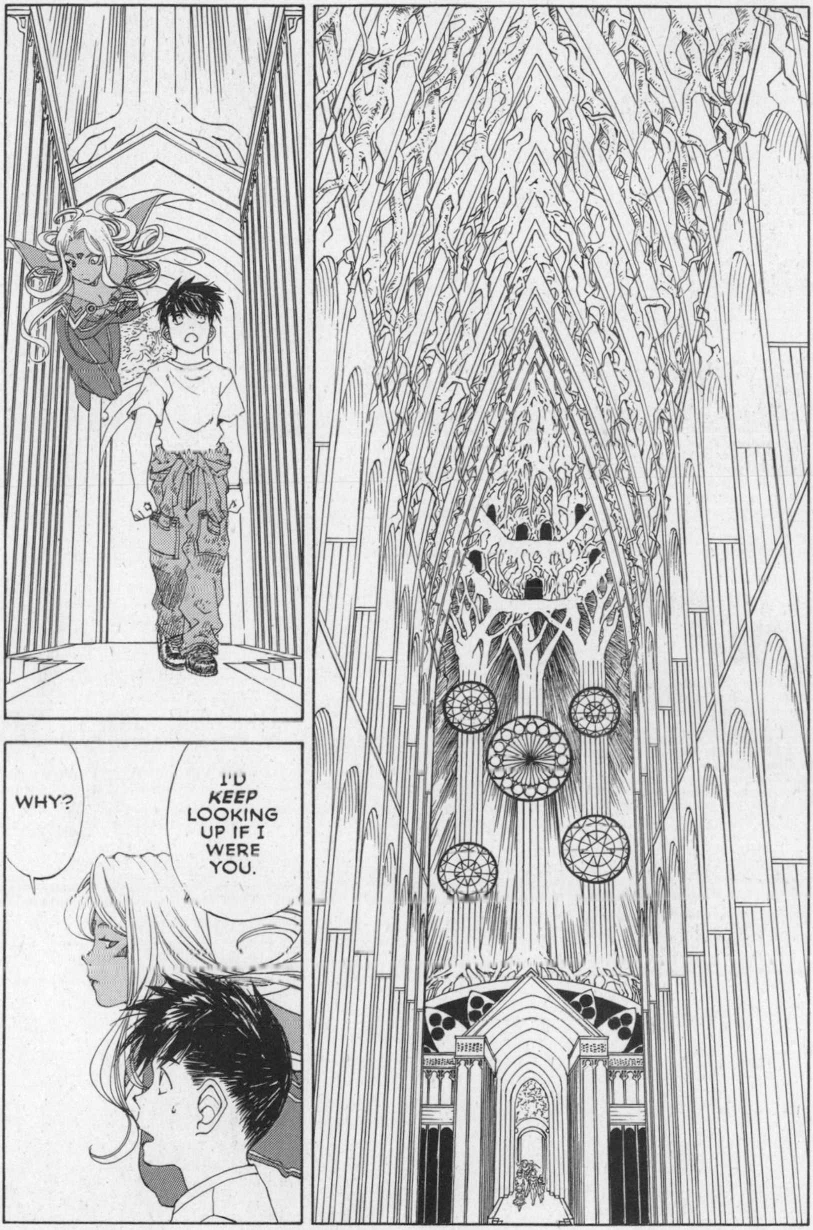
I'D *KEEP* LOOKING UP IF I WERE YOU.
WHY?

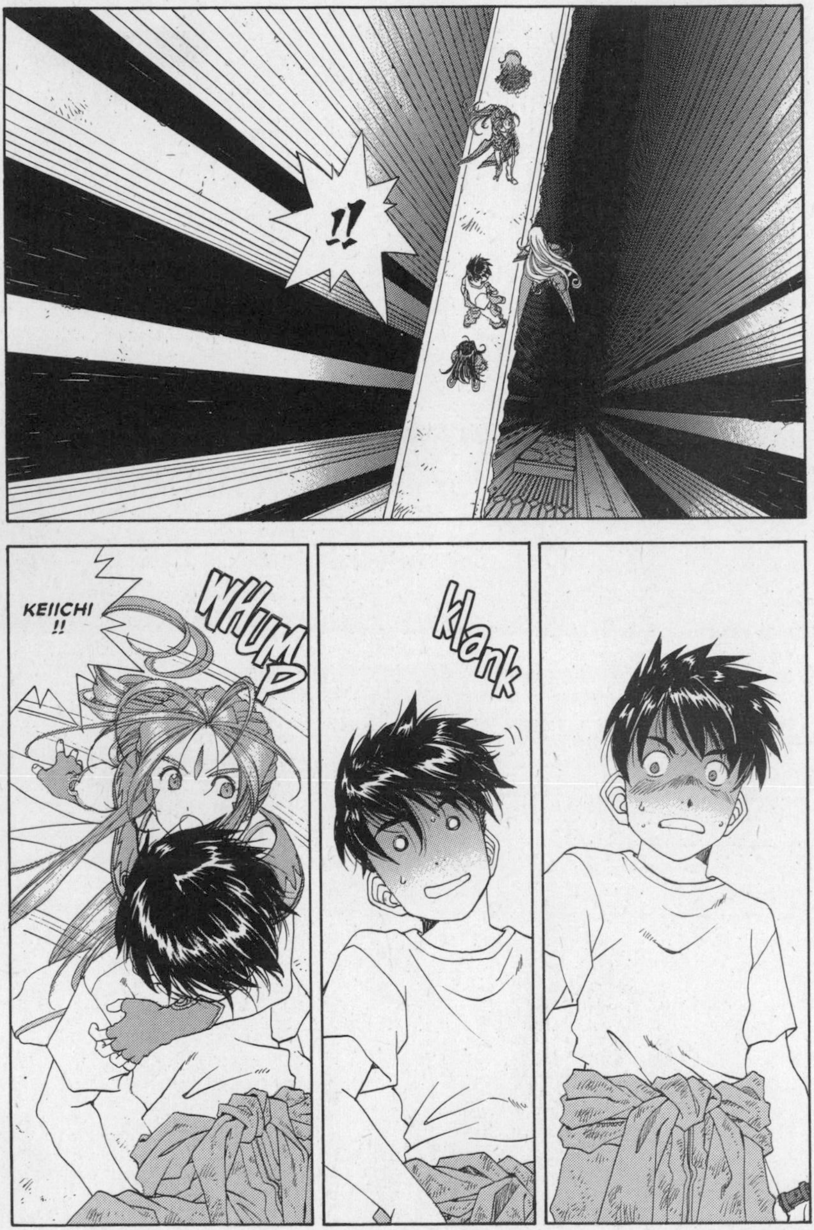
!!
klank
WHUMP
KEIICHI !!

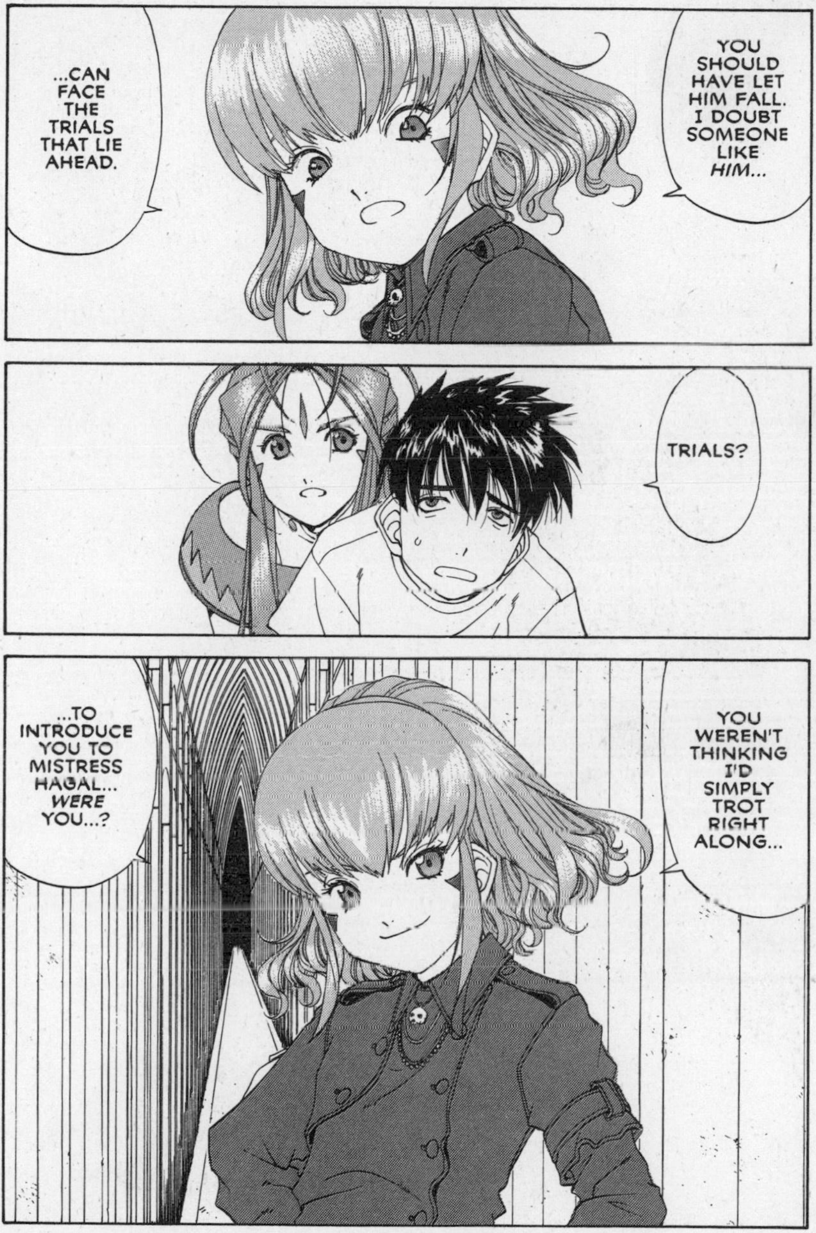
YOU SHOULD HAVE LET HIM FALL. I DOUBT SOMEONE LIKE *HIM*...
...CAN FACE THE TRIALS THAT LIE AHEAD.
TRIALS?
YOU WEREN'T THINKING I'D SIMPLY TROT RIGHT ALONG...
...TO INTRODUCE YOU TO MISTRESS HAGAL... *WERE* YOU...?

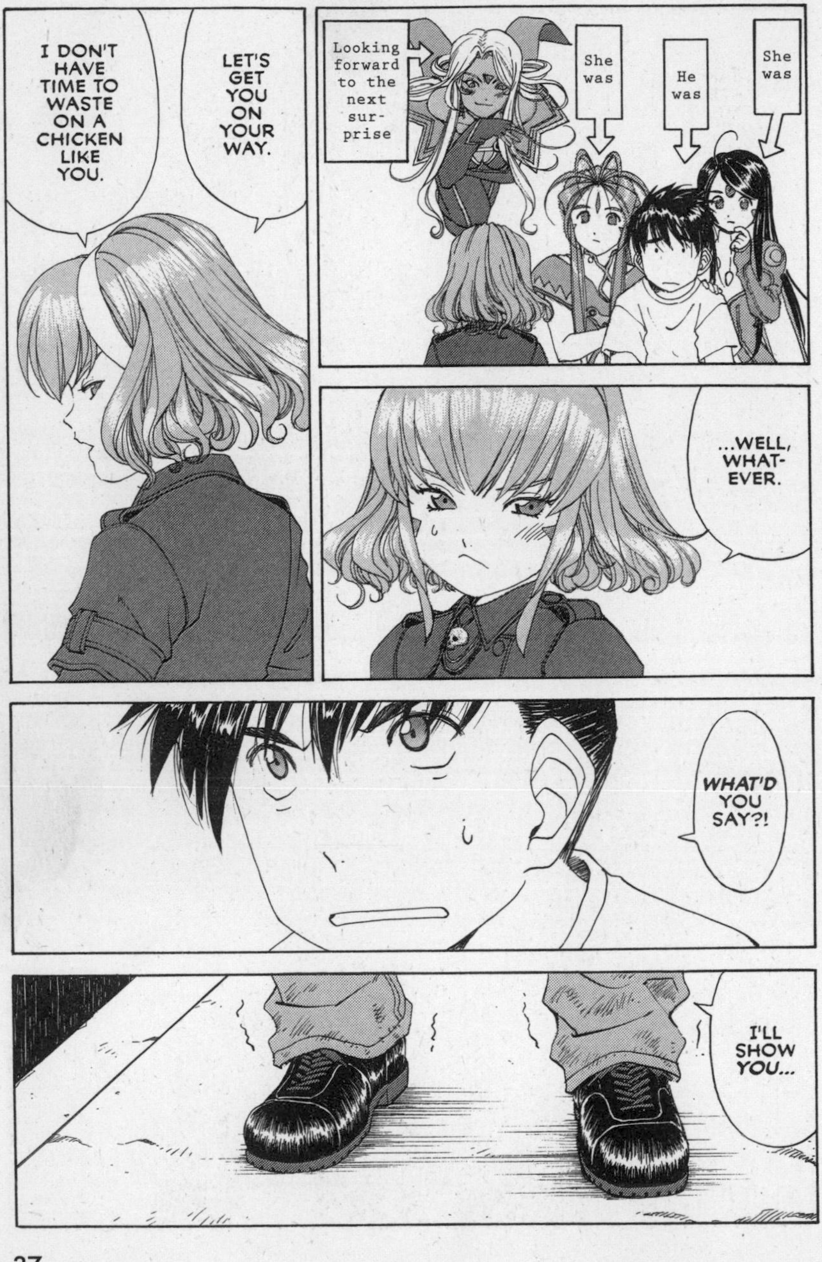

She was
He was
She was
Looking forward to the next sur-prise
...WELL, WHATEVER.
LET'S GET YOU ON YOUR WAY.
I DON'T HAVE TIME TO WASTE ON A CHICKEN LIKE YOU.
WHAT'D YOU SAY?!
I'LL SHOW YOU...

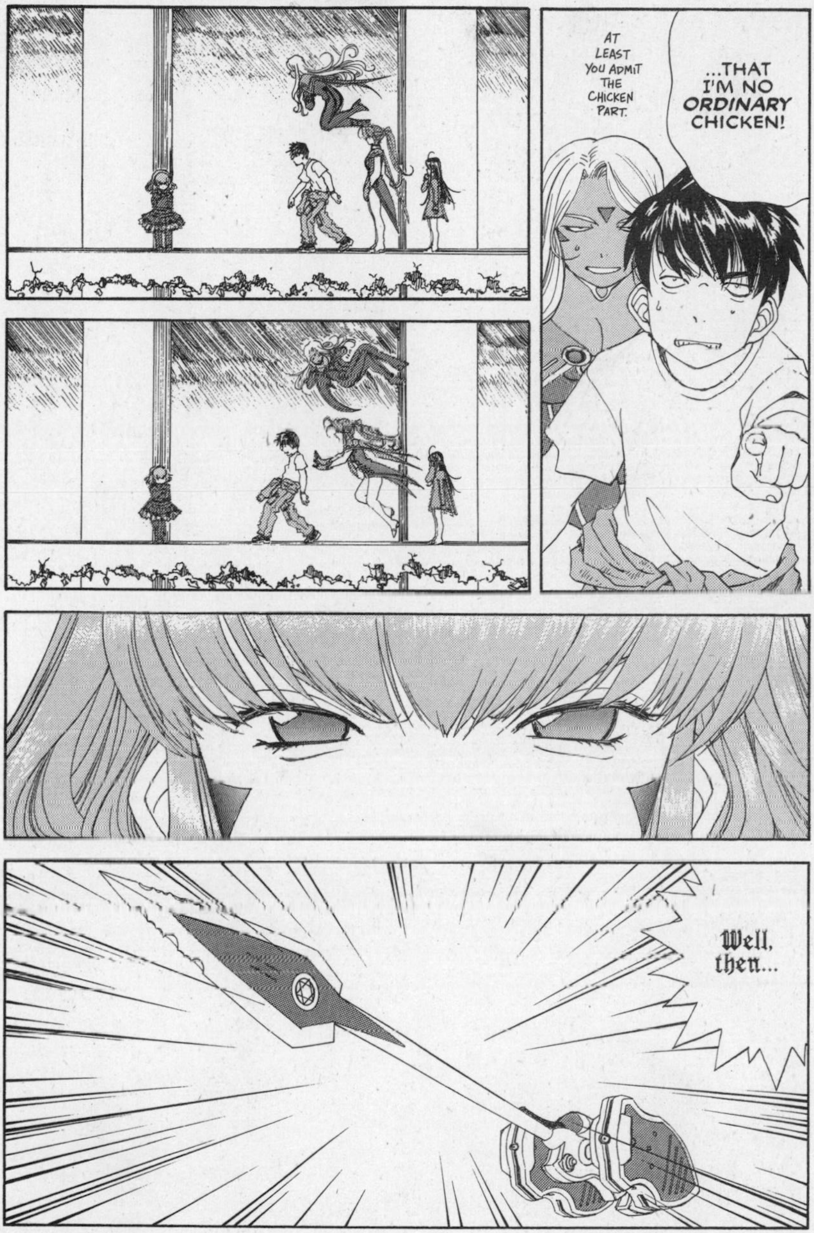
...THAT I'M NO ORDINARY CHICKEN!
AT LEAST YOU ADMIT THE CHICKEN PART.
Well, then...

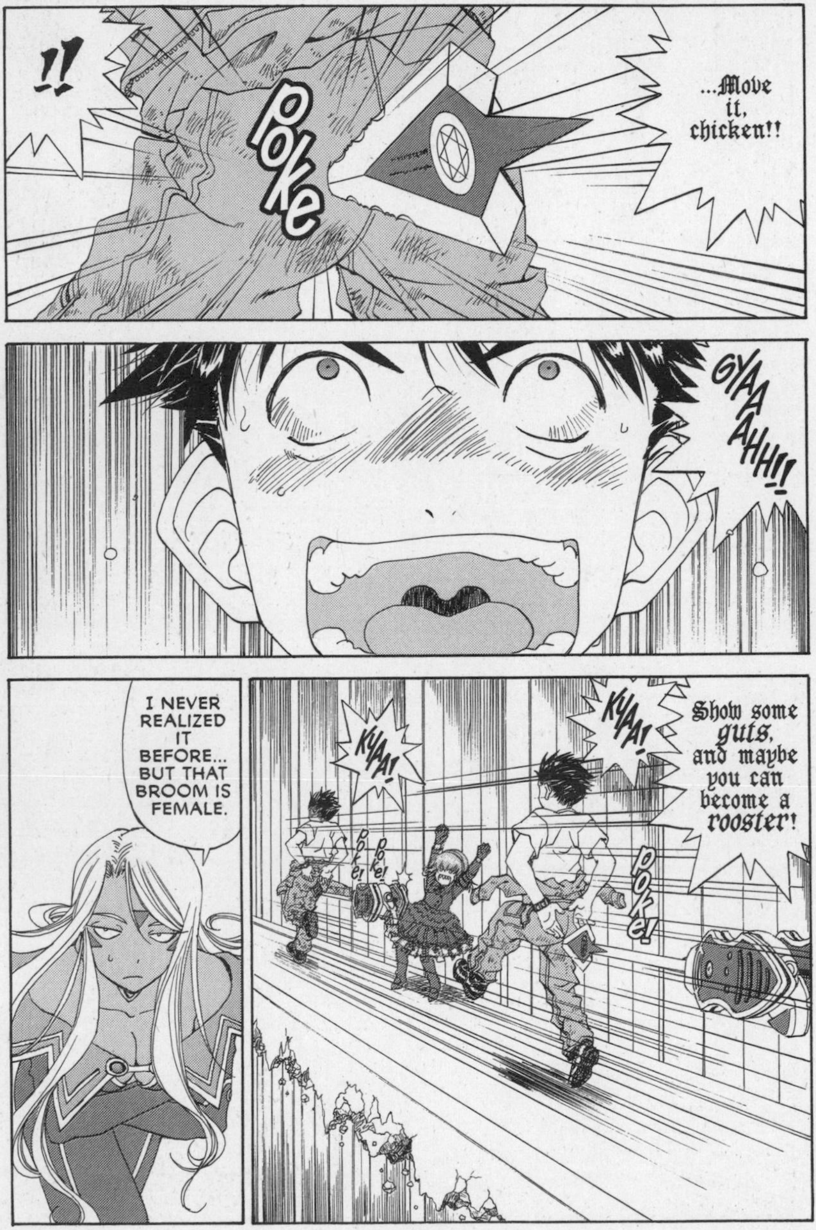
...Move it, chicken!!
poke
!!
GYAAAHH!!
Show some guts, and maybe you can become a rooster!
KYAA!
KYAA!
poke!
poke!
poke!
I NEVER REALIZED IT BEFORE... BUT THAT BROOM IS FEMALE.

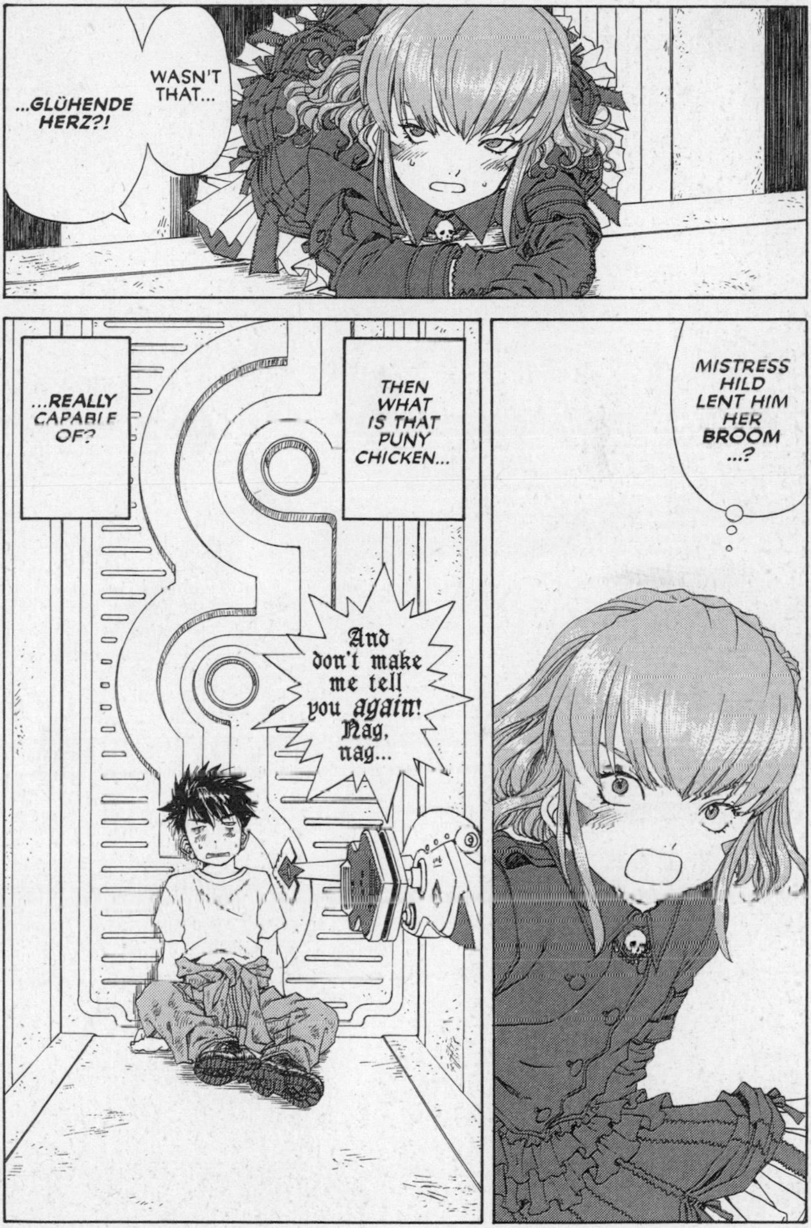
WASN'T THAT...
...GLÜHENDE HERZ?!
MISTRESS HILD LENT HIM HER BROOM ...?
THEN WHAT IS THAT PUNY CHICKEN...
...REALLY CAPABLE OF?
And don't make me tell you again! Nag, nag...

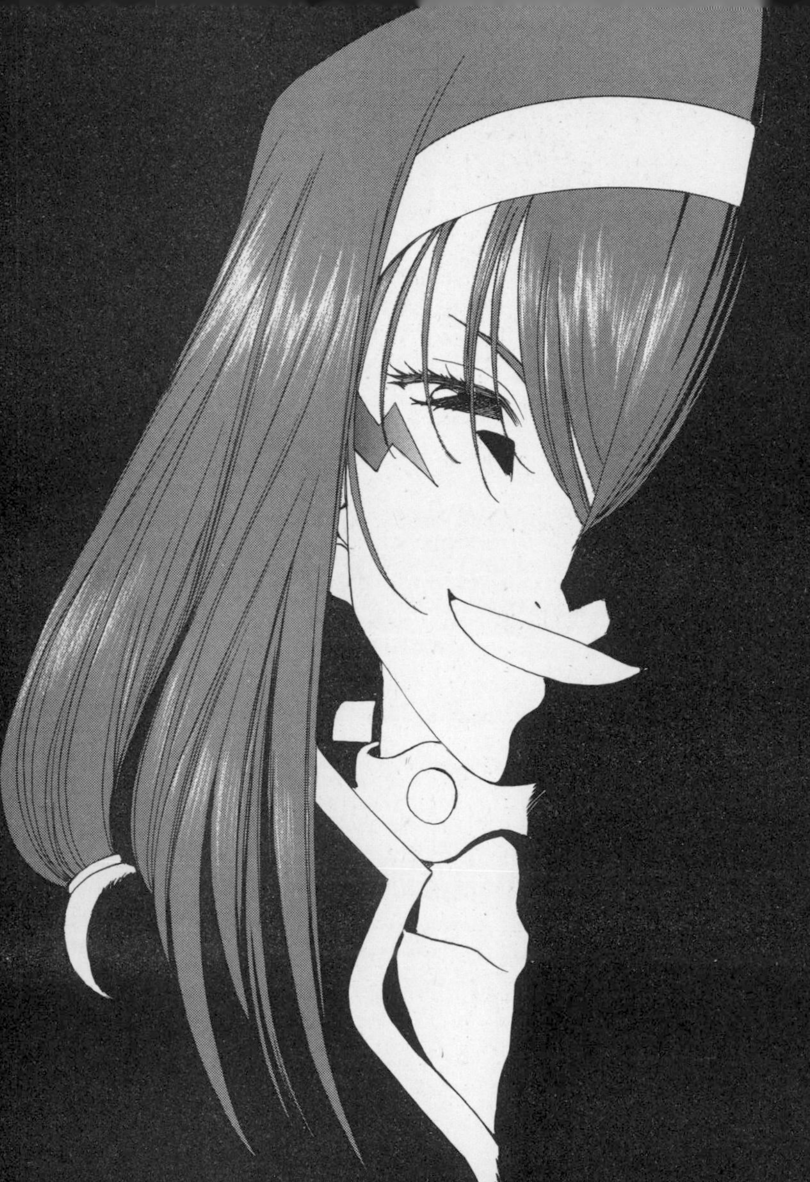

CHAPTER 252

True Darkness

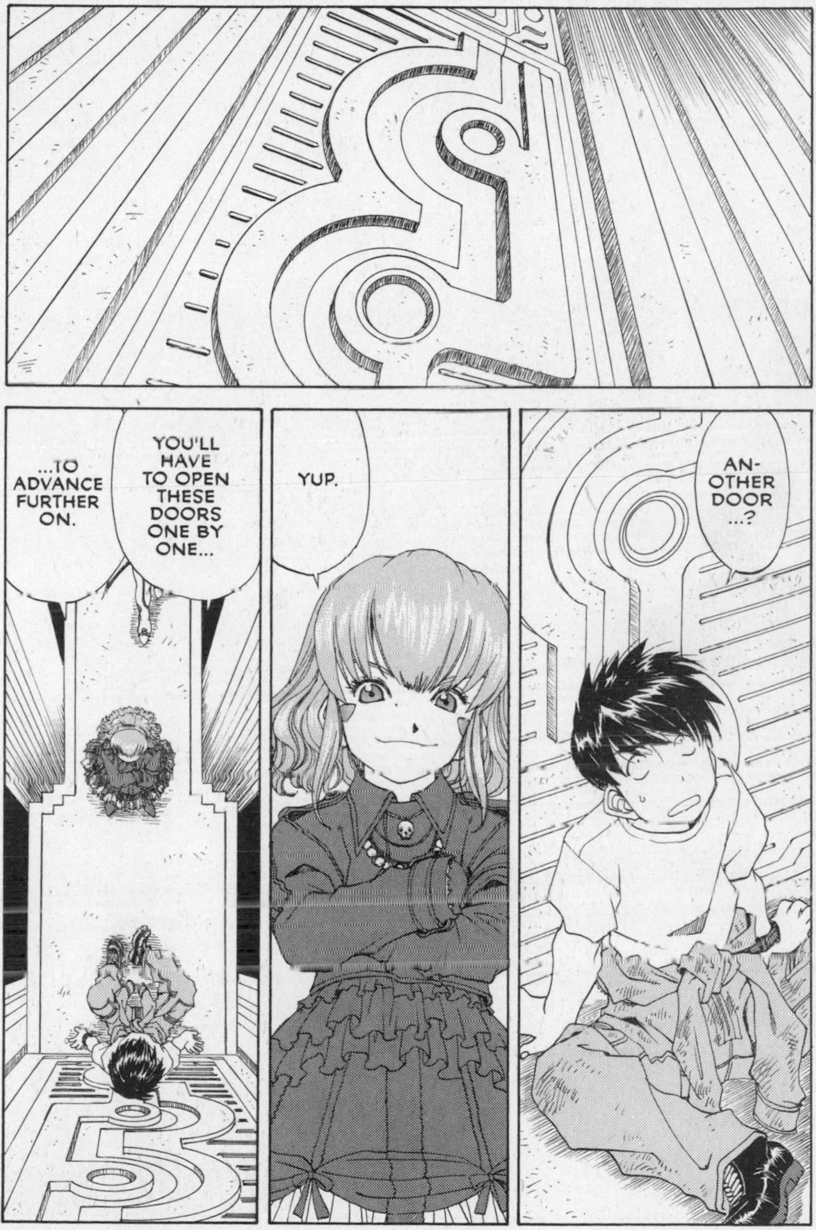
AN-OTHER DOOR ...?
YUP.
YOU'LL HAVE TO OPEN THESE DOORS ONE BY ONE...
...TO ADVANCE FURTHER ON.

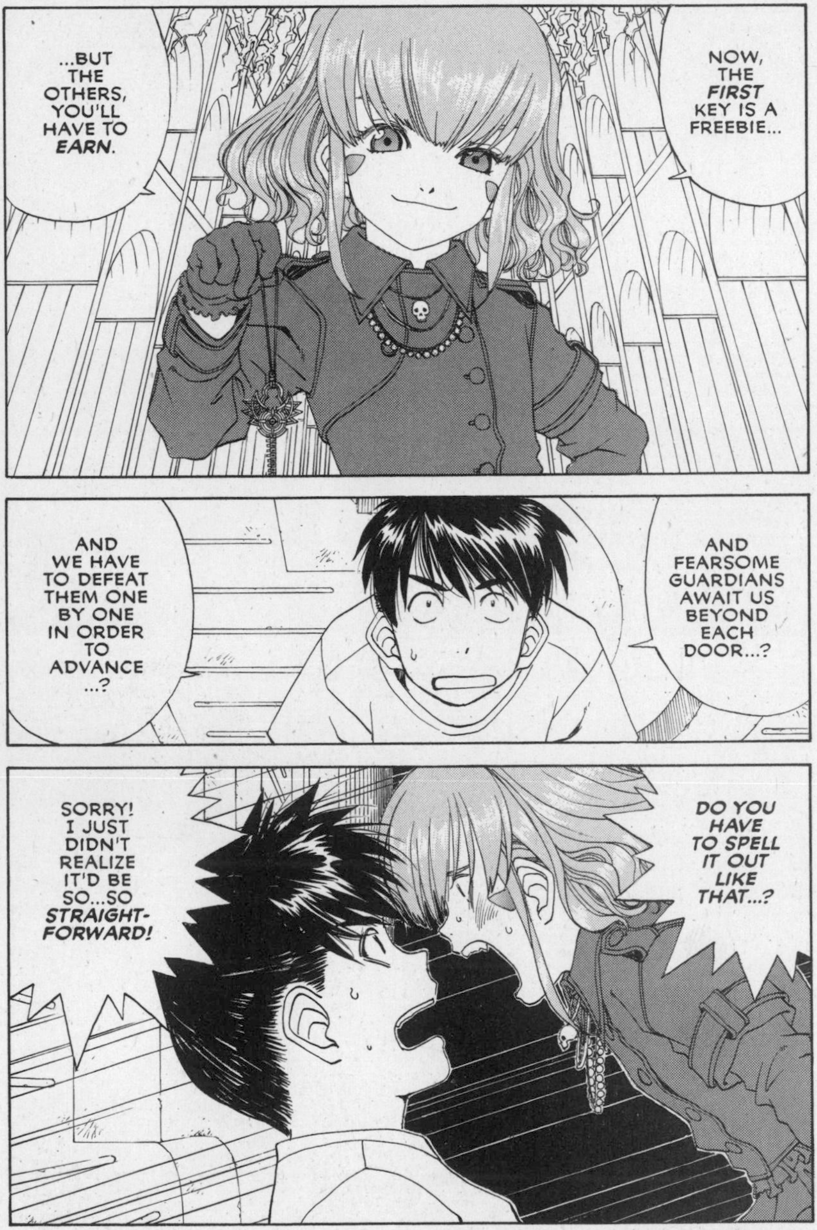
NOW, THE *FIRST* KEY IS A FREEBIE...
...BUT THE OTHERS, YOU'LL HAVE TO *EARN*.
AND FEARSOME GUARDIANS AWAIT US BEYOND EACH DOOR...?
AND WE HAVE TO DEFEAT THEM ONE BY ONE IN ORDER TO ADVANCE ...?
DO YOU HAVE TO SPELL IT OUT LIKE THAT...?
SORRY! I JUST DIDN'T REALIZE IT'D BE SO...SO *STRAIGHT-FORWARD!*

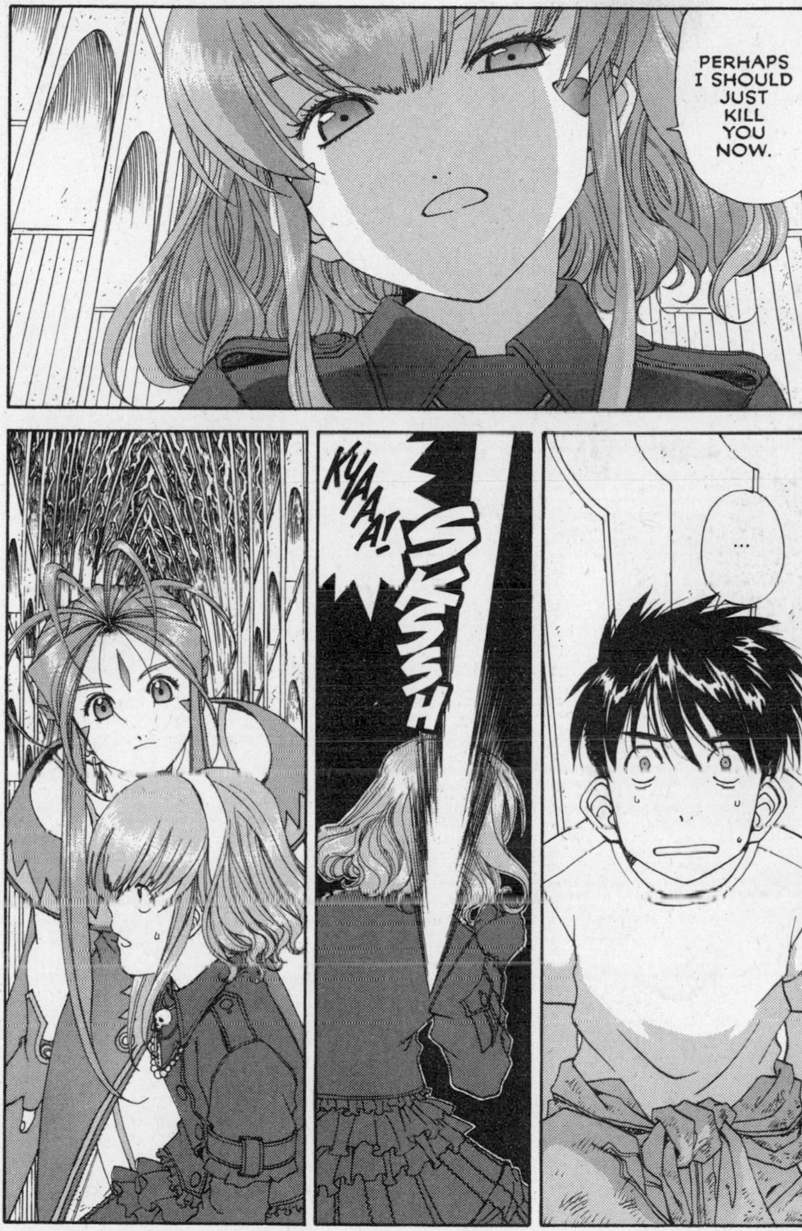
PERHAPS I SHOULD JUST KILL YOU NOW.
...
KYAAAA!
SKSSH

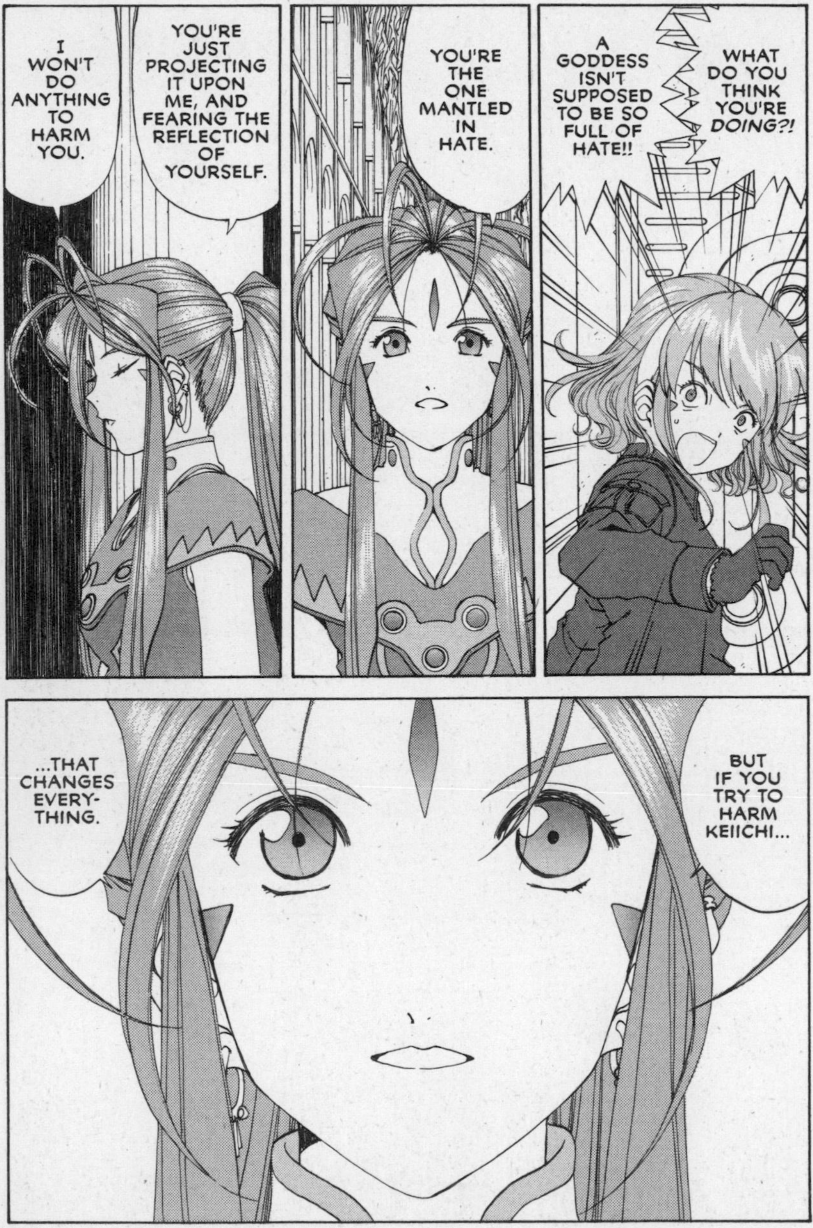
WHAT DO YOU THINK YOU'RE *DOING?!*
A GODDESS ISN'T SUPPOSED TO BE SO FULL OF HATE!!
YOU'RE THE ONE MANTLED IN HATE.
YOU'RE JUST PROJECTING IT UPON ME, AND FEARING THE REFLECTION OF YOURSELF.
I WON'T DO ANYTHING TO HARM YOU.
BUT IF YOU TRY TO HARM KEIICHI...
...THAT CHANGES EVERY-THING.

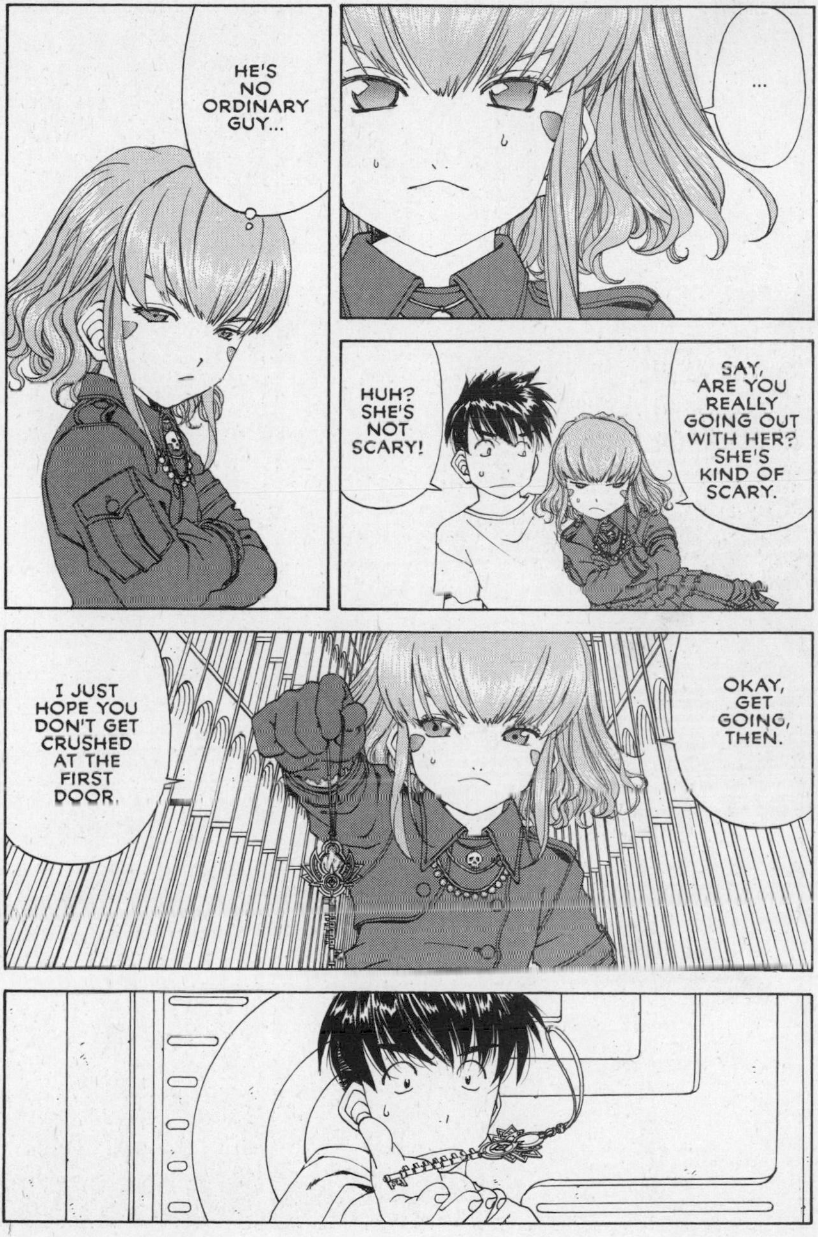
...
SAY, ARE YOU REALLY GOING OUT WITH HER? SHE'S KIND OF SCARY.
HUH? SHE'S NOT SCARY!
HE'S NO ORDINARY GUY...
OKAY, GET GOING, THEN.
I JUST HOPE YOU DON'T GET CRUSHED AT THE FIRST DOOR.

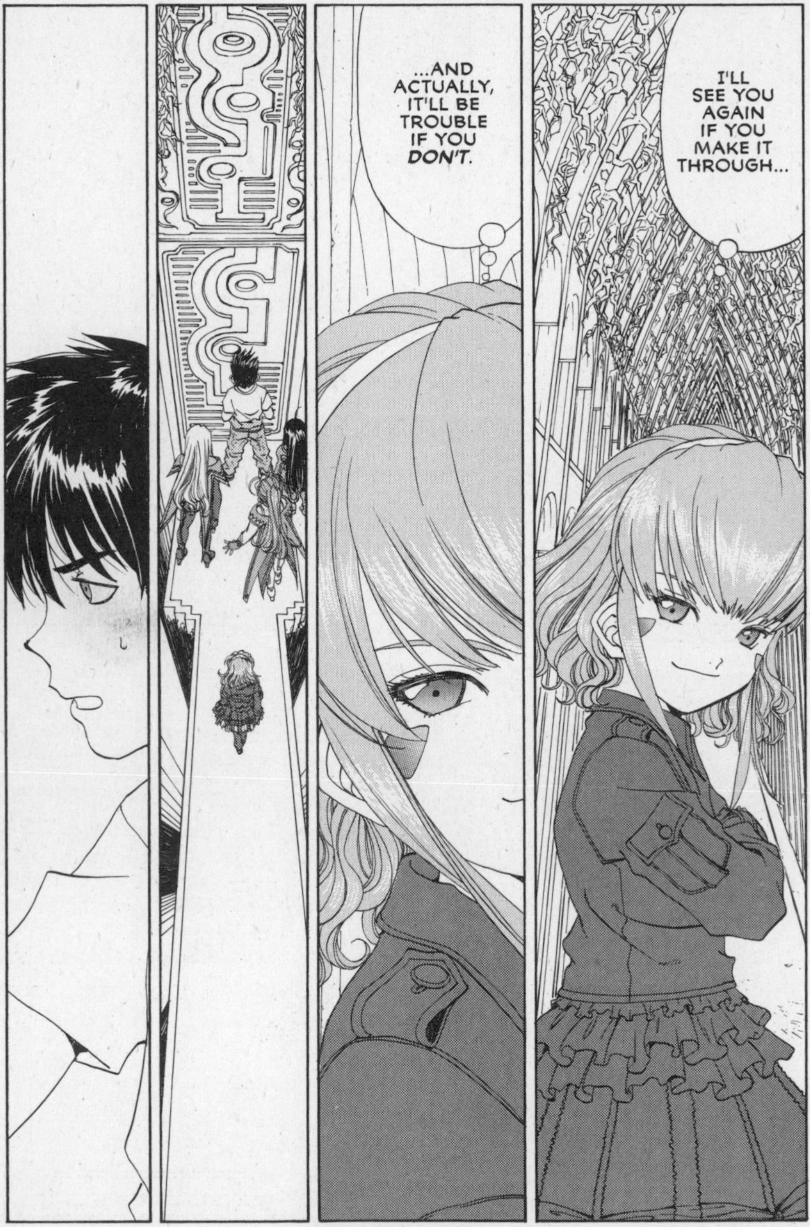
I'LL SEE YOU AGAIN IF YOU MAKE IT THROUGH...
...AND ACTUALLY, IT'LL BE TROUBLE IF YOU *DON'T*.

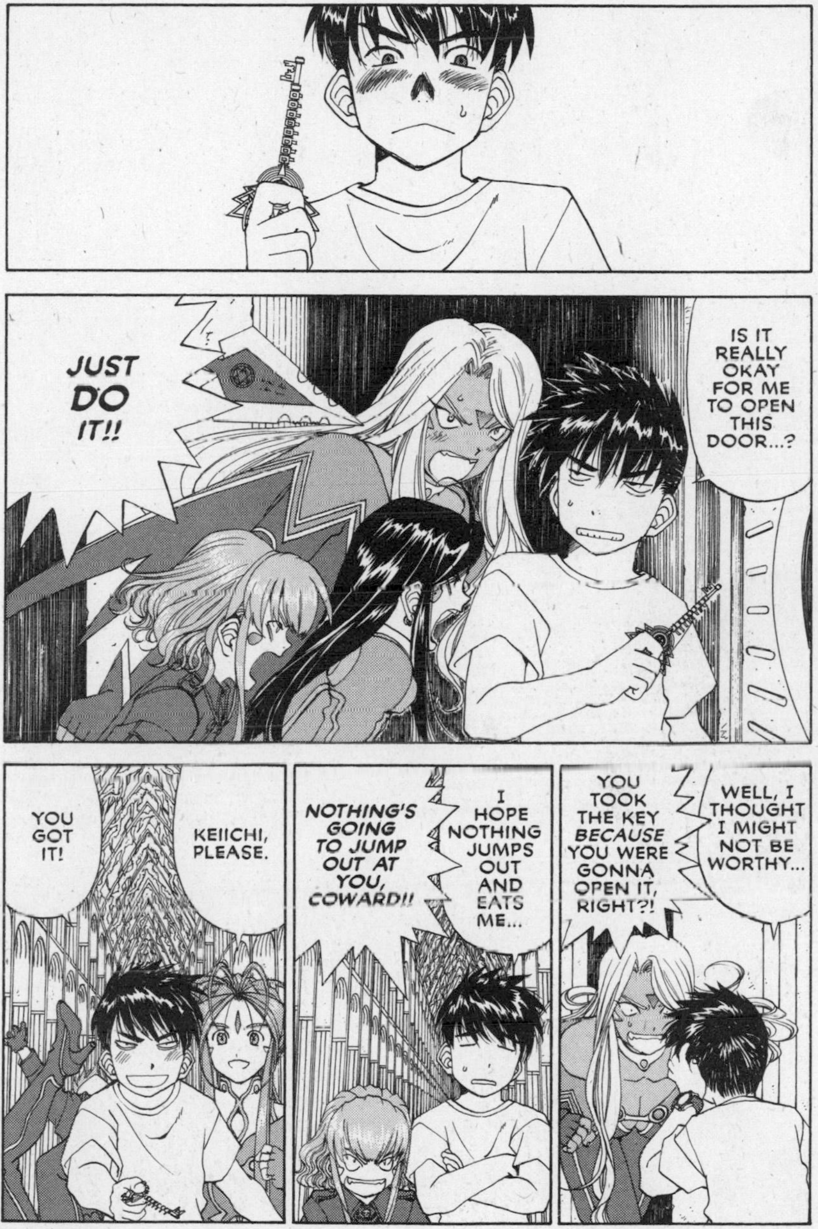
IS IT REALLY OKAY FOR ME TO OPEN THIS DOOR...?
JUST DO IT!!
WELL, I THOUGHT I MIGHT NOT BE WORTHY...
YOU TOOK THE KEY BECAUSE YOU WERE GONNA OPEN IT, RIGHT?!
I HOPE NOTHING JUMPS OUT AND EATS ME...
NOTHING'S GOING TO JUMP OUT AT YOU, COWARD!!
KEIICHI, PLEASE.
YOU GOT IT!

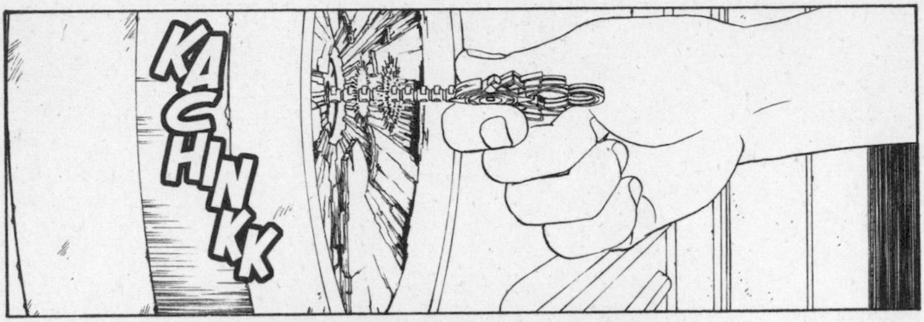
KACHINKK
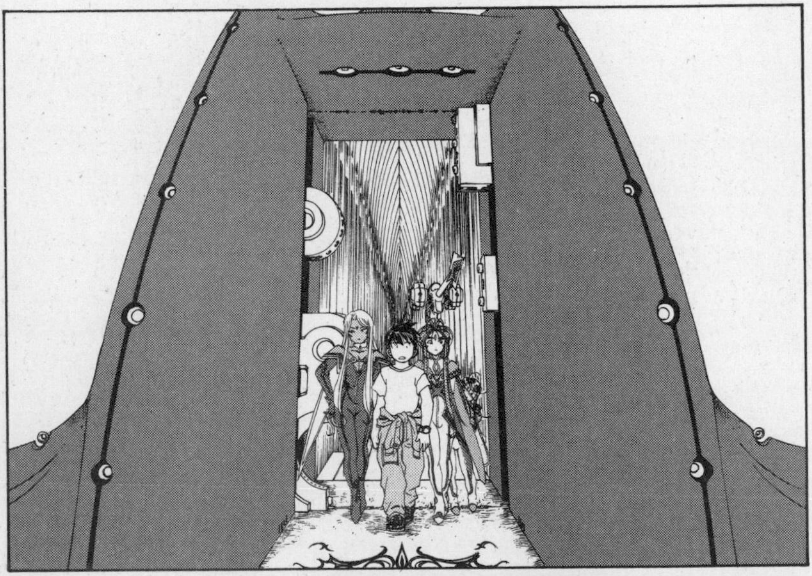
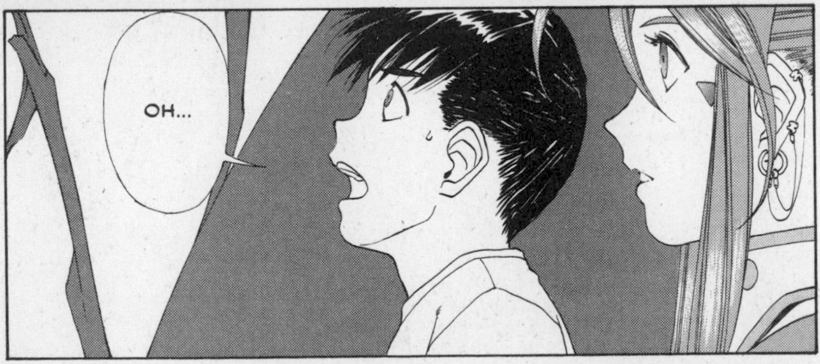
OH...

...WOW.
WHAT'S THAT...?

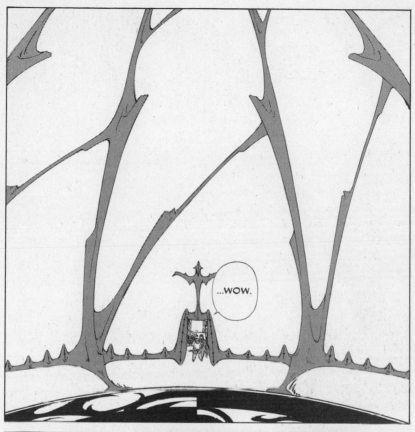

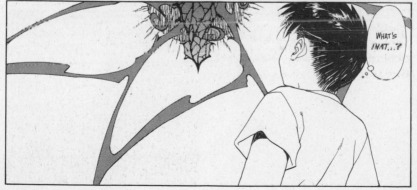

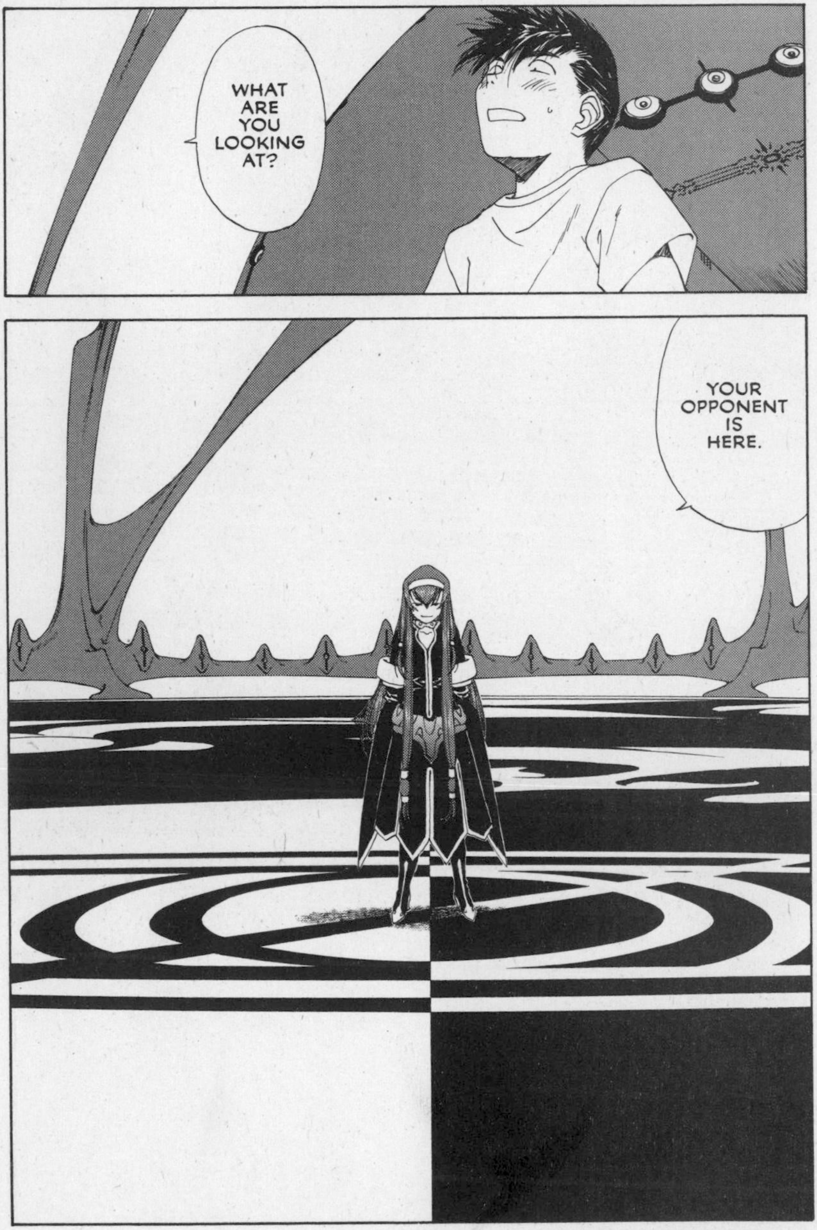
WHAT ARE YOU LOOKING AT?
YOUR OPPONENT IS HERE.

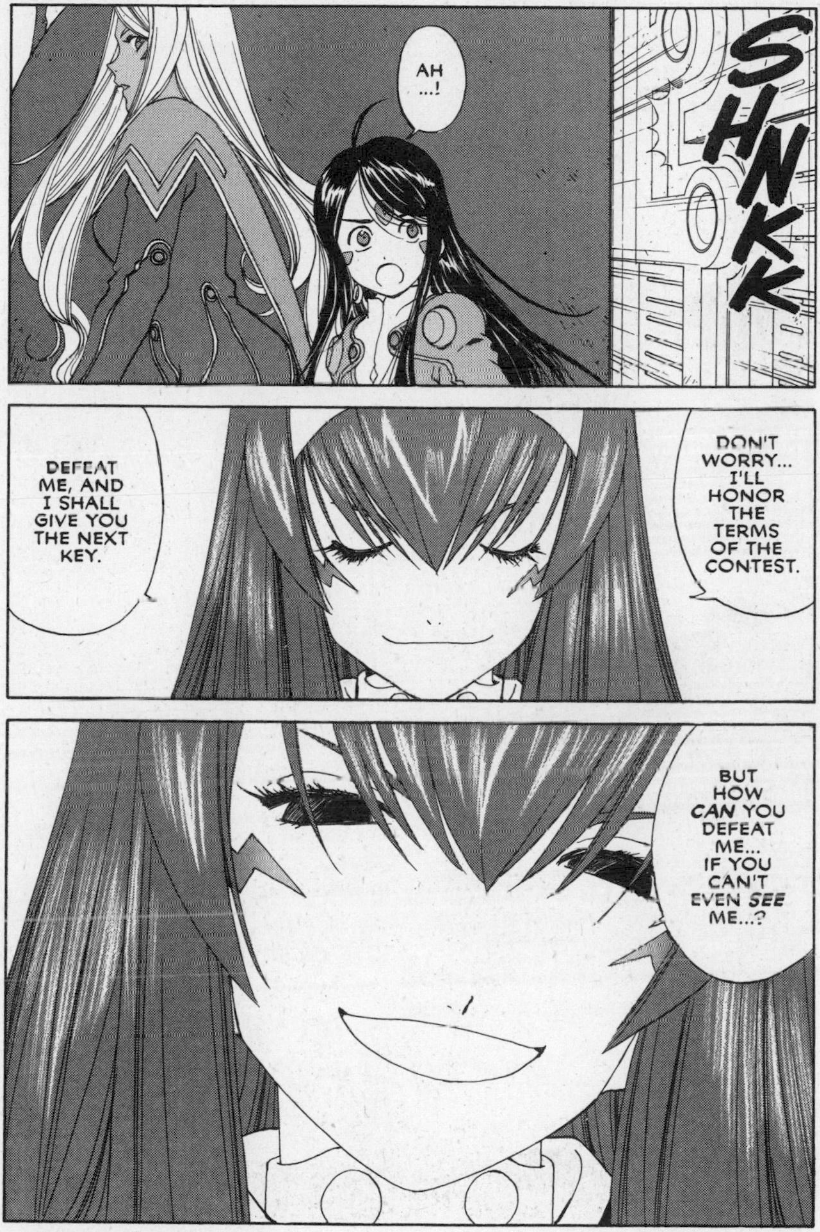
SHNKK
AH ...!
DON'T WORRY... I'LL HONOR THE TERMS OF THE CONTEST.
DEFEAT ME, AND I SHALL GIVE YOU THE NEXT KEY.
BUT HOW *CAN* YOU DEFEAT ME... IF YOU CAN'T EVEN *SEE* ME...?

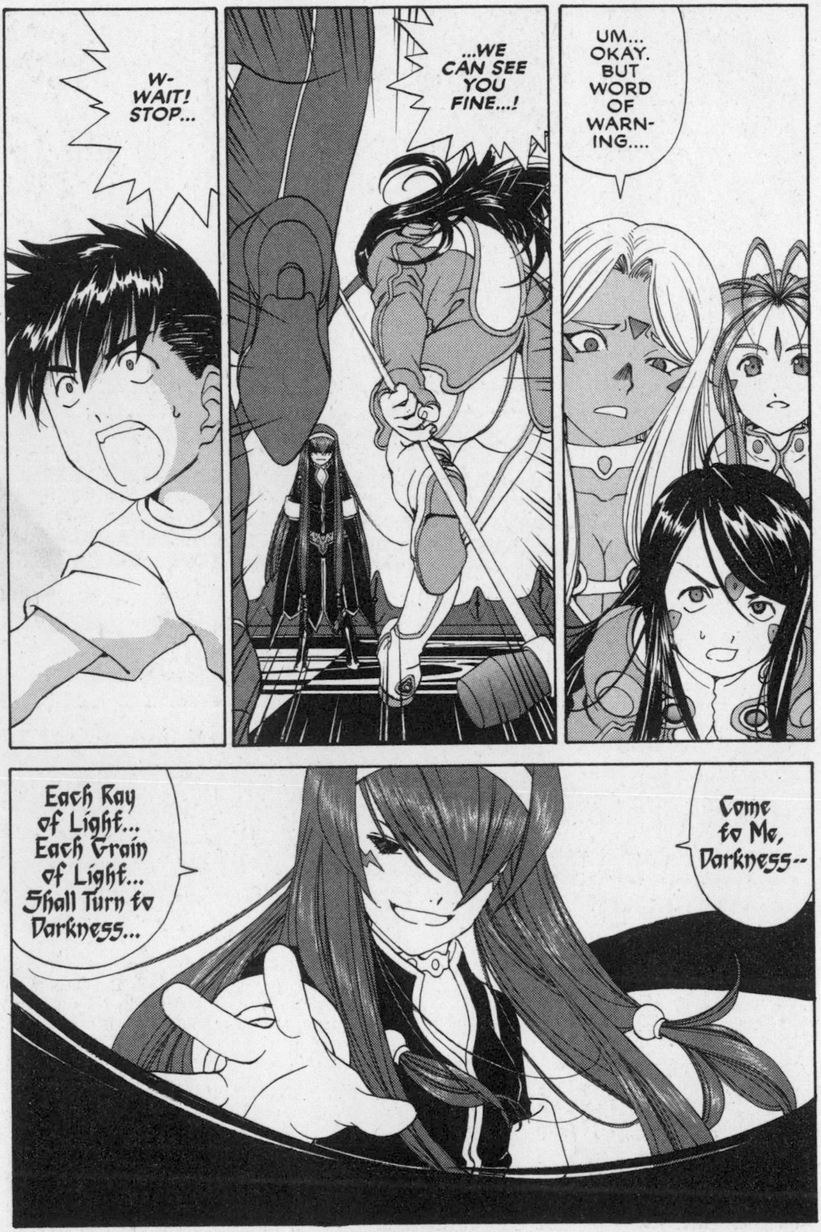
UM... OKAY. BUT WORD OF WARNING....
...WE CAN SEE YOU FINE...!
W-WAIT! STOP...
Come to Me, Darkness--
Each Ray of Light... Each Grain of Light... Shall Turn to Darkness...

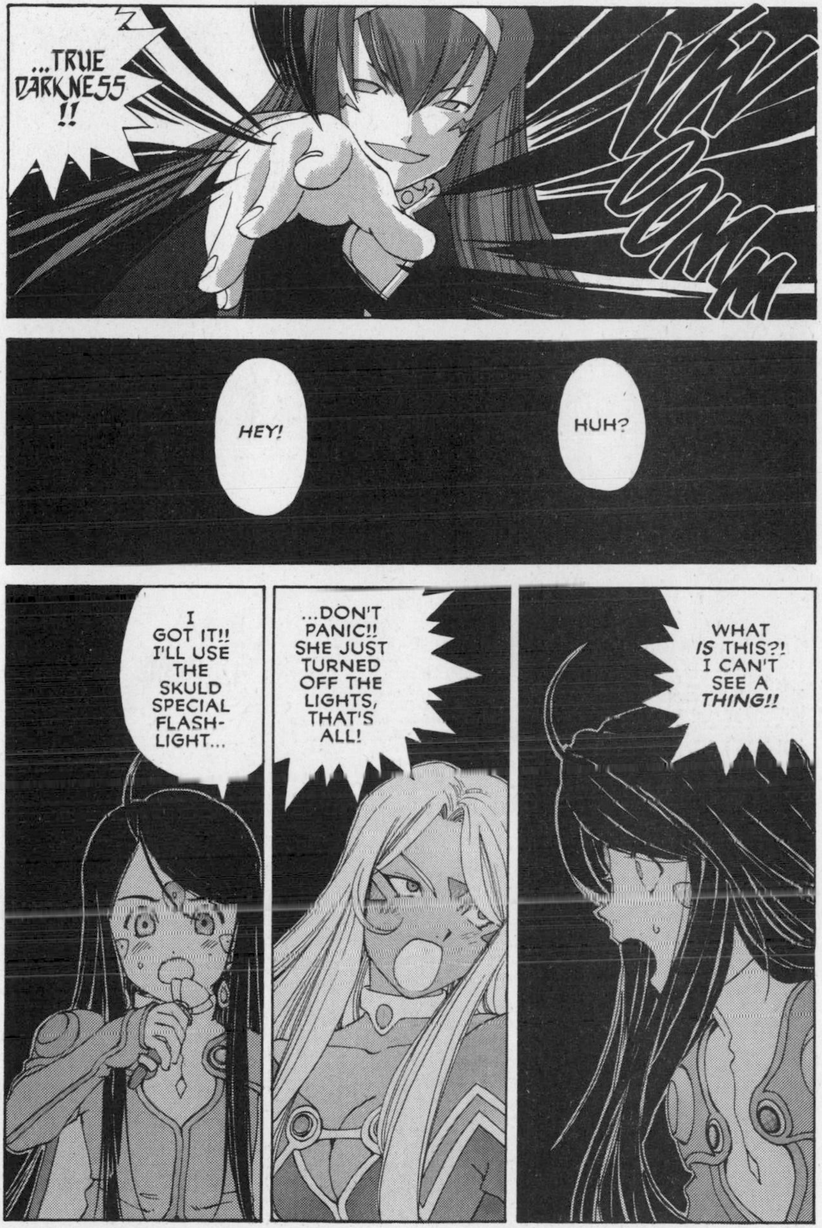
...TRUE DARKNESS!!
HUH?
HEY!
WHAT *IS* THIS?! I CAN'T SEE A *THING!!*
...DON'T PANIC!! SHE JUST TURNED OFF THE LIGHTS, THAT'S ALL!
I GOT IT!! I'LL USE THE SKULD SPECIAL FLASH-LIGHT...

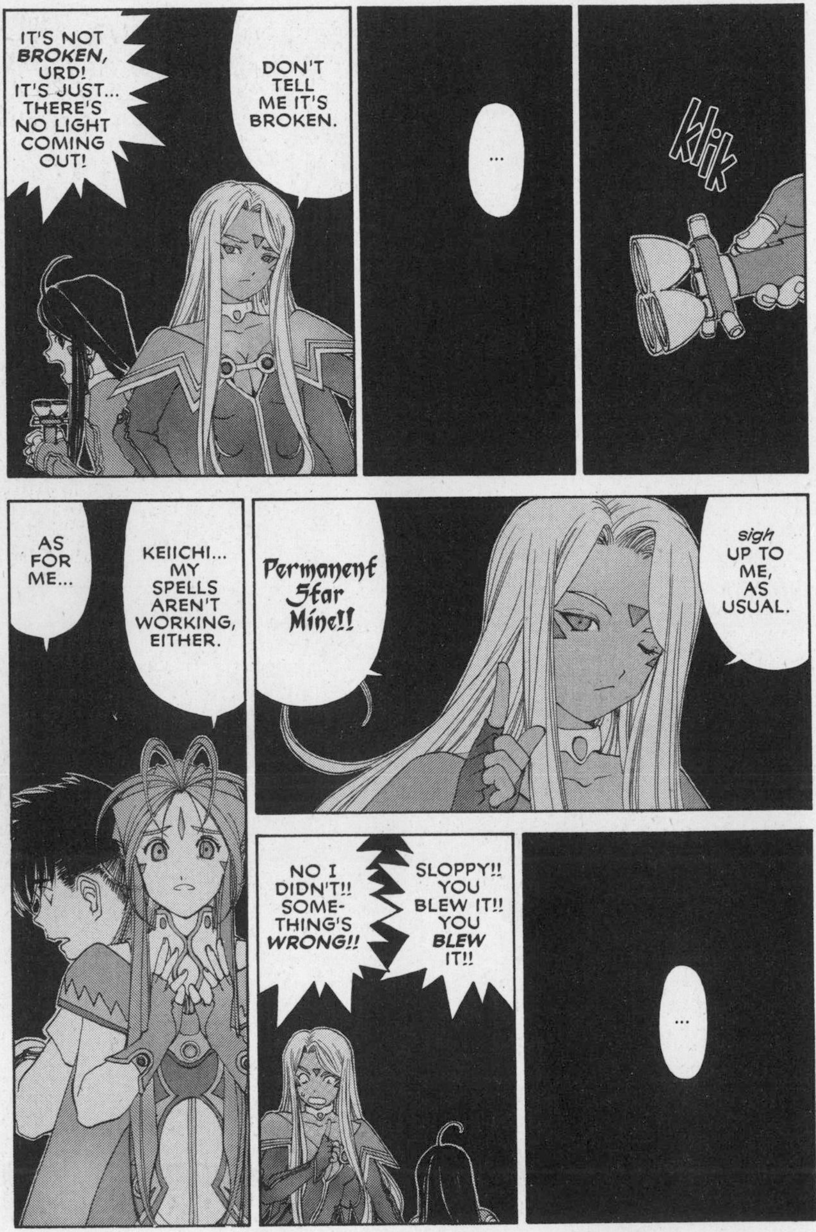
klik
...
DON'T TELL ME IT'S BROKEN.
IT'S NOT BROKEN, URD! IT'S JUST... THERE'S NO LIGHT COMING OUT!
sigh UP TO ME, AS USUAL.
Permanent Star Mine!!
...
SLOPPY!! YOU BLEW IT!! YOU BLEW IT!!
NO I DIDN'T!! SOME-THING'S WRONG!!
KEIICHI... MY SPELLS AREN'T WORKING, EITHER.
AS FOR ME...

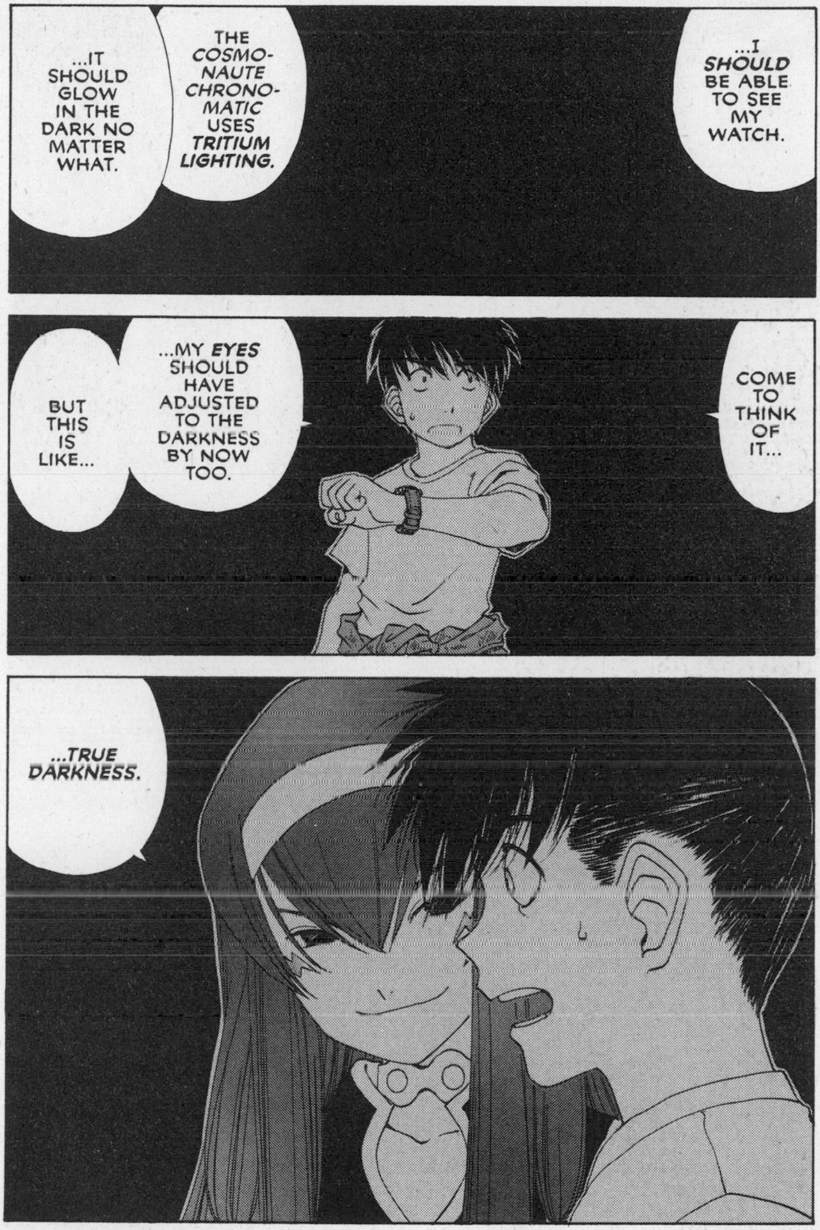
...I SHOULD BE ABLE TO SEE MY WATCH.
THE COSMONAUTE CHRONOMATIC USES TRITIUM LIGHTING.
...IT SHOULD GLOW IN THE DARK NO MATTER WHAT.
COME TO THINK OF IT...
...MY EYES SHOULD HAVE ADJUSTED TO THE DARKNESS BY NOW TOO.
BUT THIS IS LIKE...
...TRUE DARKNESS.

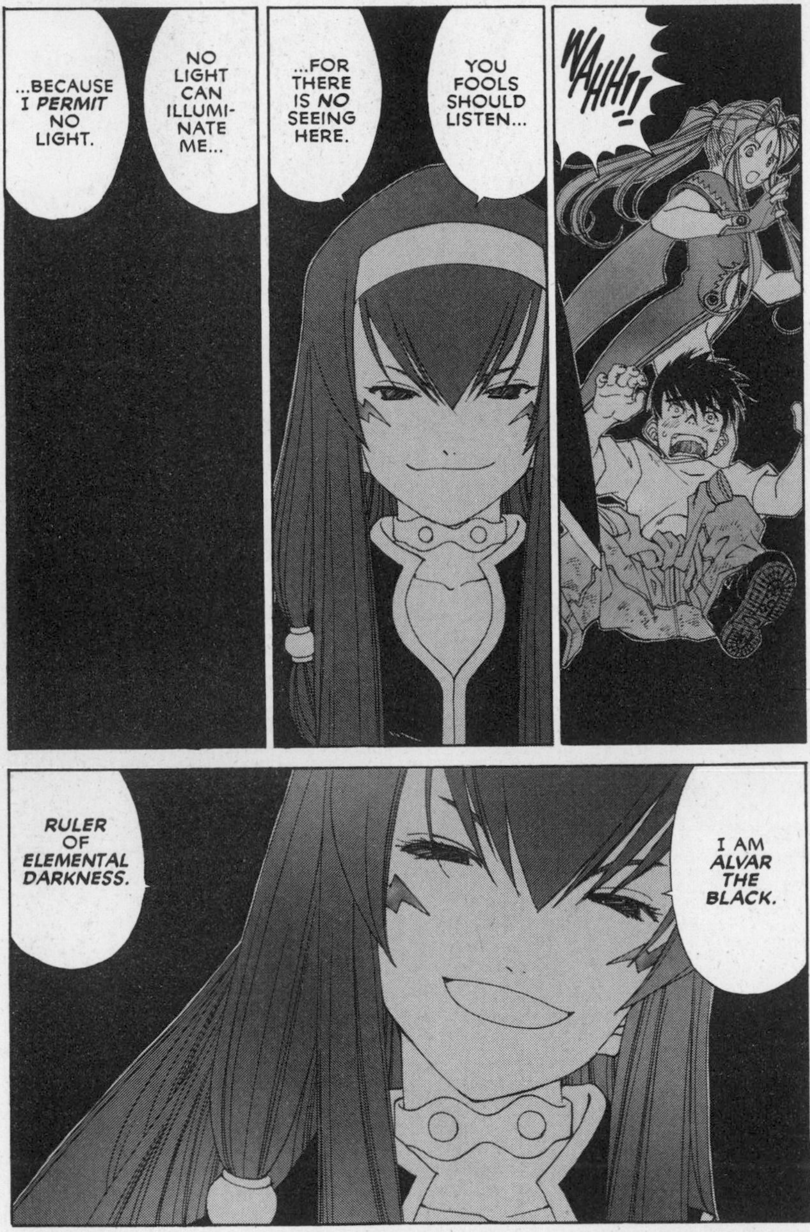
WAHHH!!
YOU FOOLS SHOULD LISTEN...
...FOR THERE IS NO SEEING HERE.
NO LIGHT CAN ILLUMINATE ME...
...BECAUSE I PERMIT NO LIGHT.
I AM ALVAR THE BLACK.
RULER OF ELEMENTAL DARKNESS.

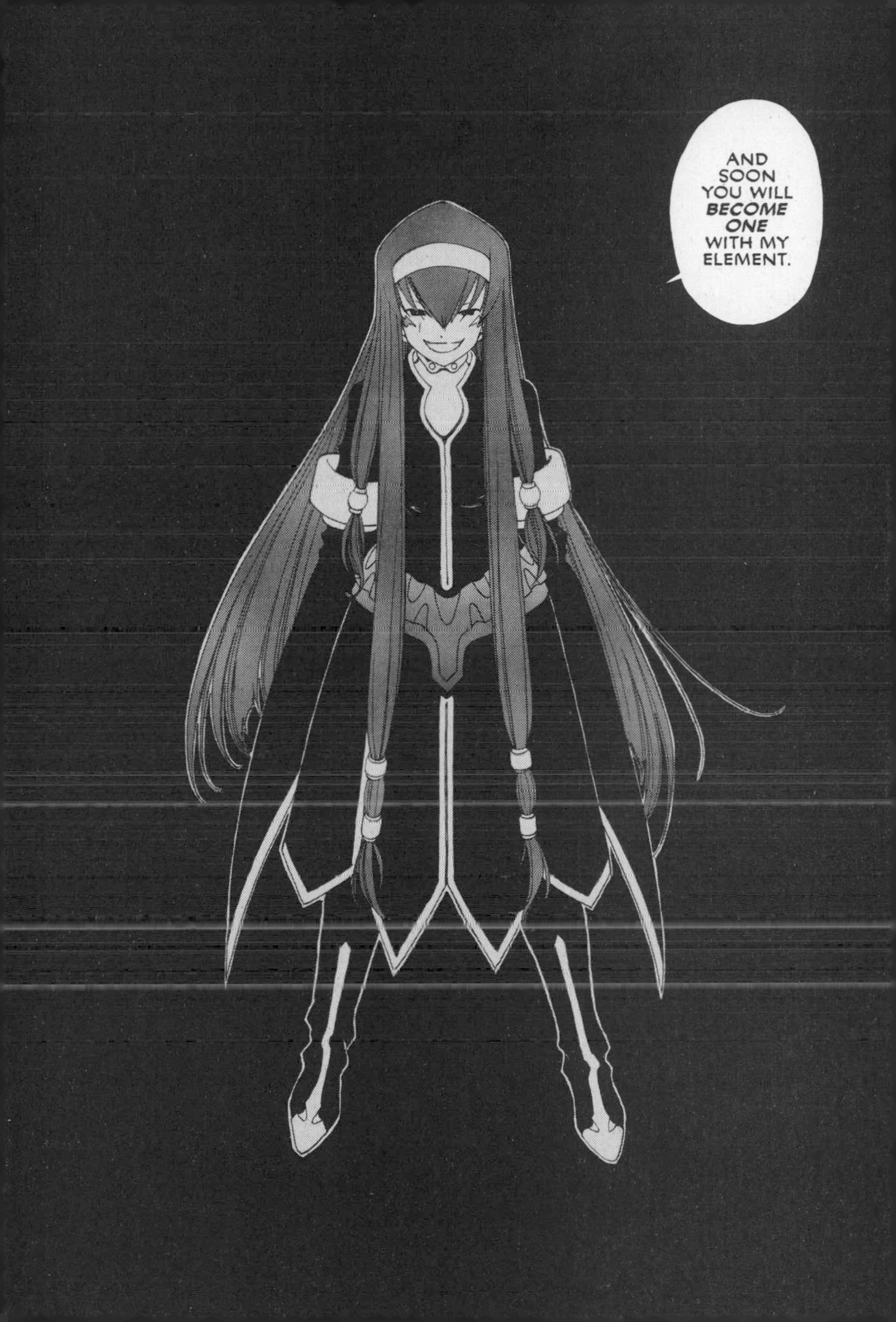
AND SOON YOU WILL ***BECOME ONE*** WITH MY ELEMENT.

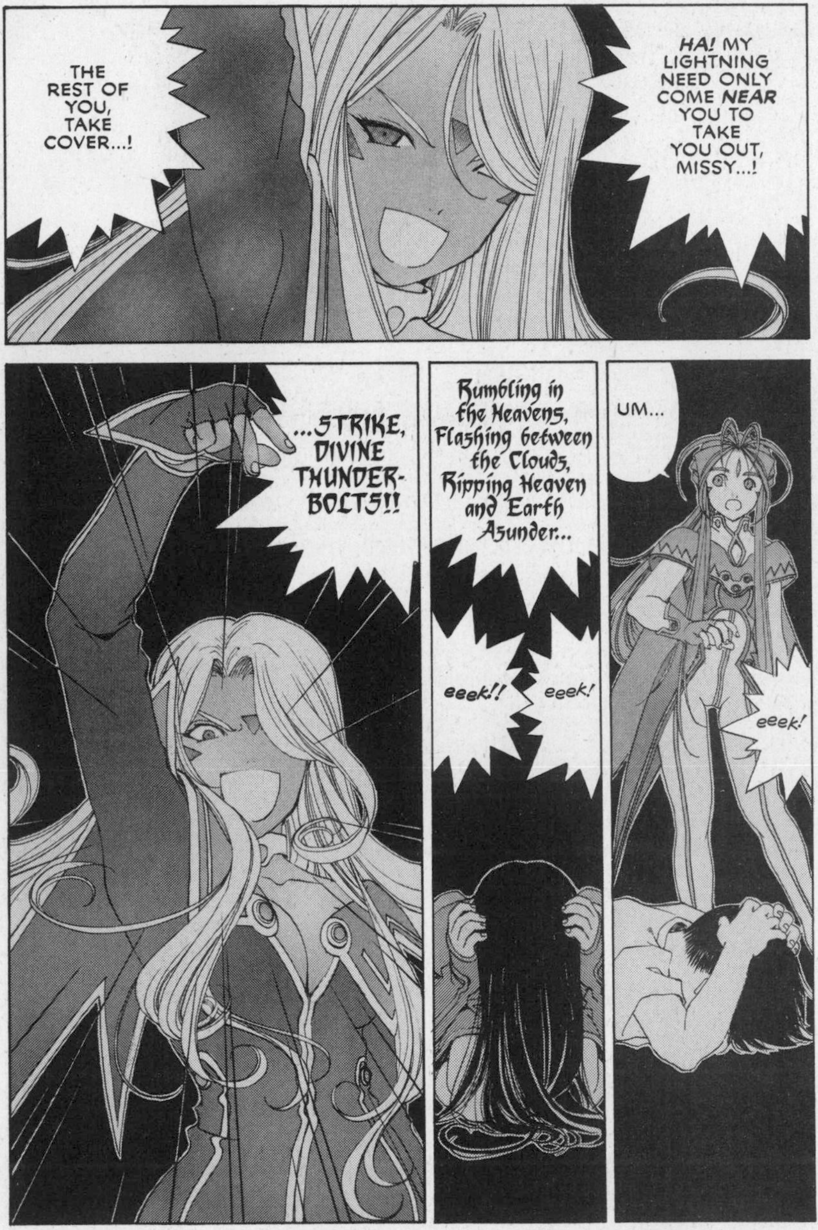
HA! MY LIGHTNING NEED ONLY COME NEAR YOU TO TAKE YOU OUT, MISSY...!
THE REST OF YOU, TAKE COVER...!
UM...
eeek!
Rumbling in the Heavens, Flashing between the Clouds, Ripping Heaven and Earth Asunder...
eeek!
eeek!!
...STRIKE, DIVINE THUNDER-BOLTS!!

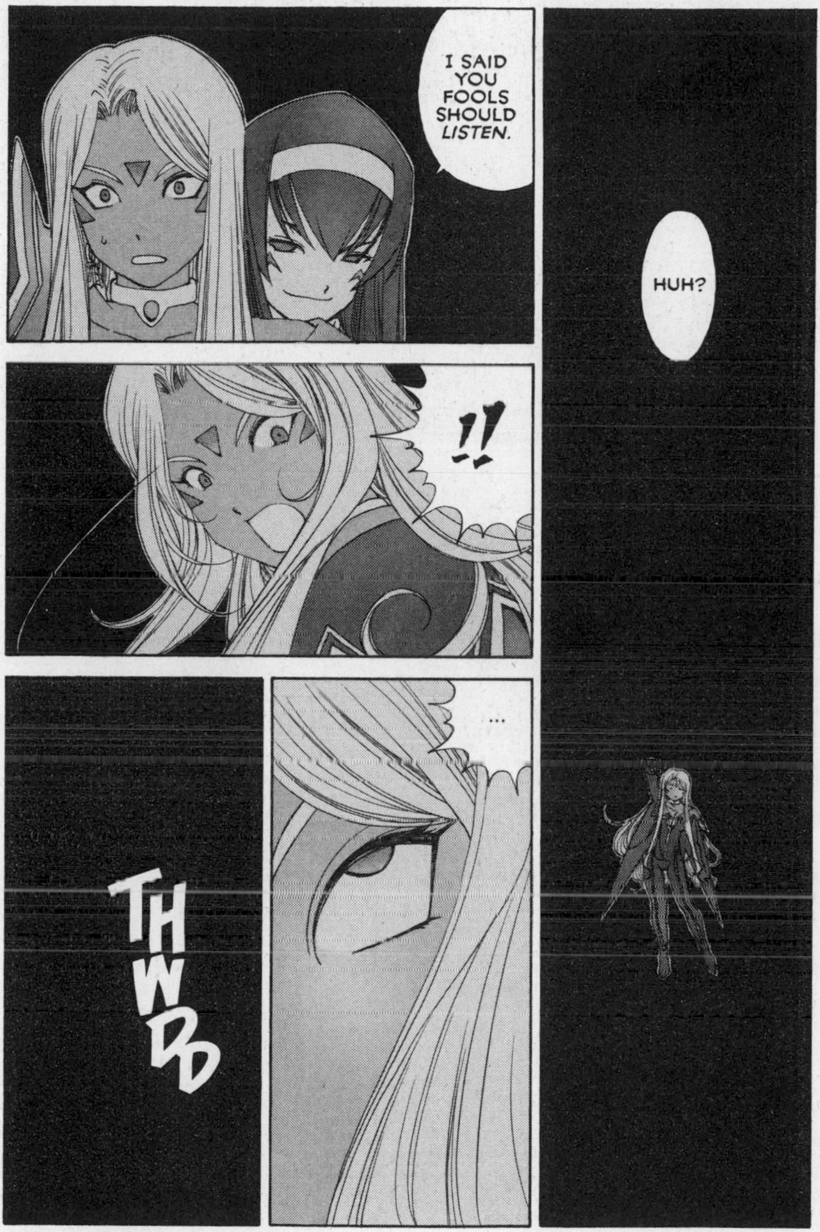

HUH?
I SAID YOU FOOLS SHOULD *LISTEN.*
!!
...
THWDD

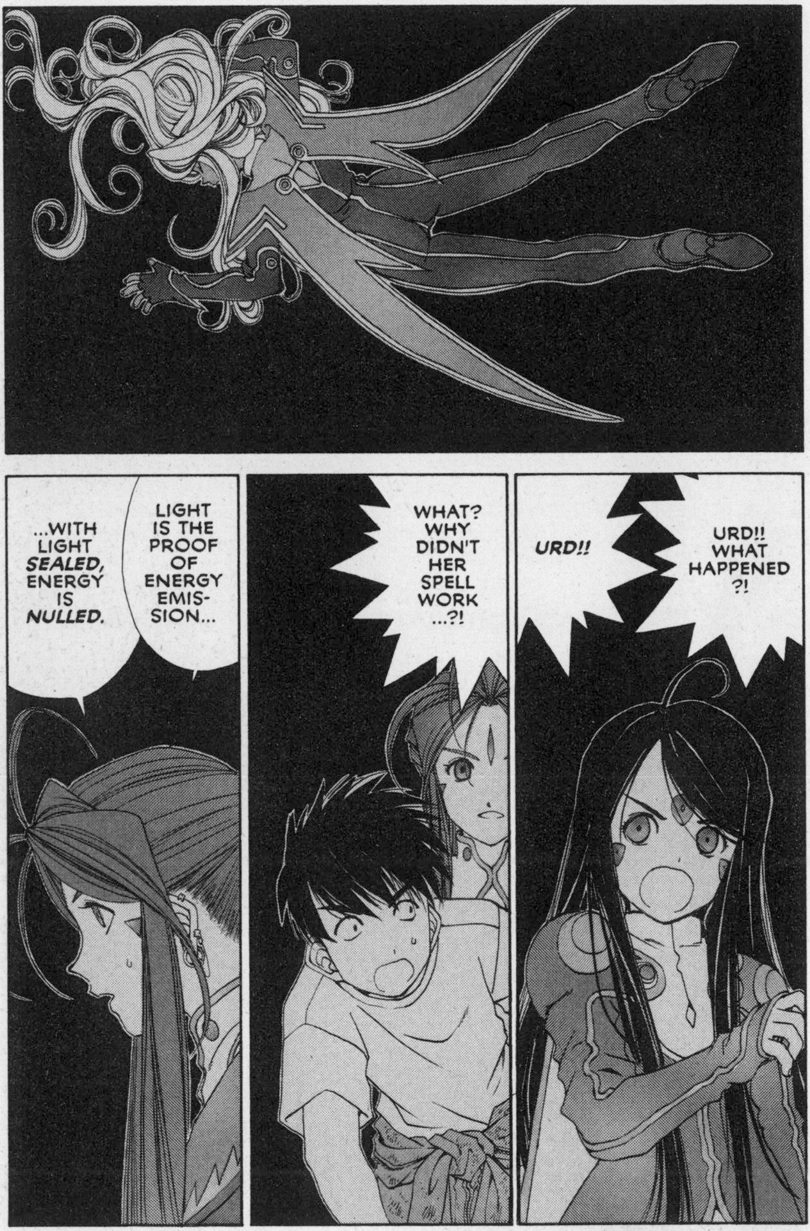
URD!! WHAT HAPPENED ?!
URD!!
WHAT? WHY DIDN'T HER SPELL WORK ...?!
LIGHT IS THE PROOF OF ENERGY EMIS-SION...
...WITH LIGHT SEALED, ENERGY IS NULLED.

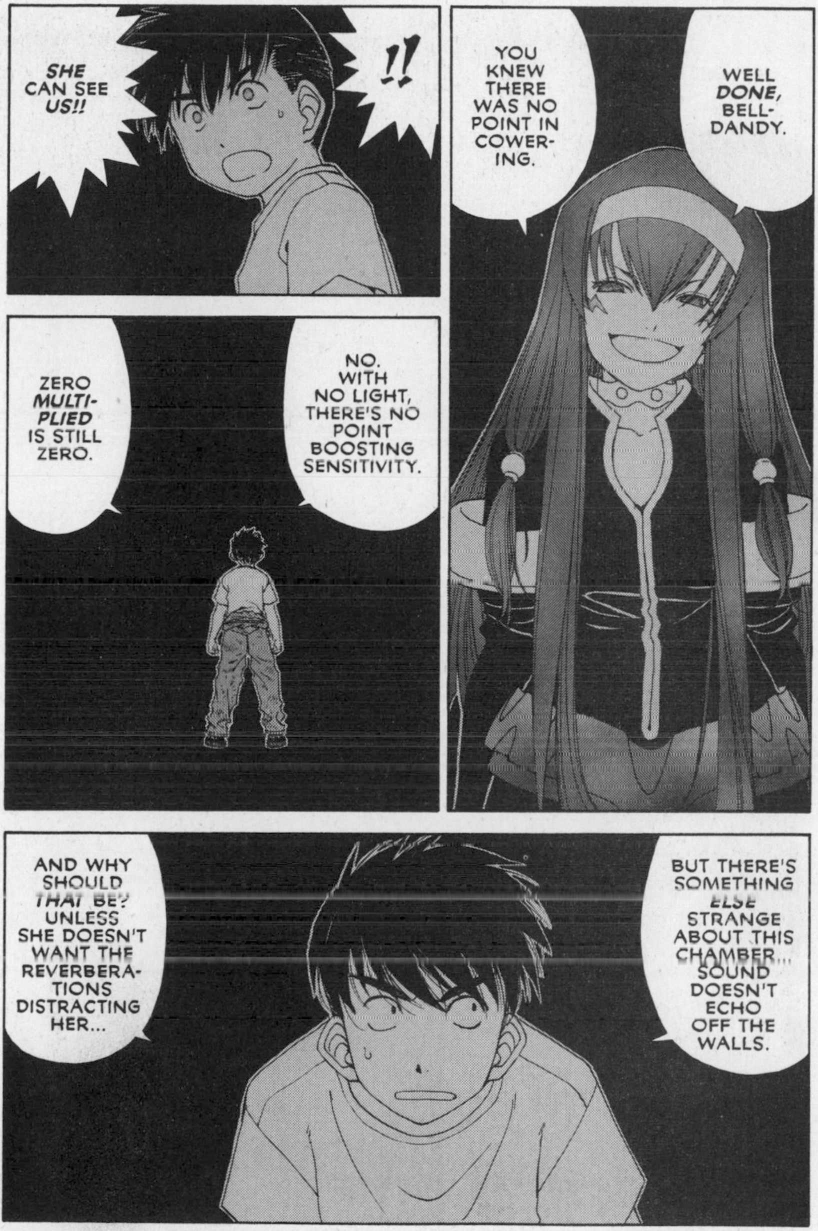
WELL DONE, BELL-DANDY.
YOU KNEW THERE WAS NO POINT IN COWER-ING.
!!
SHE CAN SEE US!!
NO. WITH NO LIGHT, THERE'S NO POINT BOOSTING SENSITIVITY.
ZERO MULTI-PLIED IS STILL ZERO.
BUT THERE'S SOMETHING ELSE STRANGE ABOUT THIS CHAMBER... SOUND DOESN'T ECHO OFF THE WALLS.
AND WHY SHOULD THAT BE? UNLESS SHE DOESN'T WANT THE REVERBERA-TIONS DISTRACTING HER...

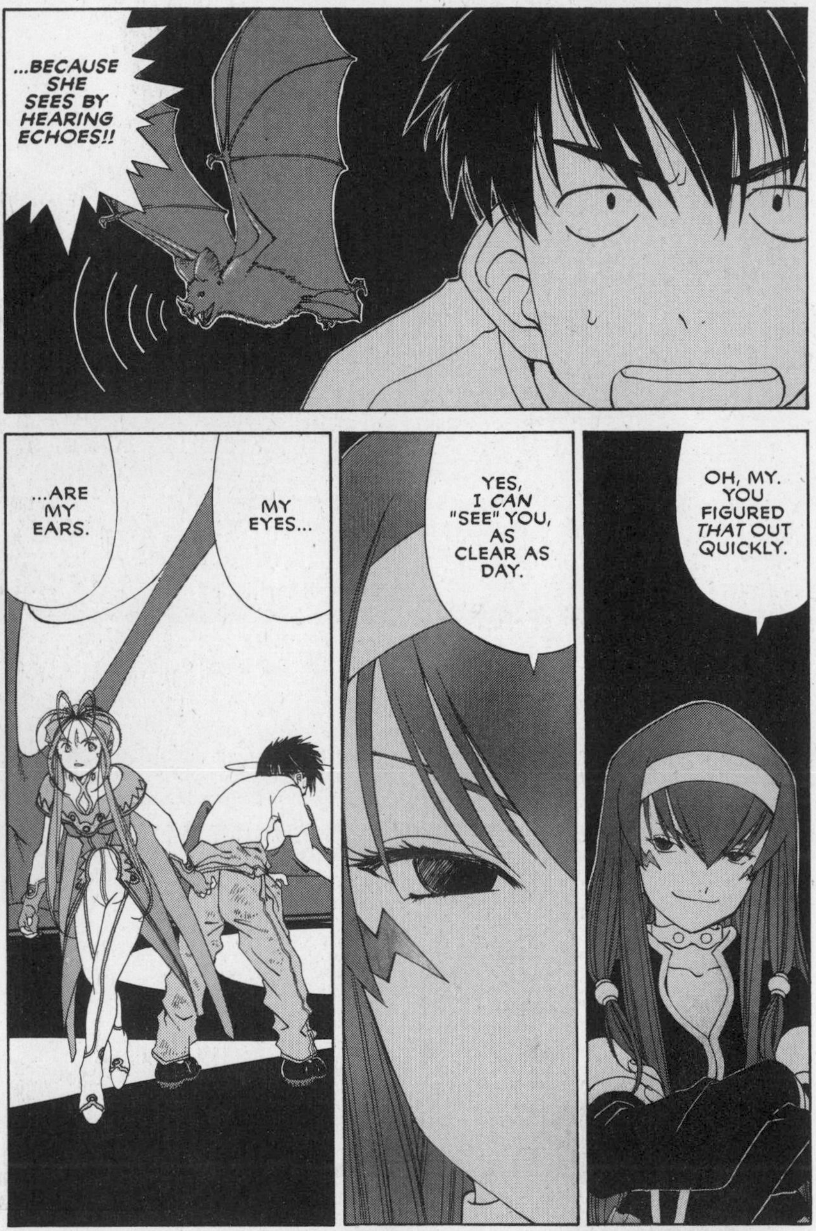
...BECAUSE SHE SEES BY HEARING ECHOES!!
OH, MY. YOU FIGURED *THAT* OUT QUICKLY.
YES, I *CAN* "SEE" YOU, AS CLEAR AS DAY.
MY EYES...
...ARE MY EARS.

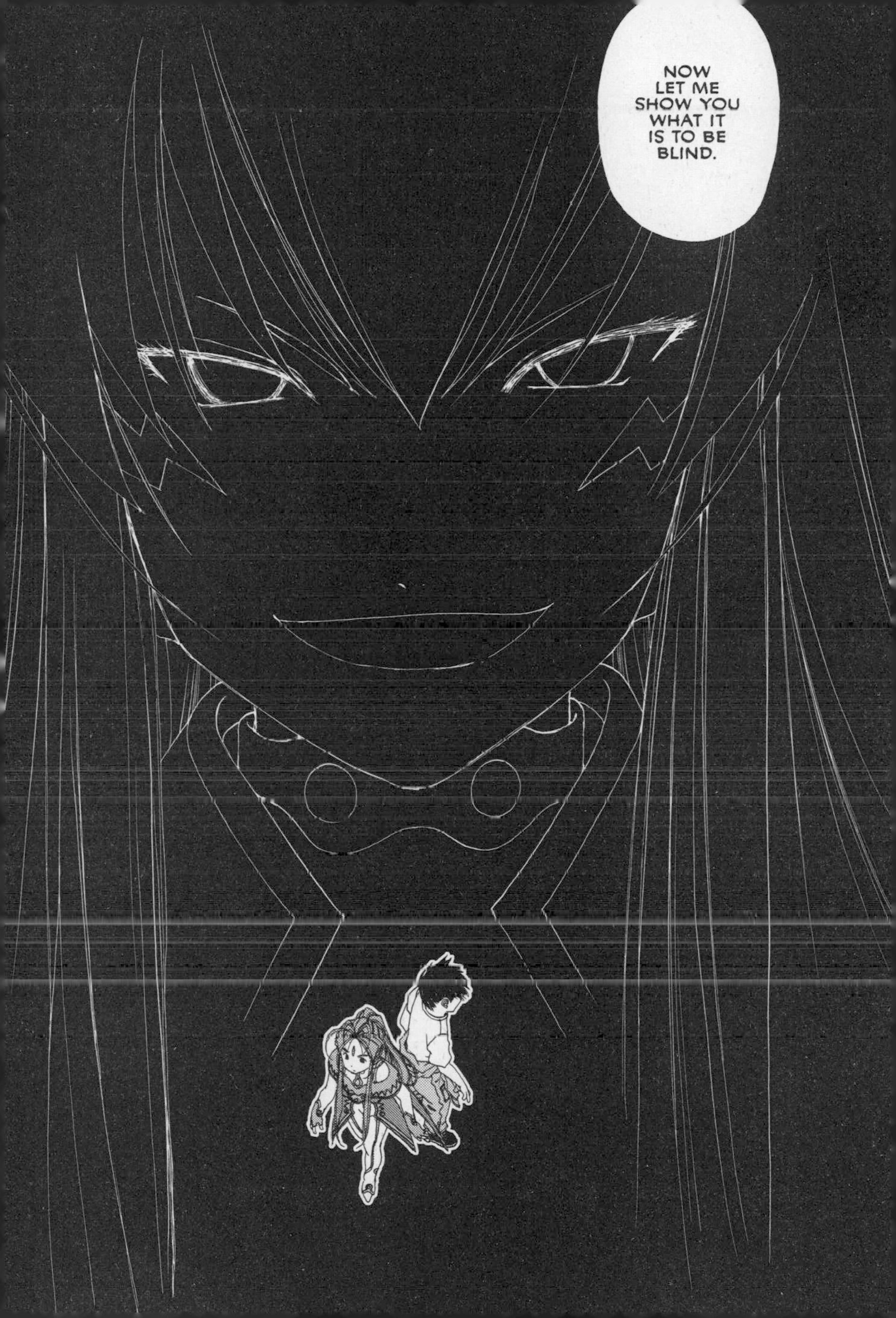
NOW LET ME SHOW YOU WHAT IT IS TO BE BLIND.

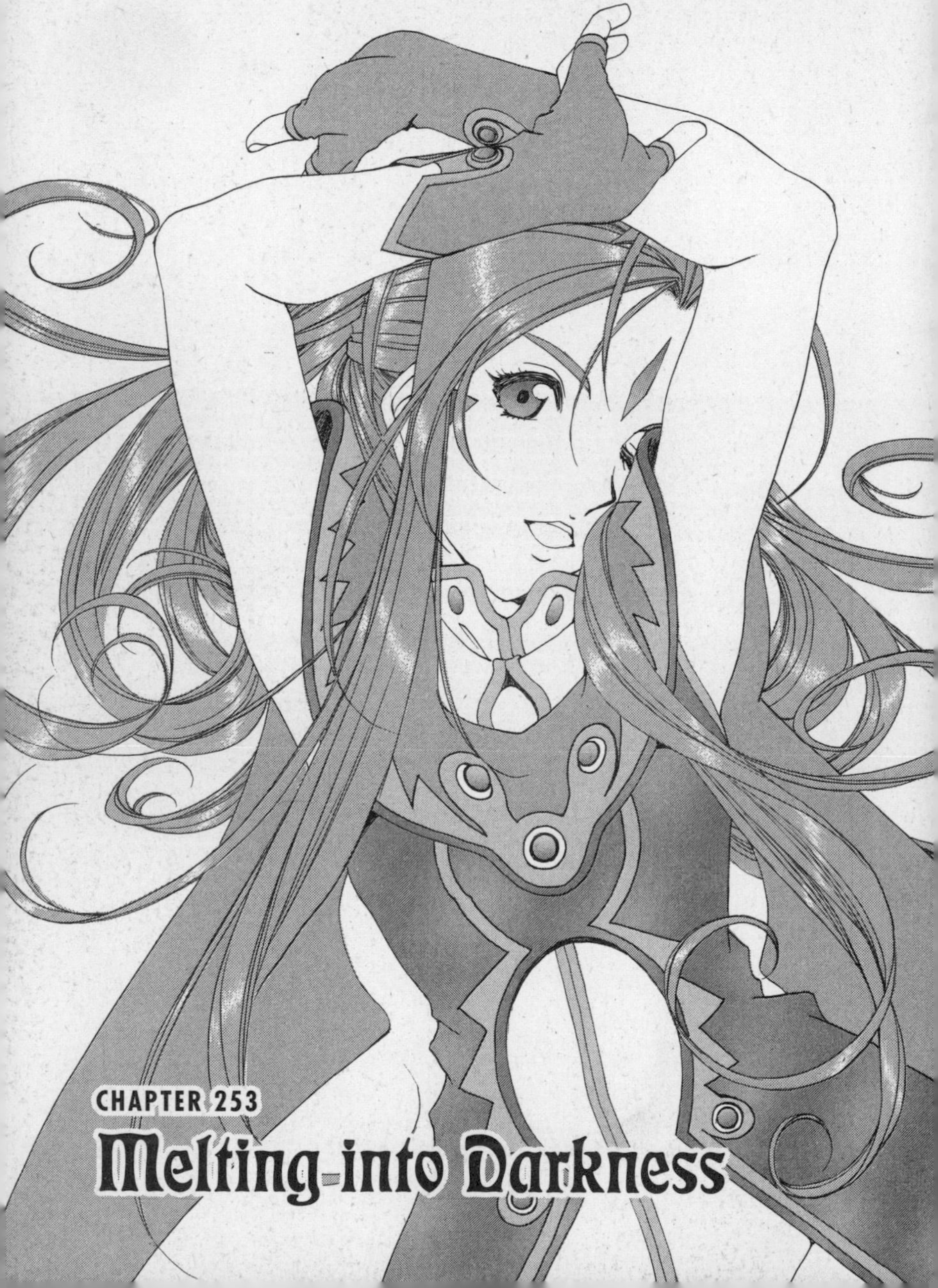

CHAPTER 253

Melting into Darkness

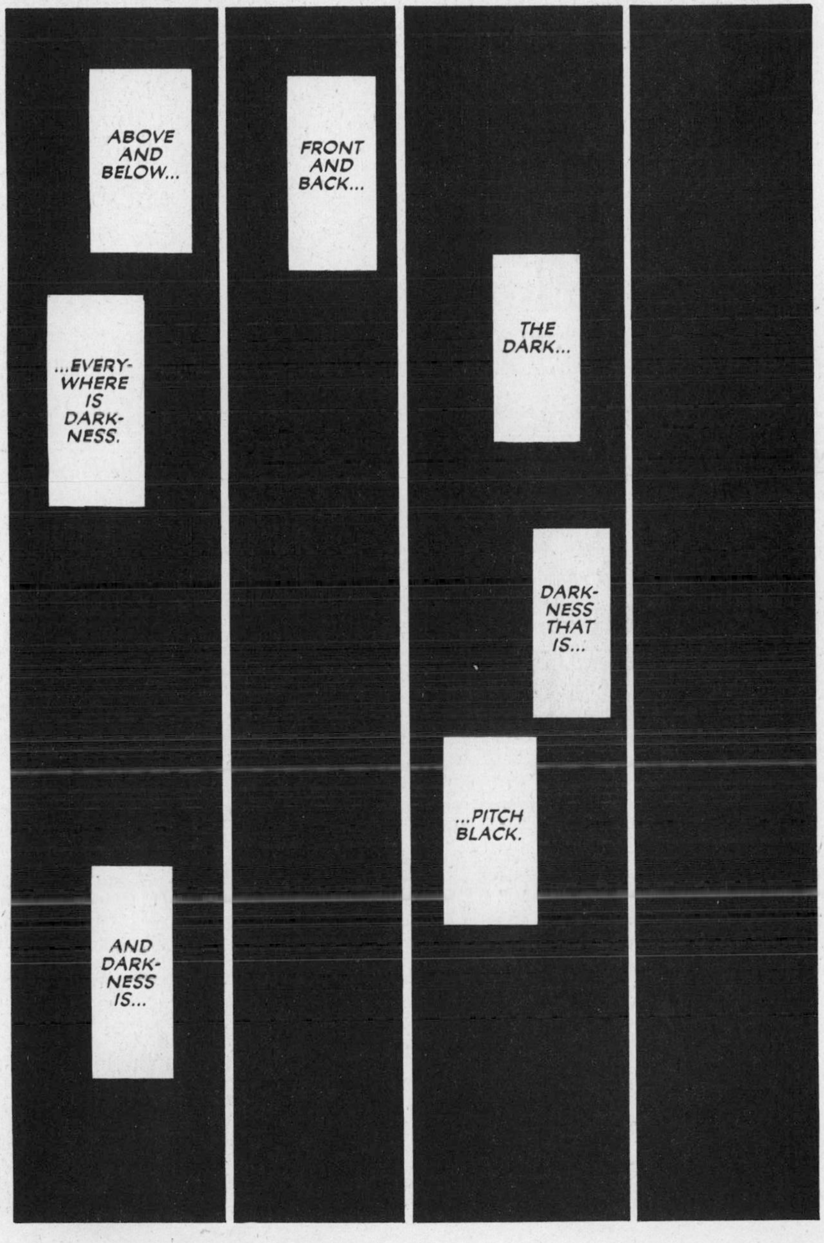
ABOVE AND BELOW...
FRONT AND BACK...
...EVERYWHERE IS DARKNESS.
AND DARKNESS IS...
THE DARK...
DARKNESS THAT IS...
...PITCH BLACK.

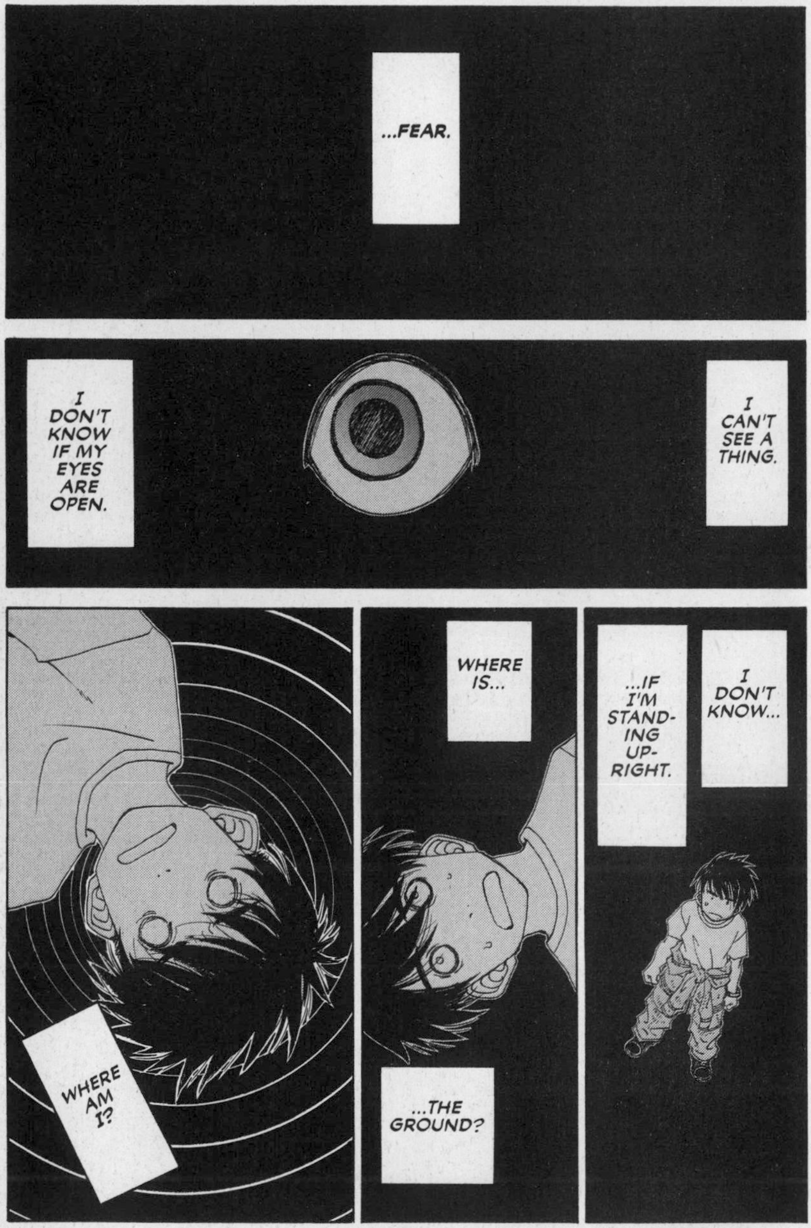
...FEAR.
I CAN'T SEE A THING.
I DON'T KNOW IF MY EYES ARE OPEN.
I DON'T KNOW...
...IF I'M STANDING UPRIGHT.
WHERE IS...
...THE GROUND?
WHERE AM I?

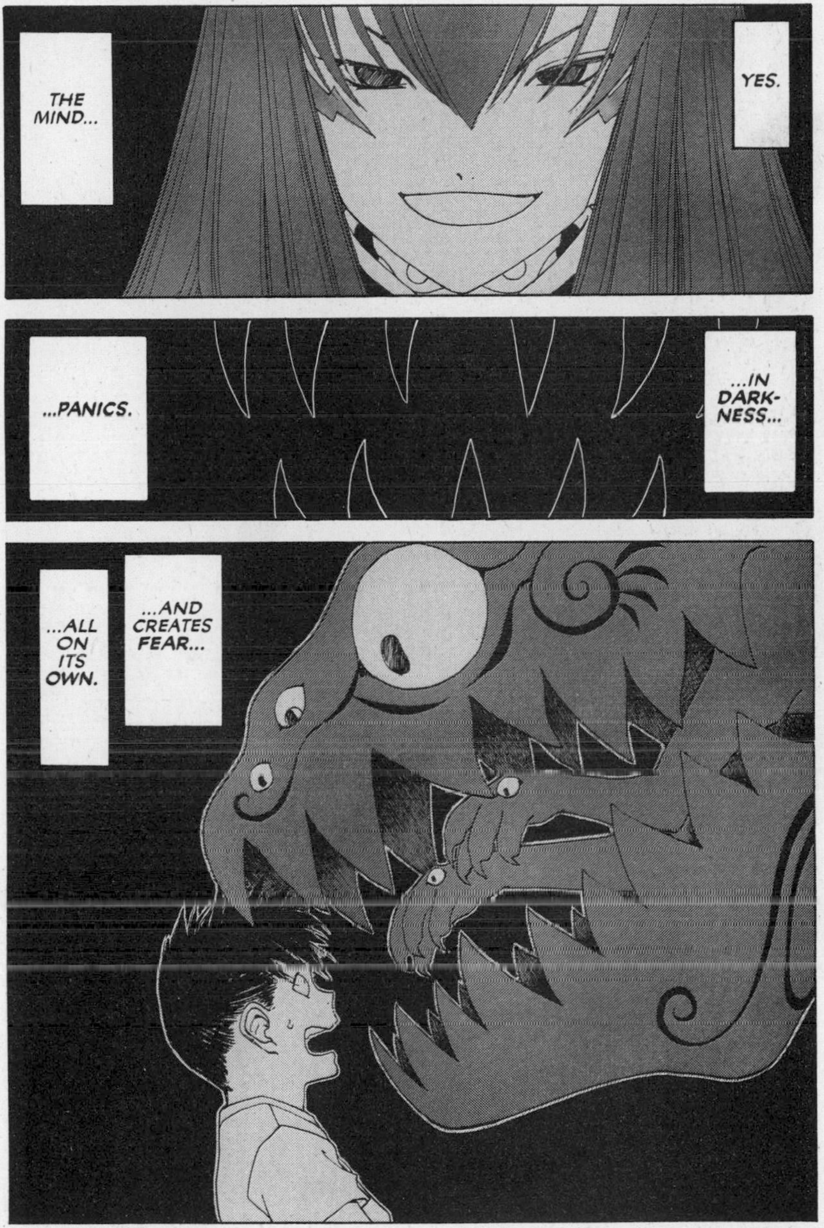
YES.
THE MIND...
...IN DARKNESS...
...PANICS.
...AND CREATES FEAR...
...ALL ON ITS OWN.

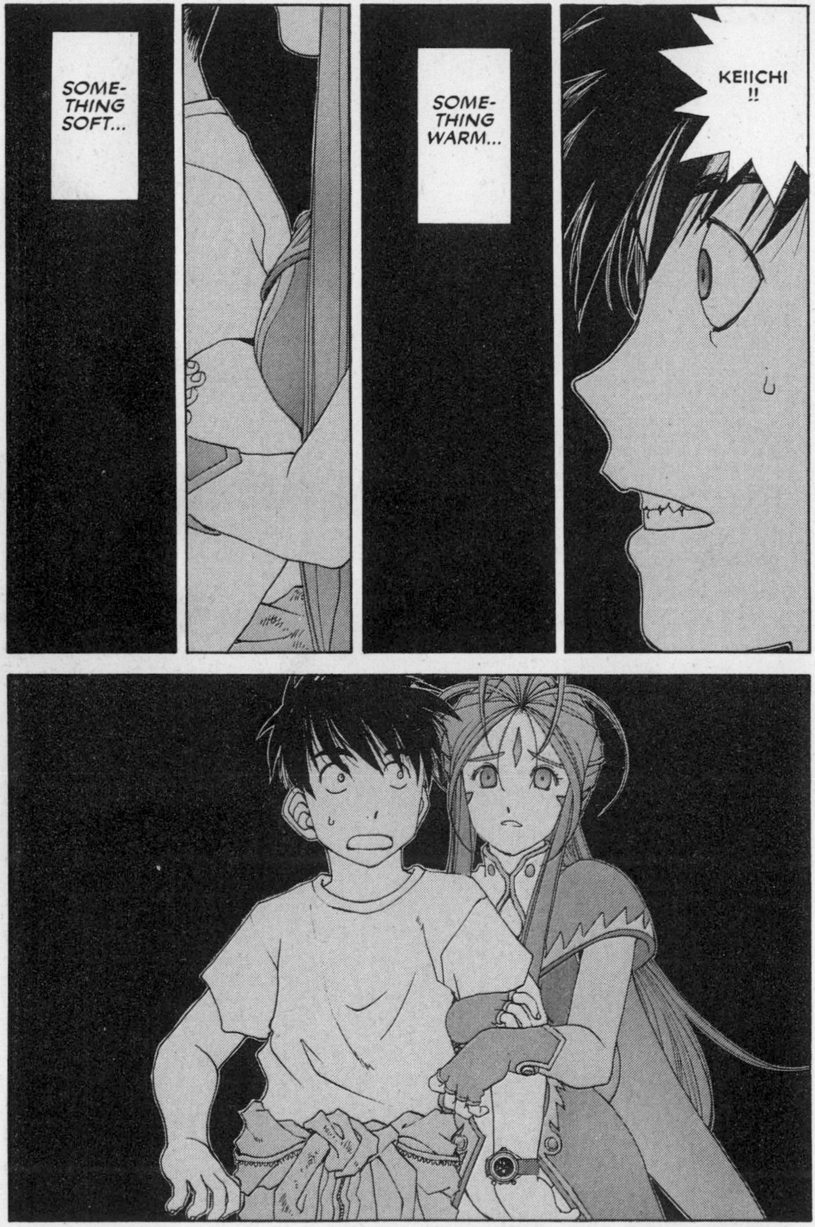
KEIICHI !!
SOME-THING WARM...
SOME-THING SOFT...

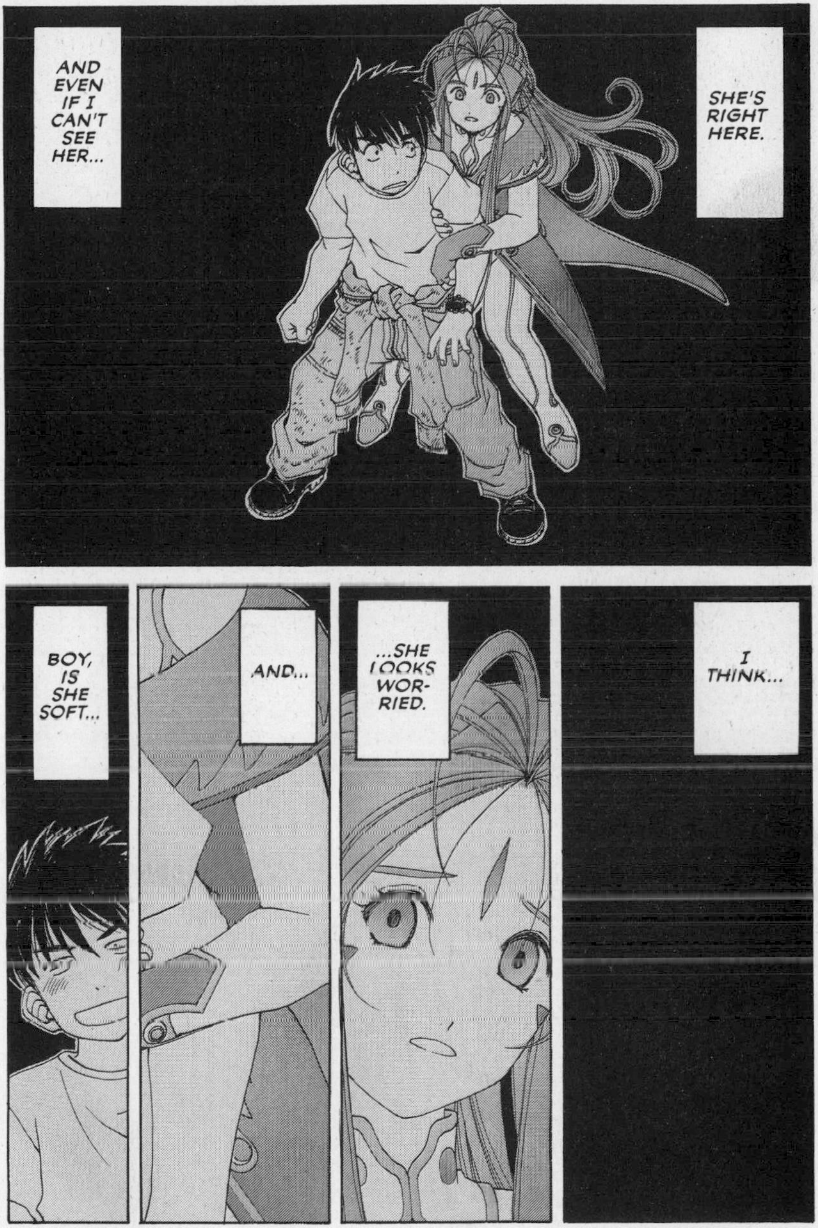
SHE'S RIGHT HERE.
AND EVEN IF I CAN'T SEE HER...
I THINK...
...SHE LOOKS WOR-RIED.
AND...
BOY, IS SHE SOFT...

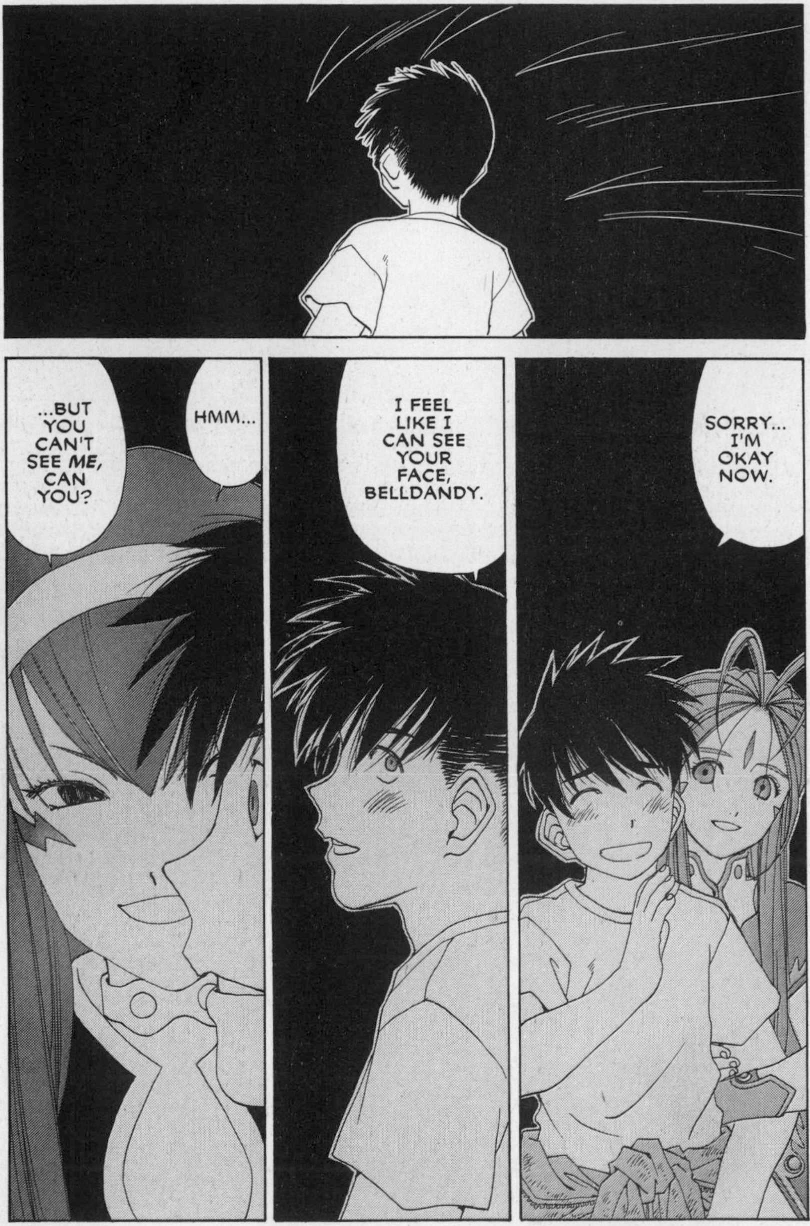
SORRY... I'M OKAY NOW.
I FEEL LIKE I CAN SEE YOUR FACE, BELLDANDY.
HMM...
...BUT YOU CAN'T SEE *ME*, CAN YOU?

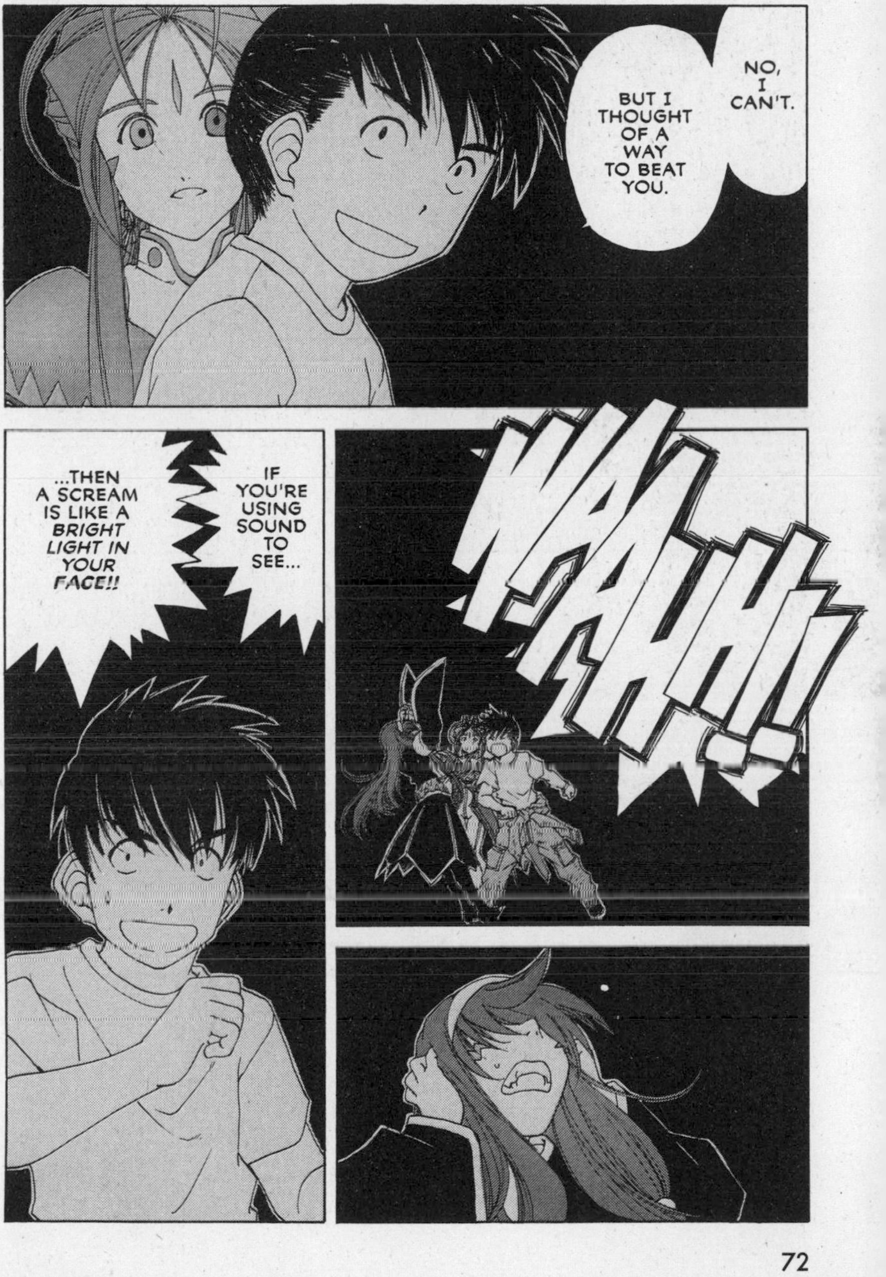
NO, I CAN'T.
BUT I THOUGHT OF A WAY TO BEAT YOU.
WAAAH!!
IF YOU'RE USING SOUND TO SEE...
...THEN A SCREAM IS LIKE A *BRIGHT LIGHT IN YOUR FACE!!*

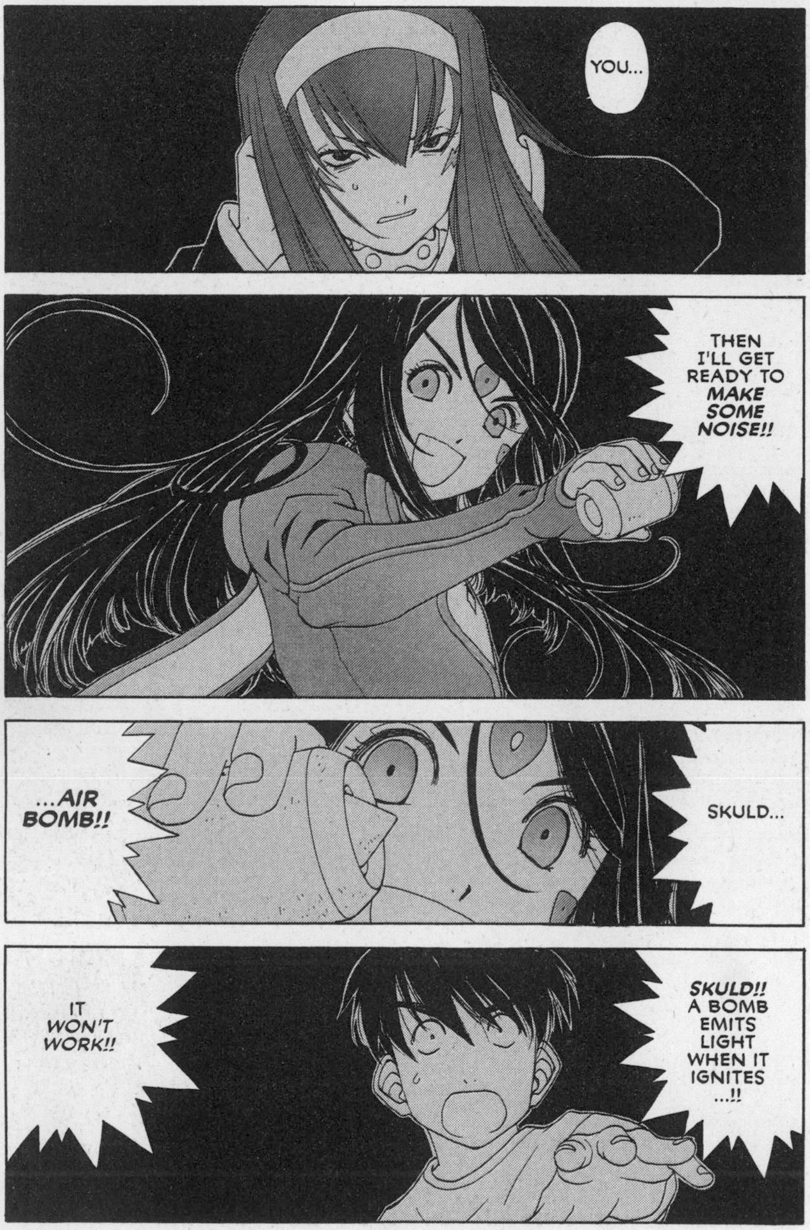
YOU...
THEN I'LL GET READY TO *MAKE SOME NOISE!!*
SKULD...
...AIR BOMB!!
SKULD!! A BOMB EMITS LIGHT WHEN IT IGNITES ...!!
IT *WON'T WORK!!*

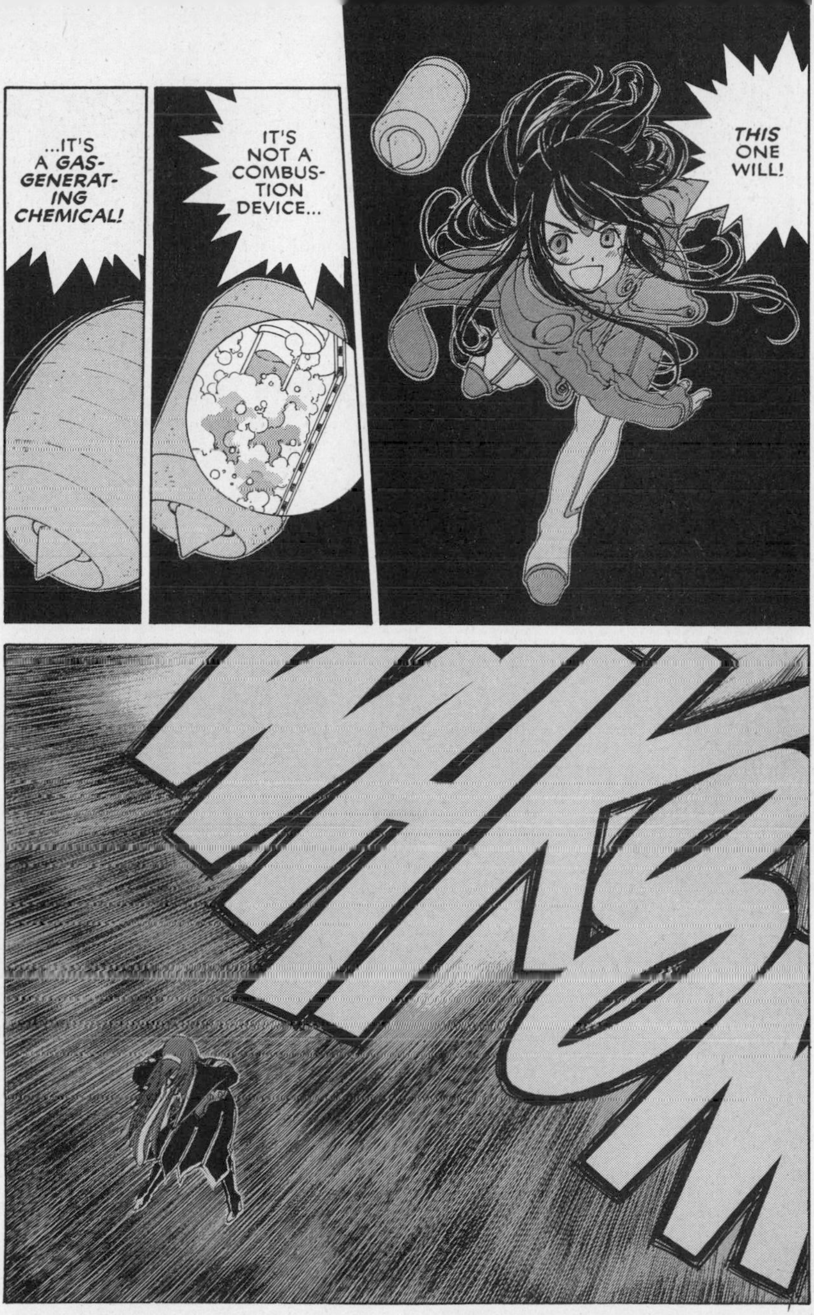
THIS ONE WILL!
IT'S NOT A COMBUSTION DEVICE...
...IT'S A GAS-GENERATING CHEMICAL!

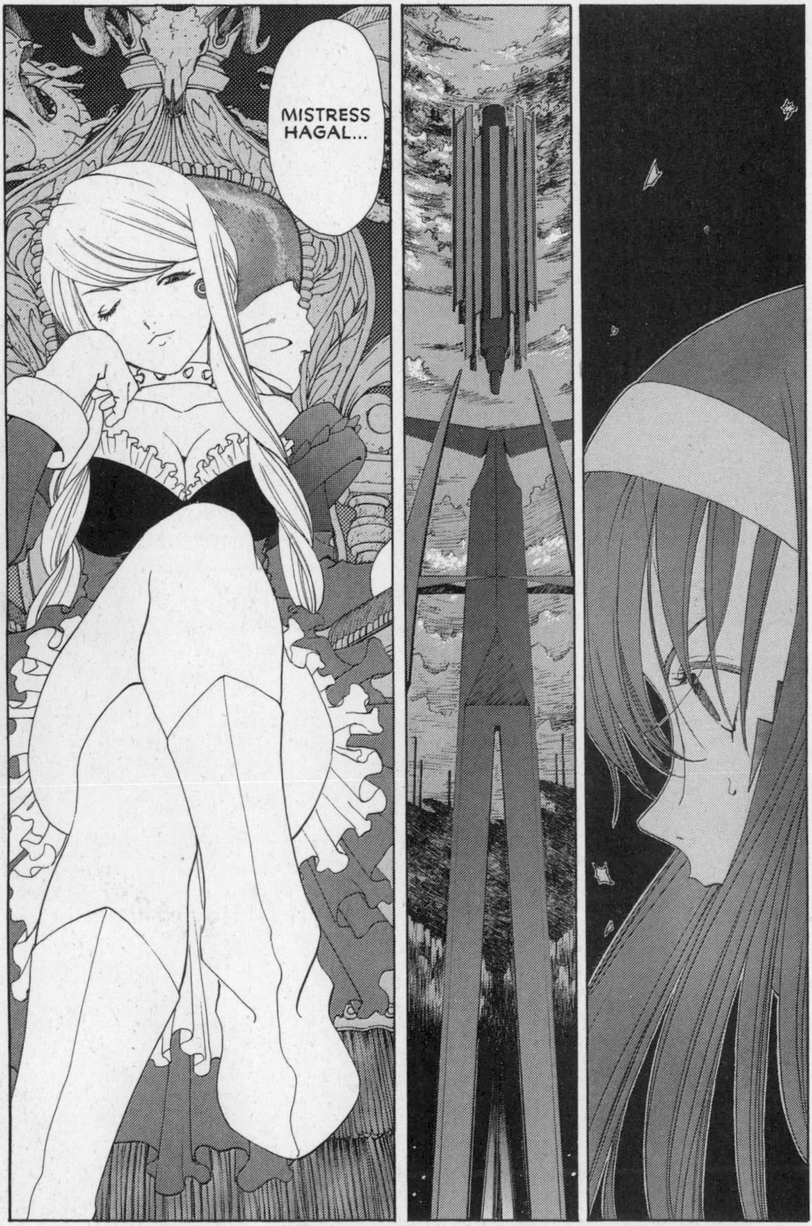
MISTRESS HAGAL...

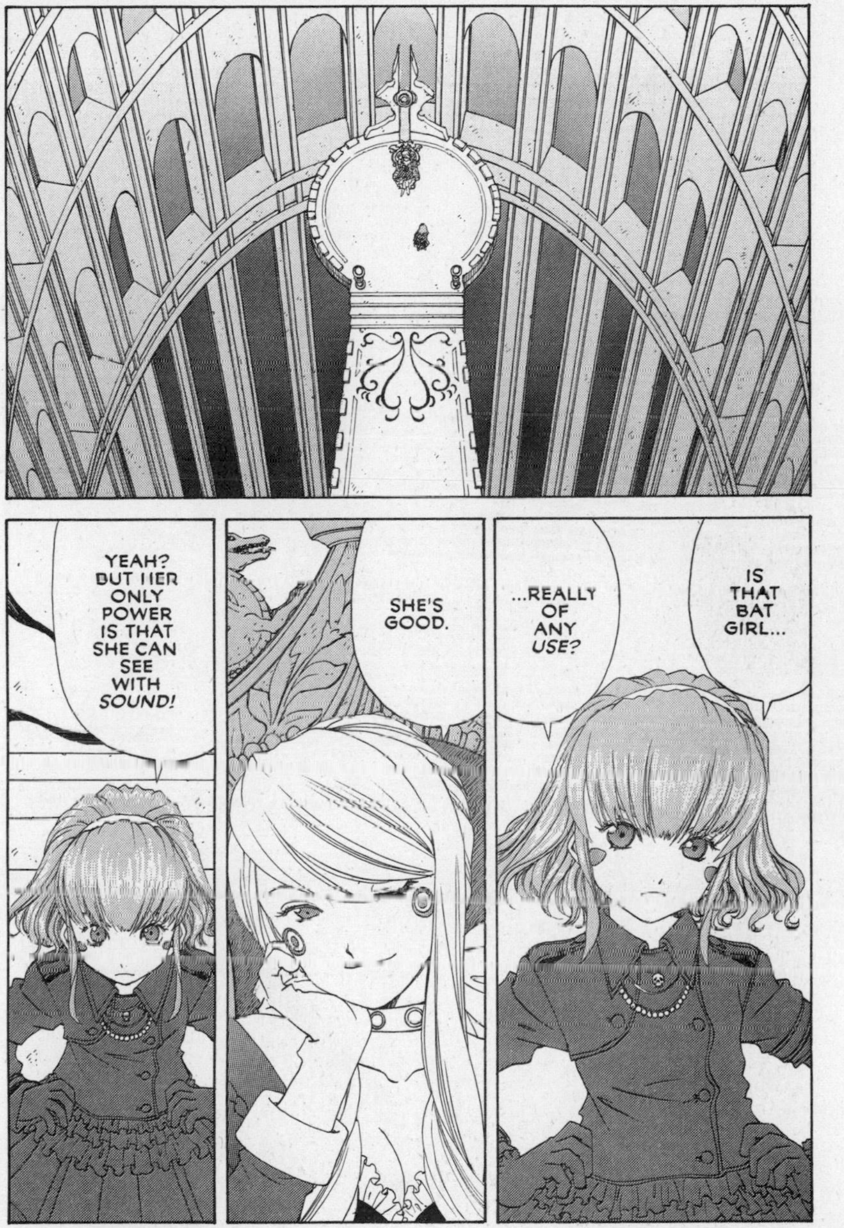
IS THAT BAT GIRL...
...REALLY OF ANY *USE?*
SHE'S GOOD.
YEAH? BUT HER ONLY POWER IS THAT SHE CAN SEE WITH *SOUND!*

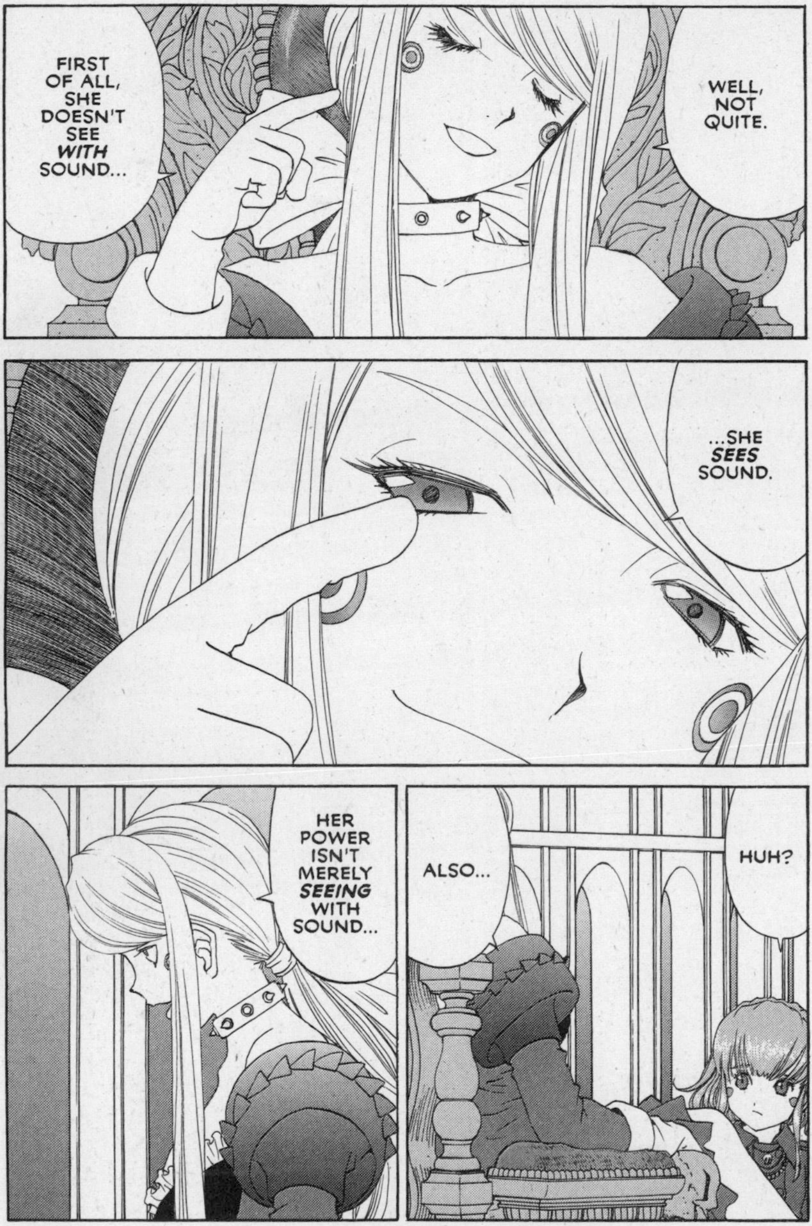
WELL, NOT QUITE.
FIRST OF ALL, SHE DOESN'T SEE *WITH* SOUND...
...SHE *SEES* SOUND.
HUH?
ALSO...
HER POWER ISN'T MERELY *SEEING* WITH SOUND...

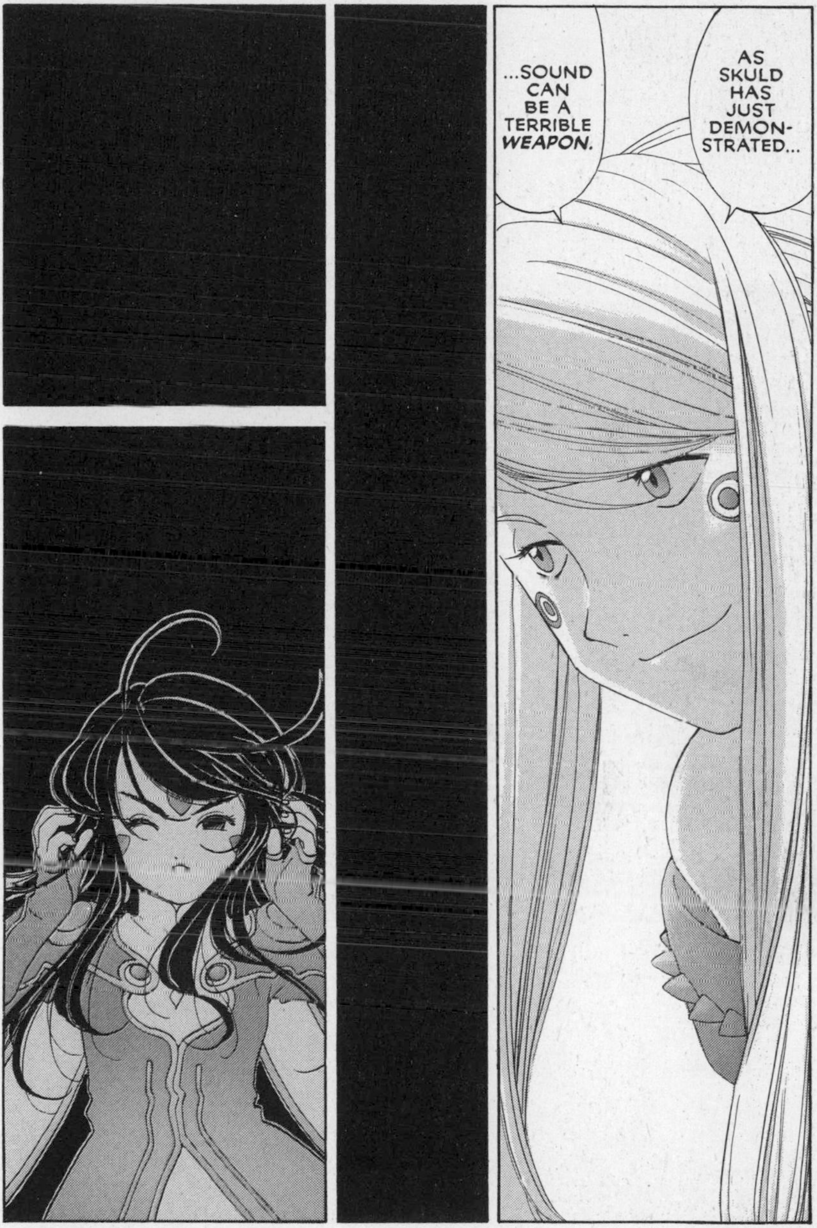
AS SKULD HAS JUST DEMON-STRATED...
...SOUND CAN BE A TERRIBLE *WEAPON.*

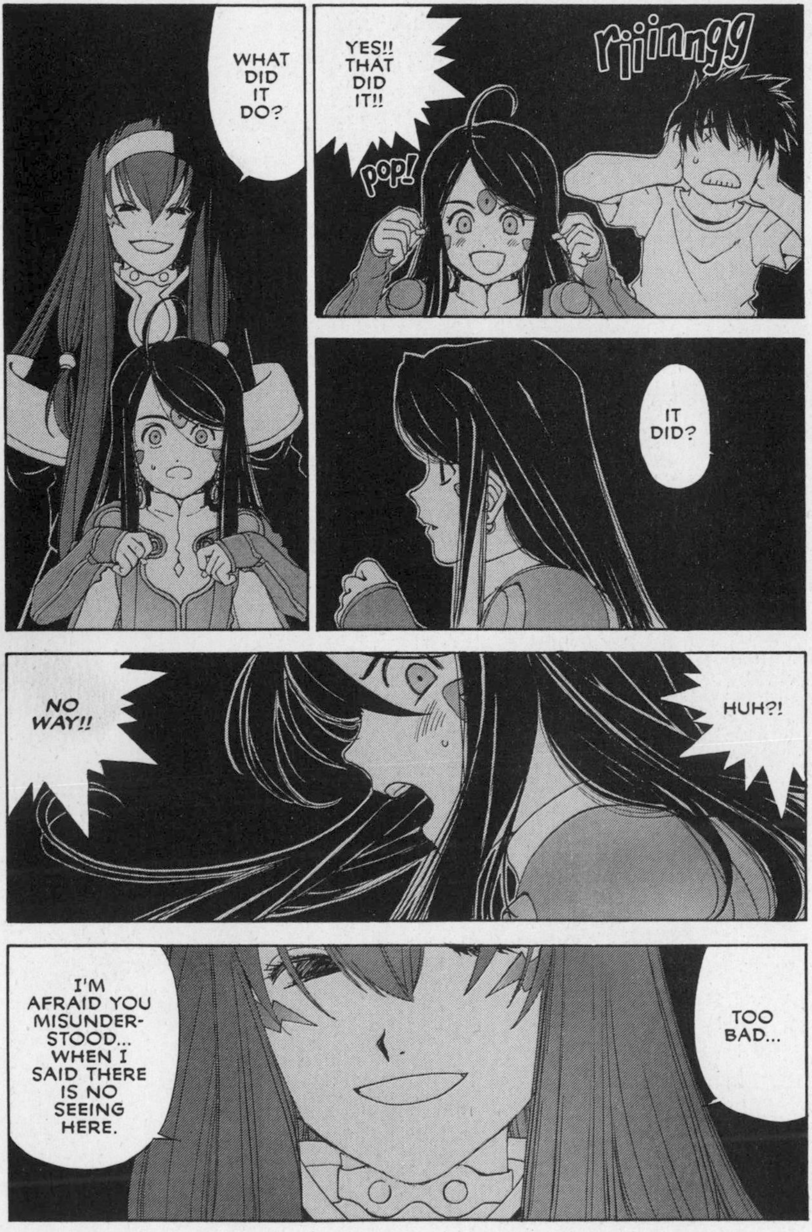
riiinngg
YES!! THAT DID IT!!
pop!
IT DID?
WHAT DID IT DO?
HUH?!
NO WAY!!
TOO BAD...
I'M AFRAID YOU MISUNDER-STOOD... WHEN I SAID THERE IS NO SEEING HERE.

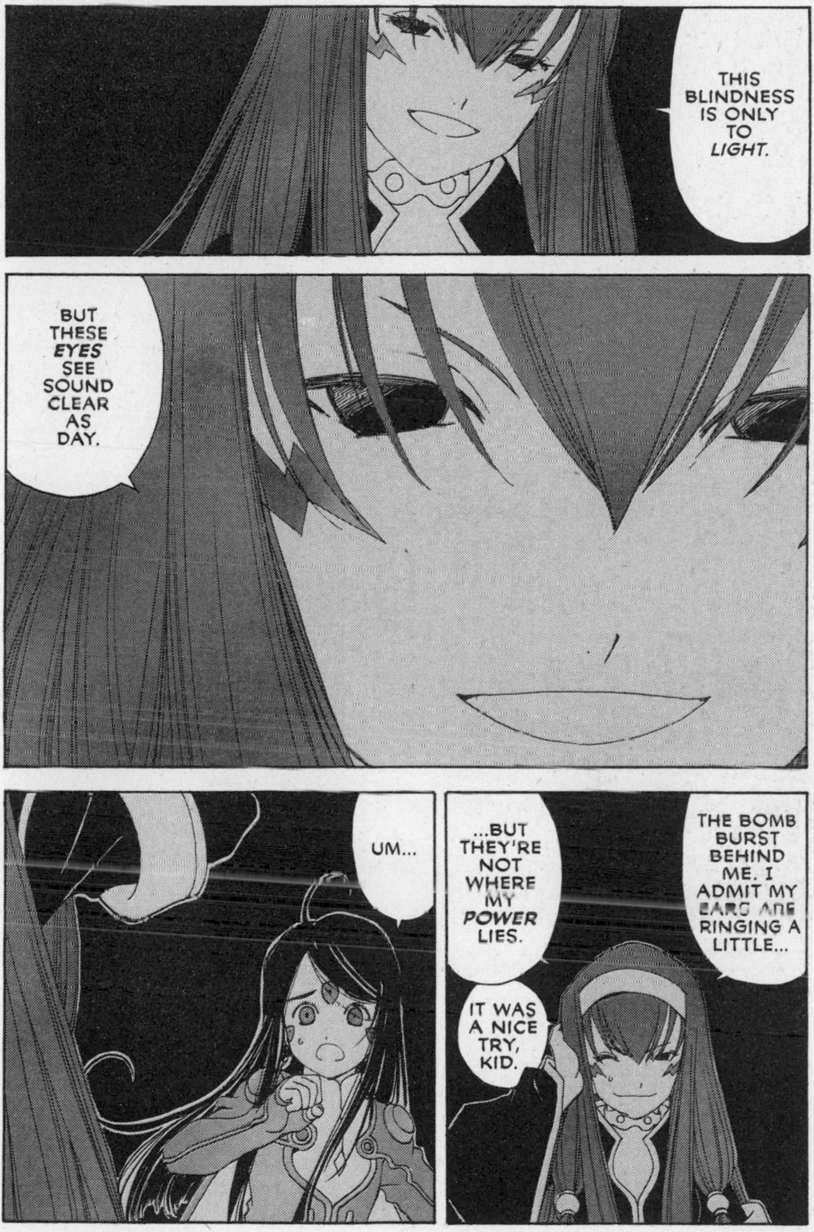
THIS BLINDNESS IS ONLY TO *LIGHT.*
BUT THESE ***EYES*** SEE SOUND CLEAR AS DAY.
THE BOMB BURST BEHIND ME. I ADMIT MY EARS ARE RINGING A LITTLE...
...BUT THEY'RE NOT WHERE MY ***POWER*** LIES.
IT WAS A NICE TRY, KID.
UM...

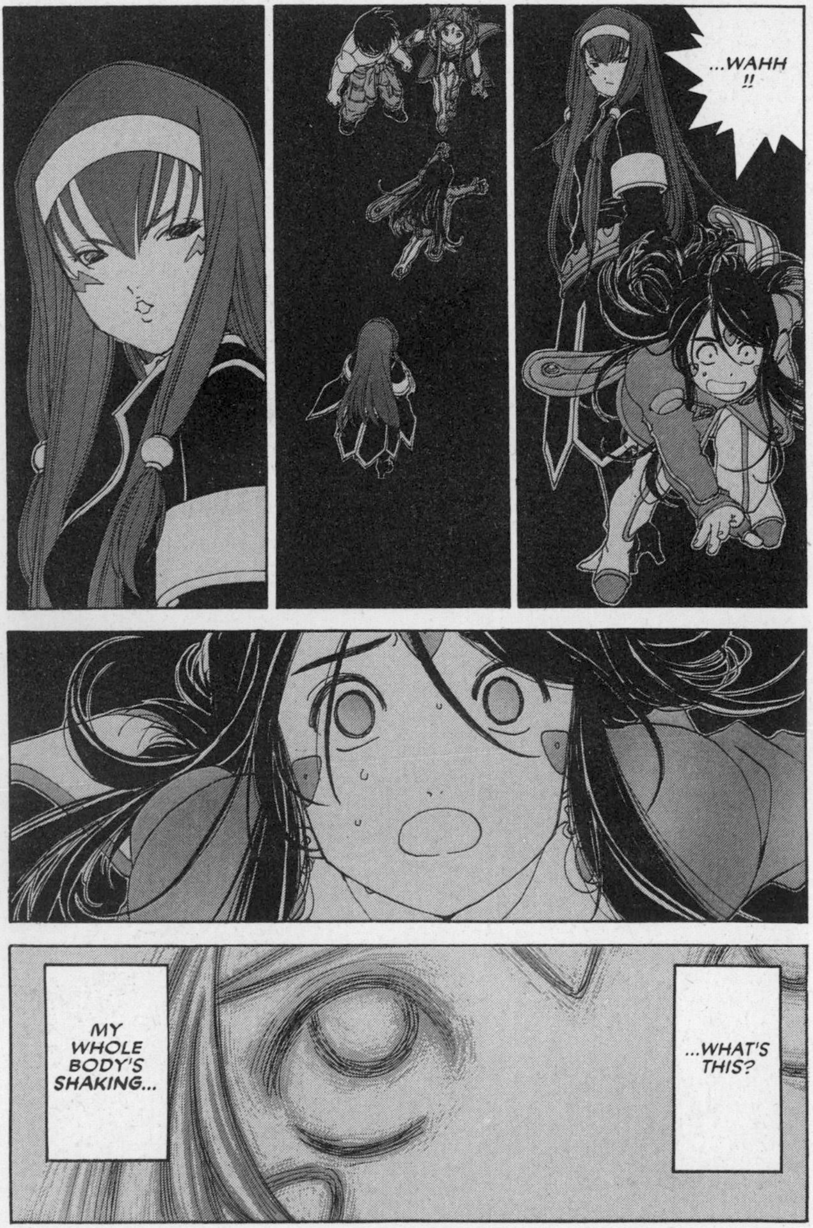
...WAHH !!
...WHAT'S THIS?
MY WHOLE BODY'S SHAKING...

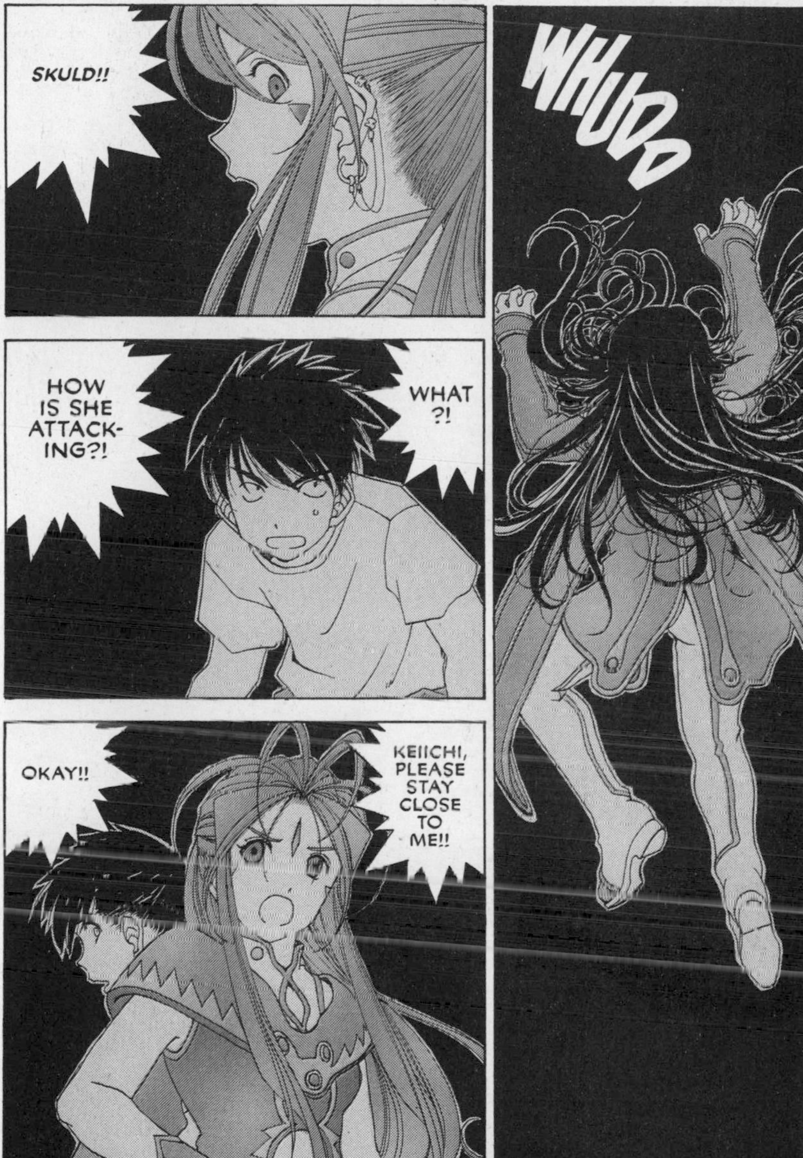
WHUDD
SKULD!!
WHAT ?!
HOW IS SHE ATTACK-ING?!
KEIICHI, PLEASE STAY CLOSE TO ME!!
OKAY!!

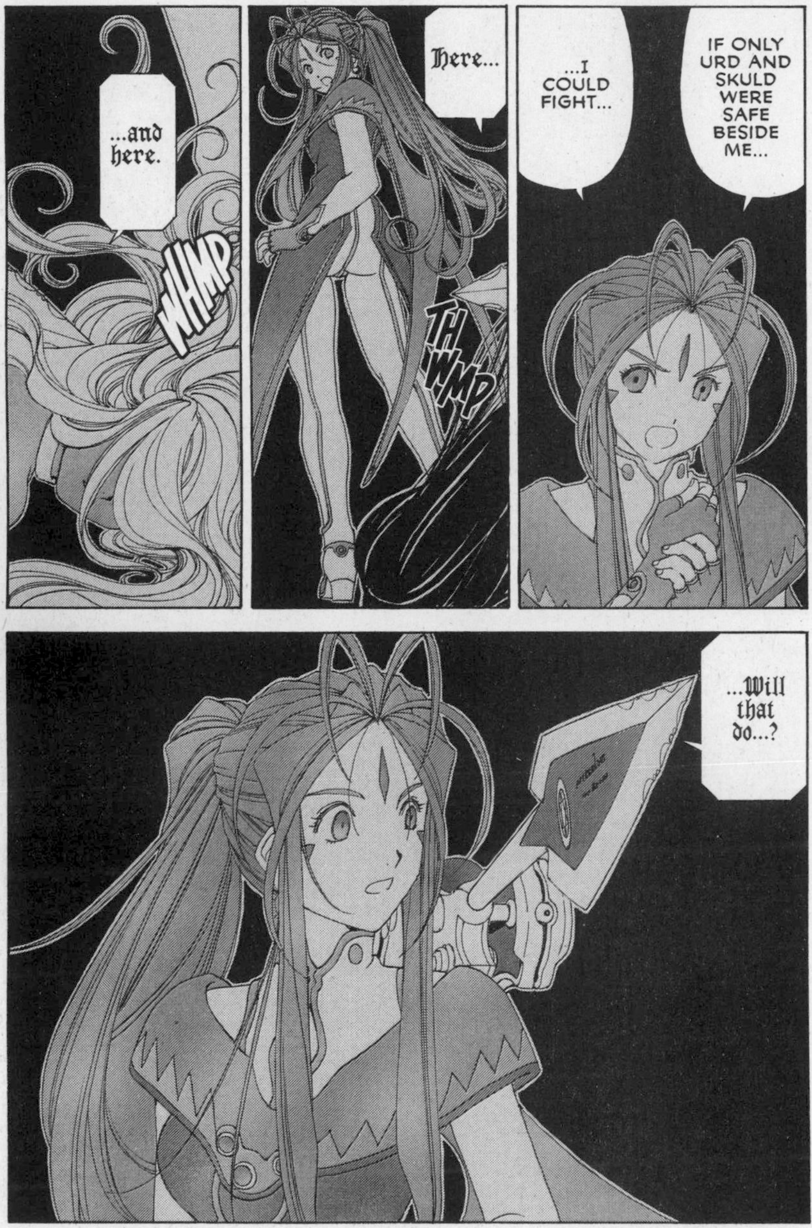
IF ONLY URD AND SKULD WERE SAFE BESIDE ME...
...I COULD FIGHT...
Here...
THWMP
...and here.
WHMP
...Will that do...?

YOU CAN SEE?!
No better than you.
I'm going on my coordinates.
Based on my pre-memorized map...
...I can determine where you and I are located.

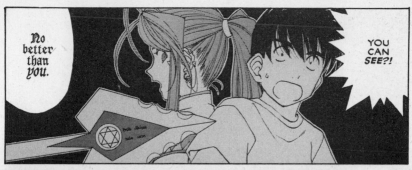

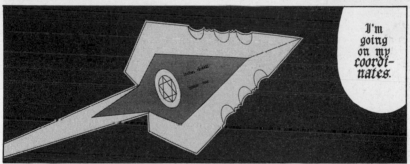

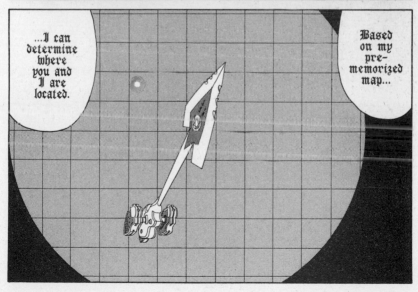

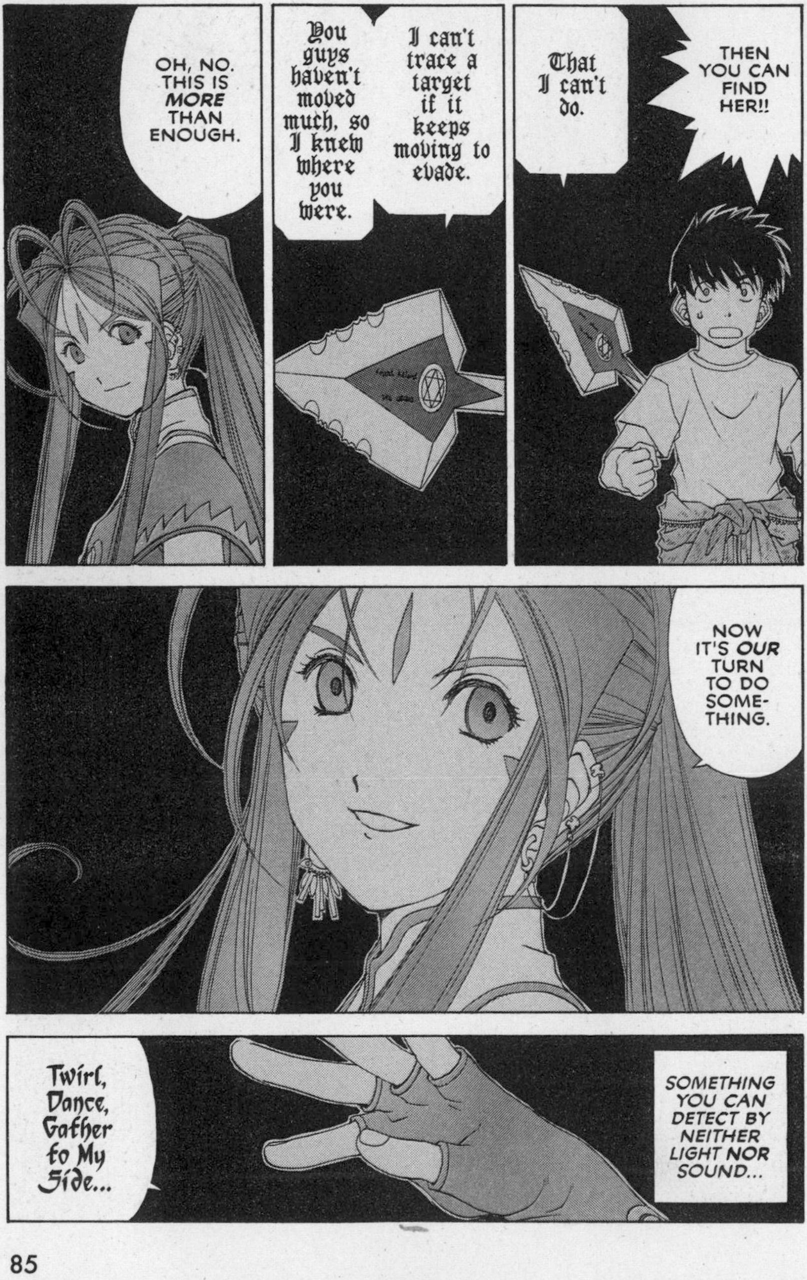
THEN YOU CAN FIND HER!!
That I can't do.
I can't trace a target if it keeps moving to evade.
You guys haven't moved much, so I knew where you were.
OH, NO. THIS IS MORE THAN ENOUGH.
NOW IT'S OUR TURN TO DO SOME-THING.
SOMETHING YOU CAN DETECT BY NEITHER LIGHT NOR SOUND...
Twirl, Dance, Gather to My Side...

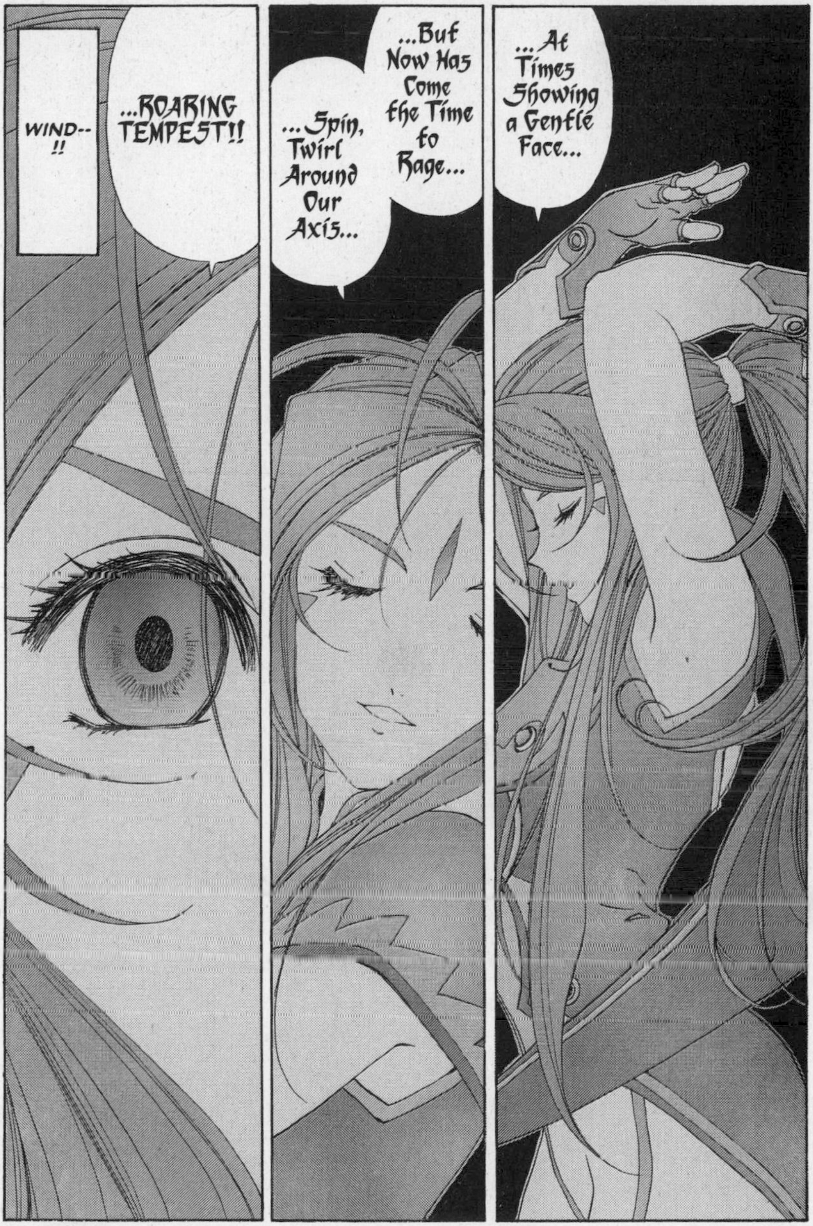
...At Times Showing a Gentle Face...
...But Now Has Come the Time to Rage...
...Spin, Twirl Around Our Axis...
...ROARING TEMPEST!!
WIND--!!

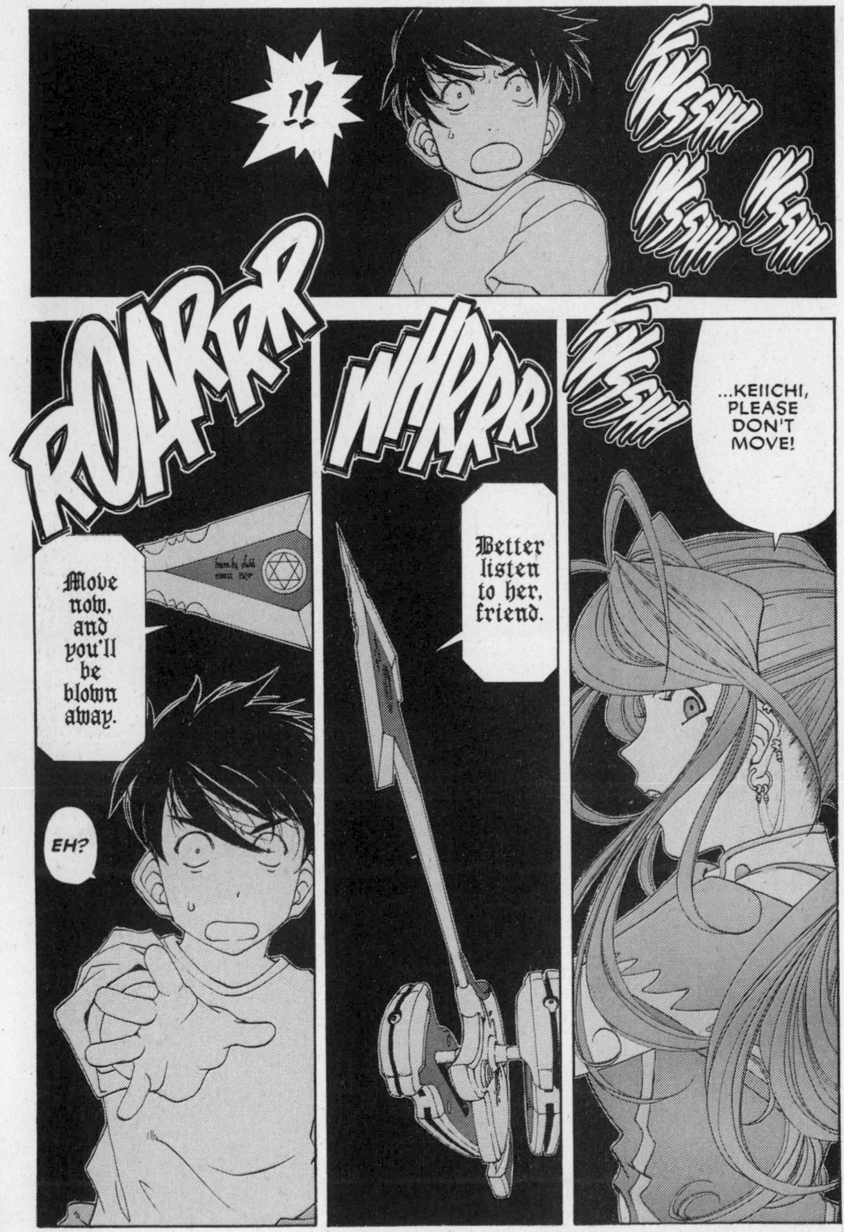
FWSSH
WSSH
WSSH
!!
FWSSH
...KEIICHI, PLEASE DON'T MOVE!
WHRRR
Better listen to her, friend.
ROARRR
Move now, and you'll be blown away.
EH?

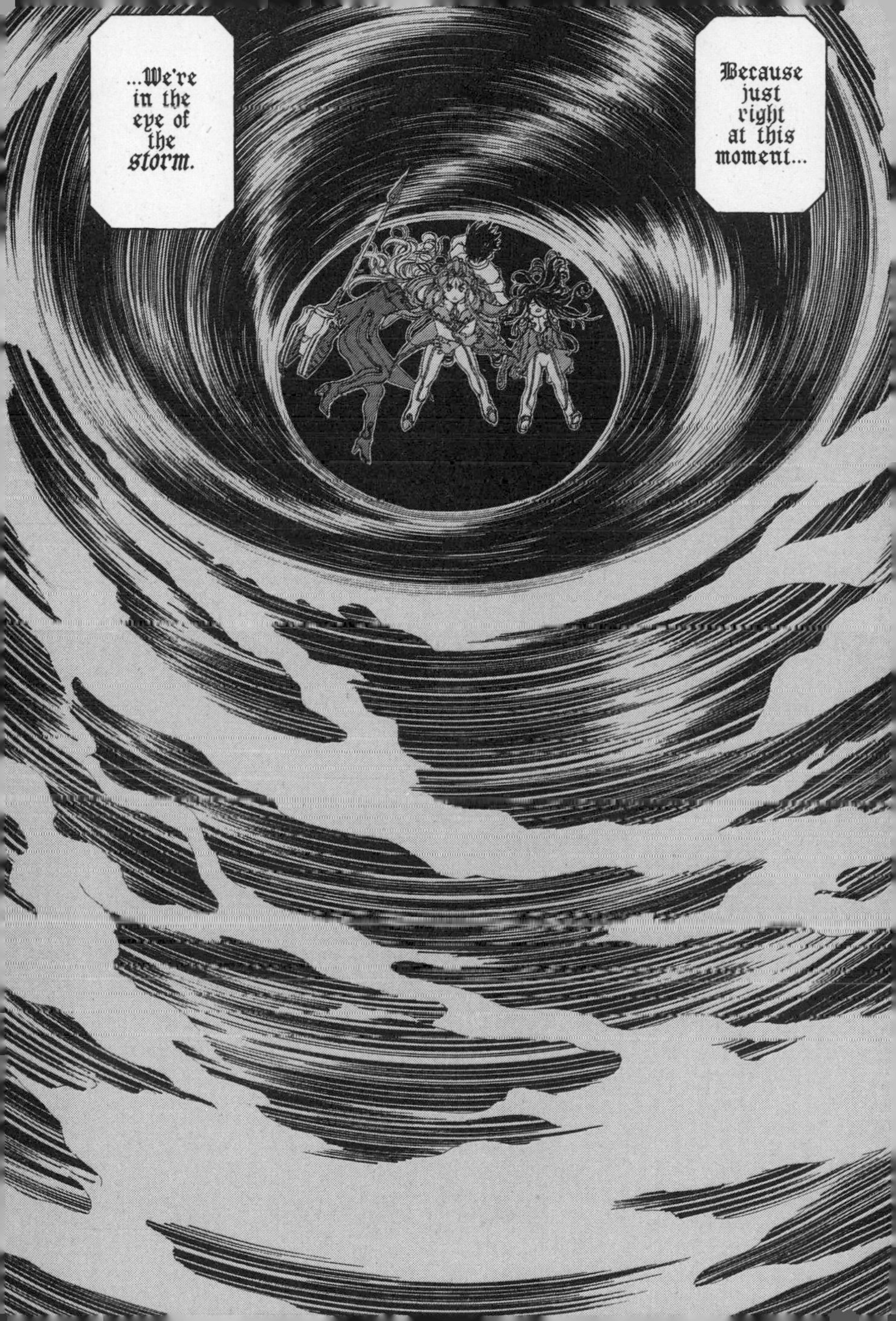
Because just right at this moment...
...We're in the eye of the storm.

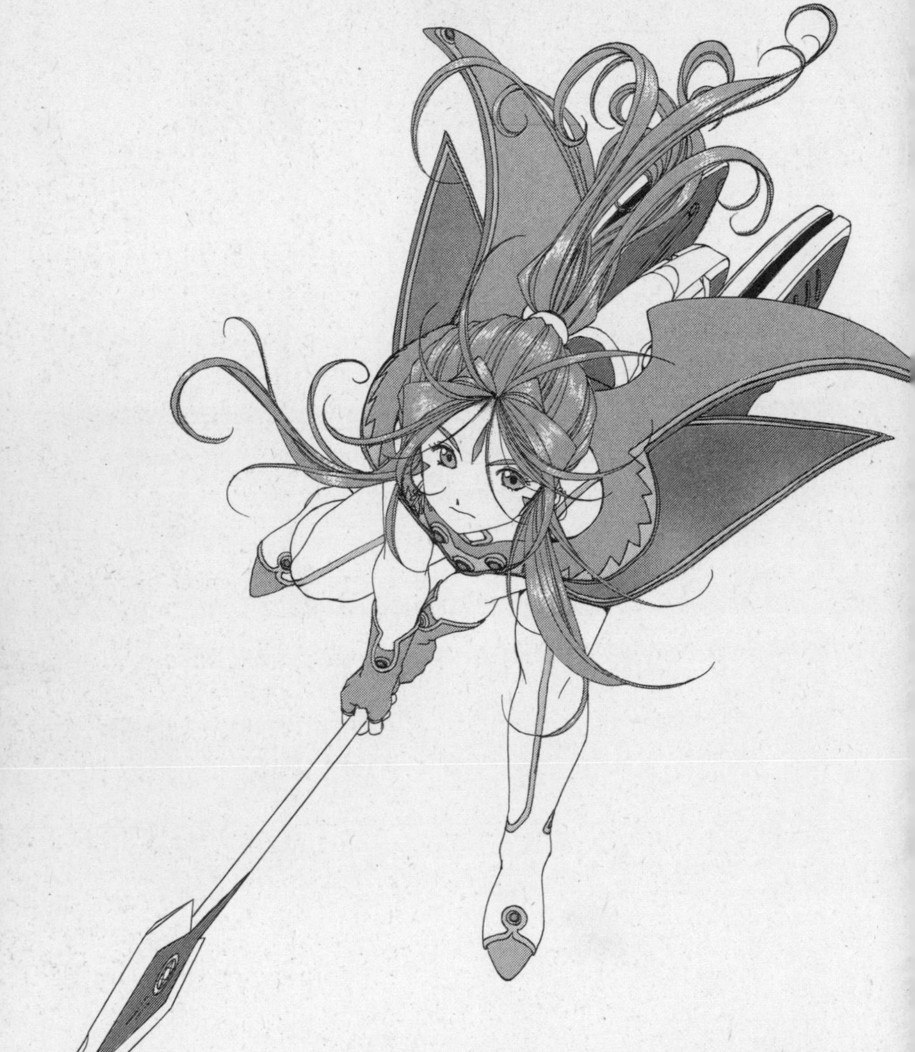

CHAPTER 254

Darkness, Shaken

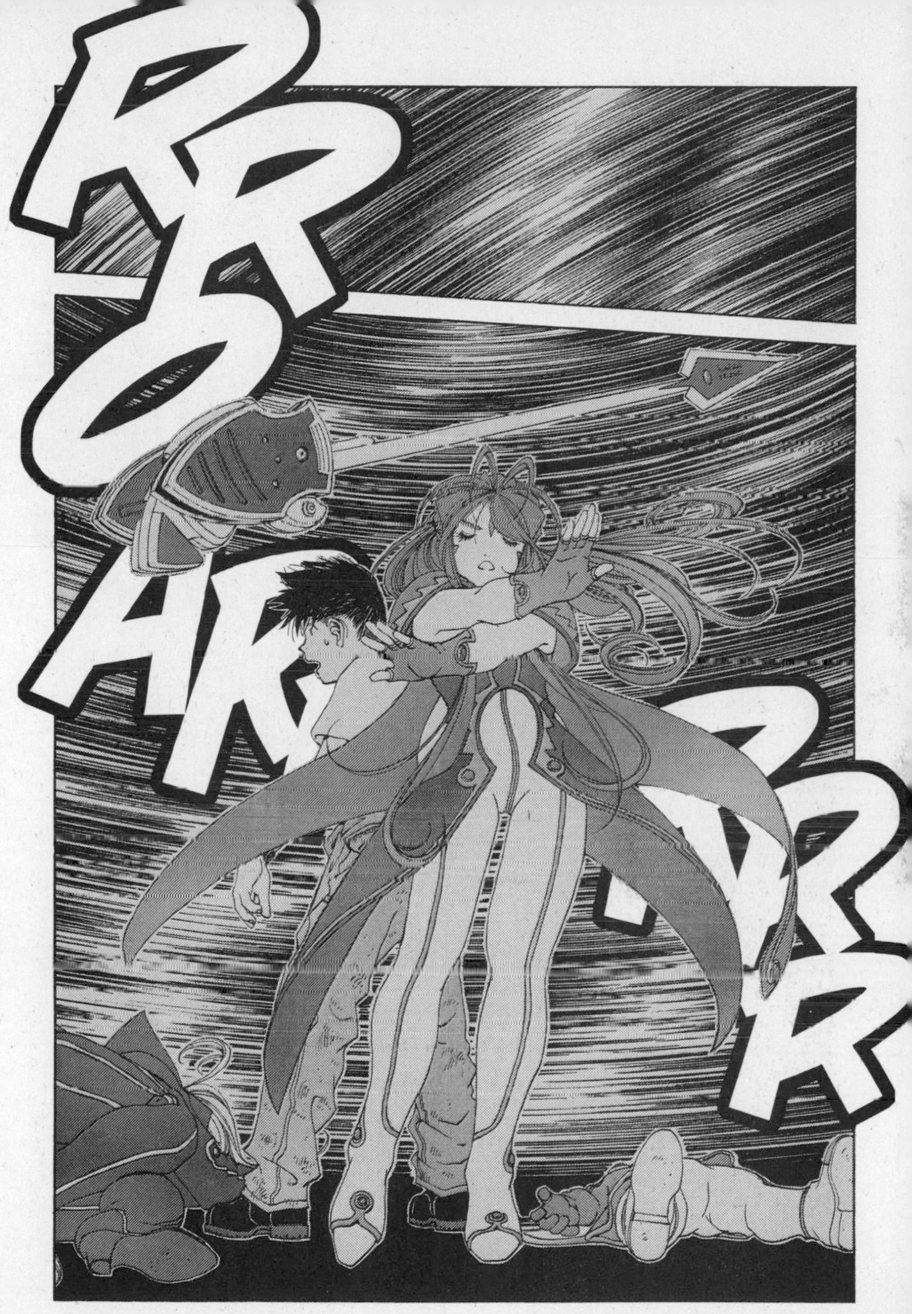
ROARRR

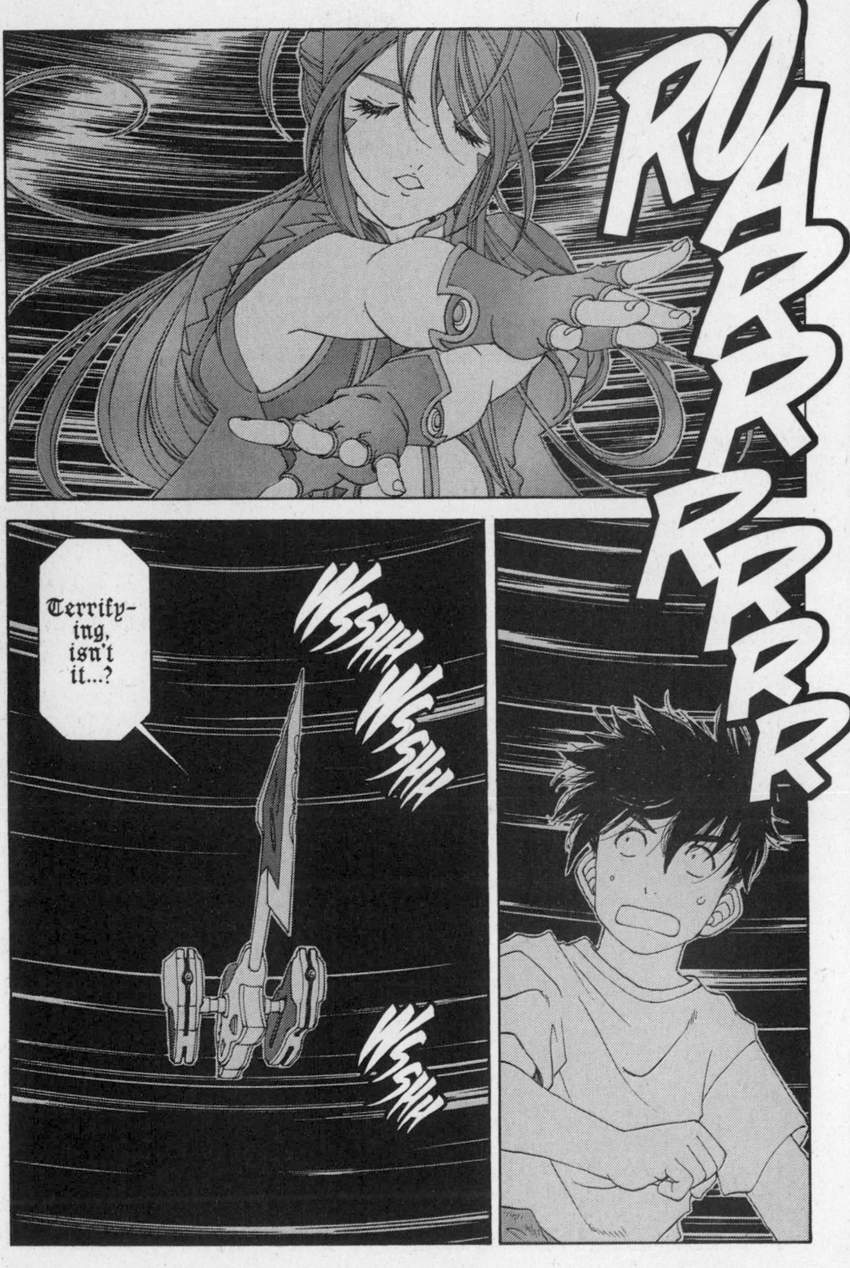
ROARRRRR
Terrifying, isn't it...?
WSSHH WSSHH
WSSHH

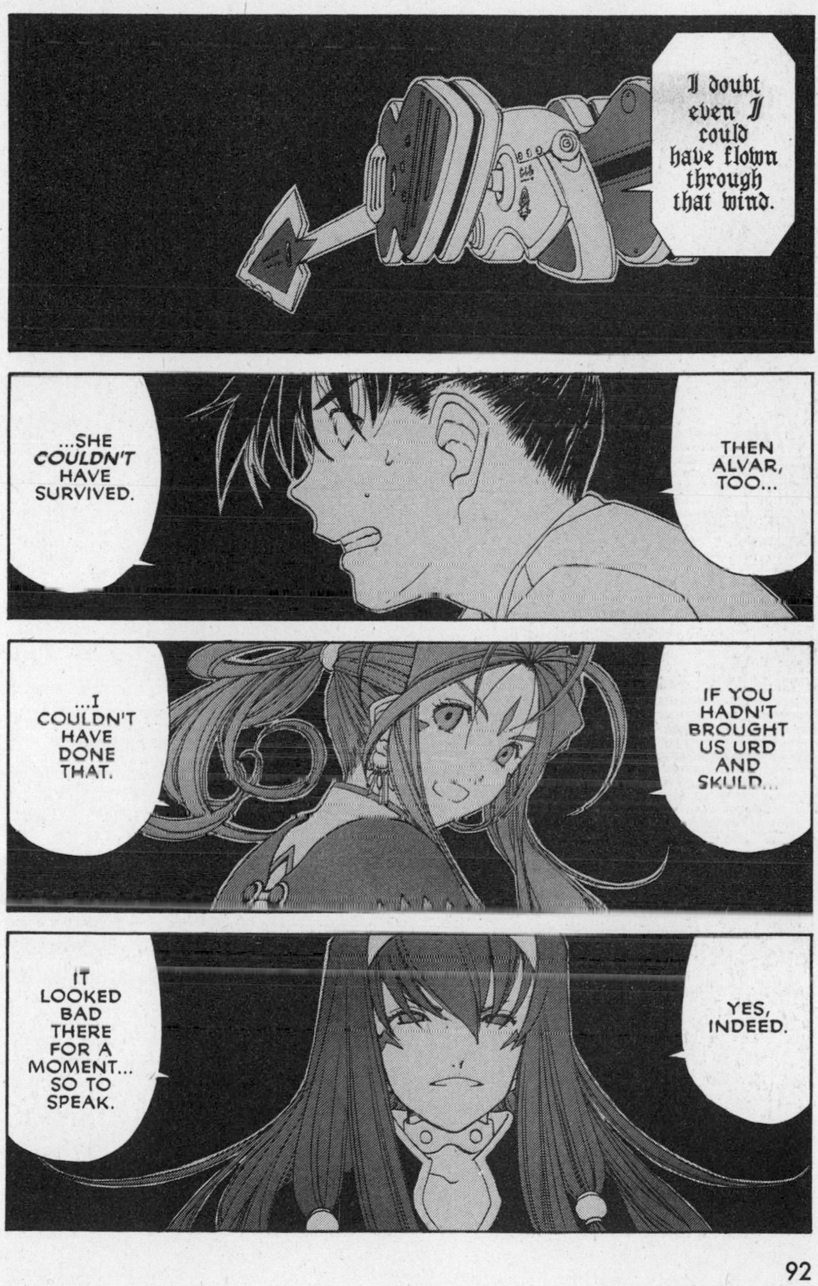
I doubt even I could have flown through that wind.
THEN ALVAR, TOO...
...SHE *COULDN'T* HAVE SURVIVED.
IF YOU HADN'T BROUGHT US URD AND SKULD...
...I COULDN'T HAVE DONE THAT.
YES, INDEED.
IT LOOKED BAD THERE FOR A MOMENT... SO TO SPEAK.

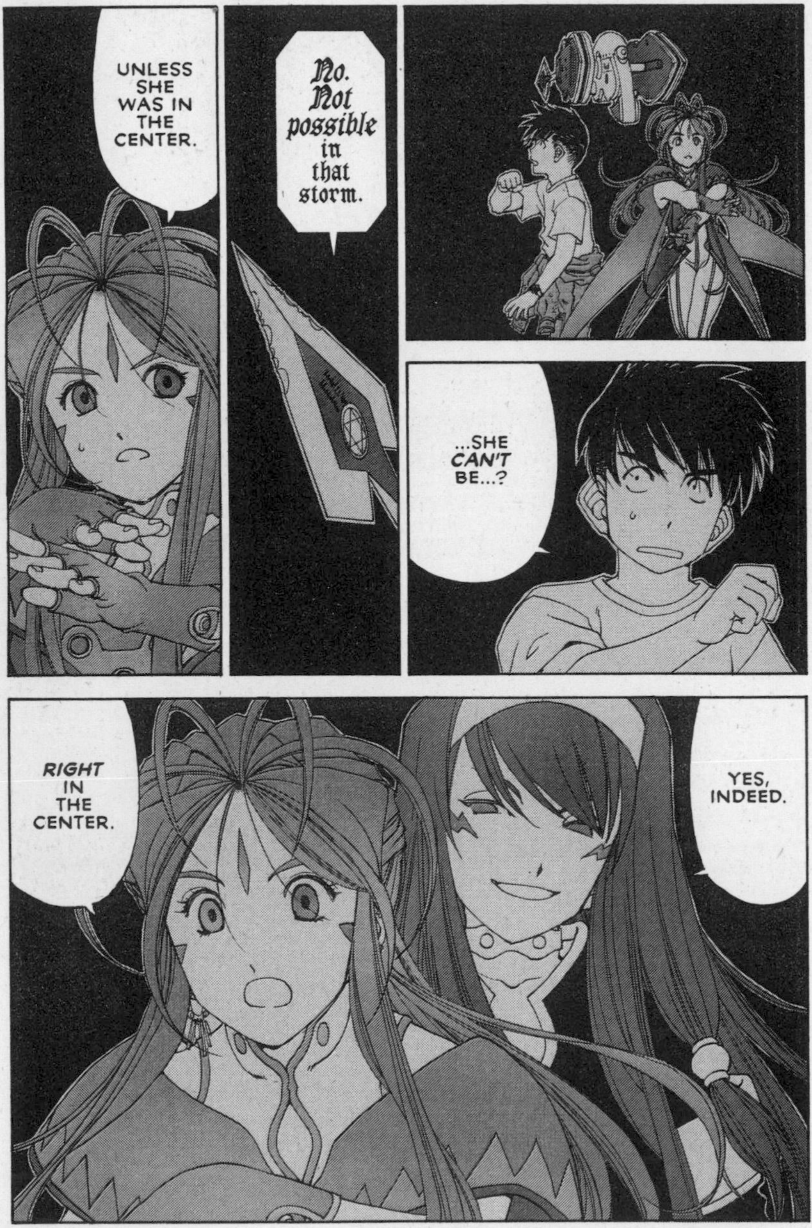
...SHE CAN'T BE...?
No. Not possible in that storm.
UNLESS SHE WAS IN THE CENTER.
YES, INDEED.
RIGHT IN THE CENTER.

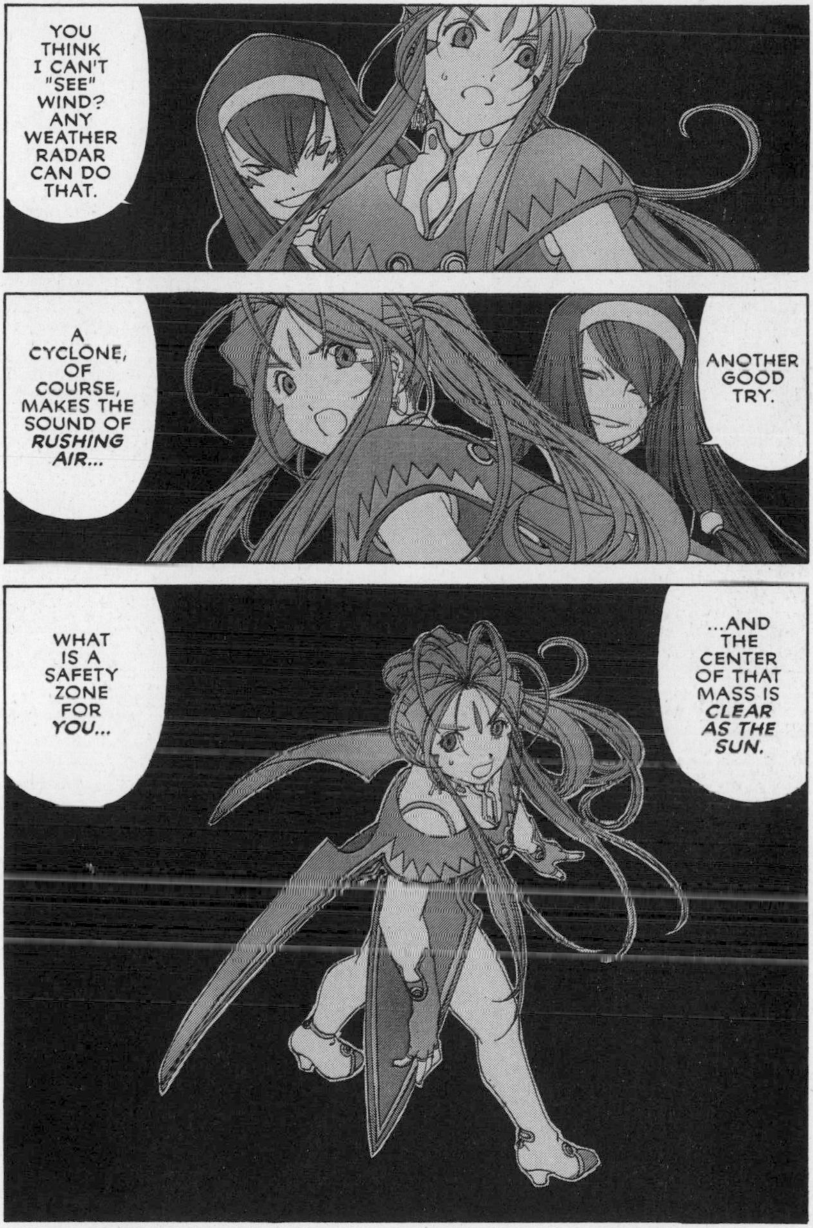
YOU THINK I CAN'T "SEE" WIND? ANY WEATHER RADAR CAN DO THAT.
A CYCLONE, OF COURSE, MAKES THE SOUND OF *RUSHING AIR*...
ANOTHER GOOD TRY.
WHAT IS A SAFETY ZONE FOR *YOU*...
...AND THE CENTER OF THAT MASS IS *CLEAR AS THE SUN.*

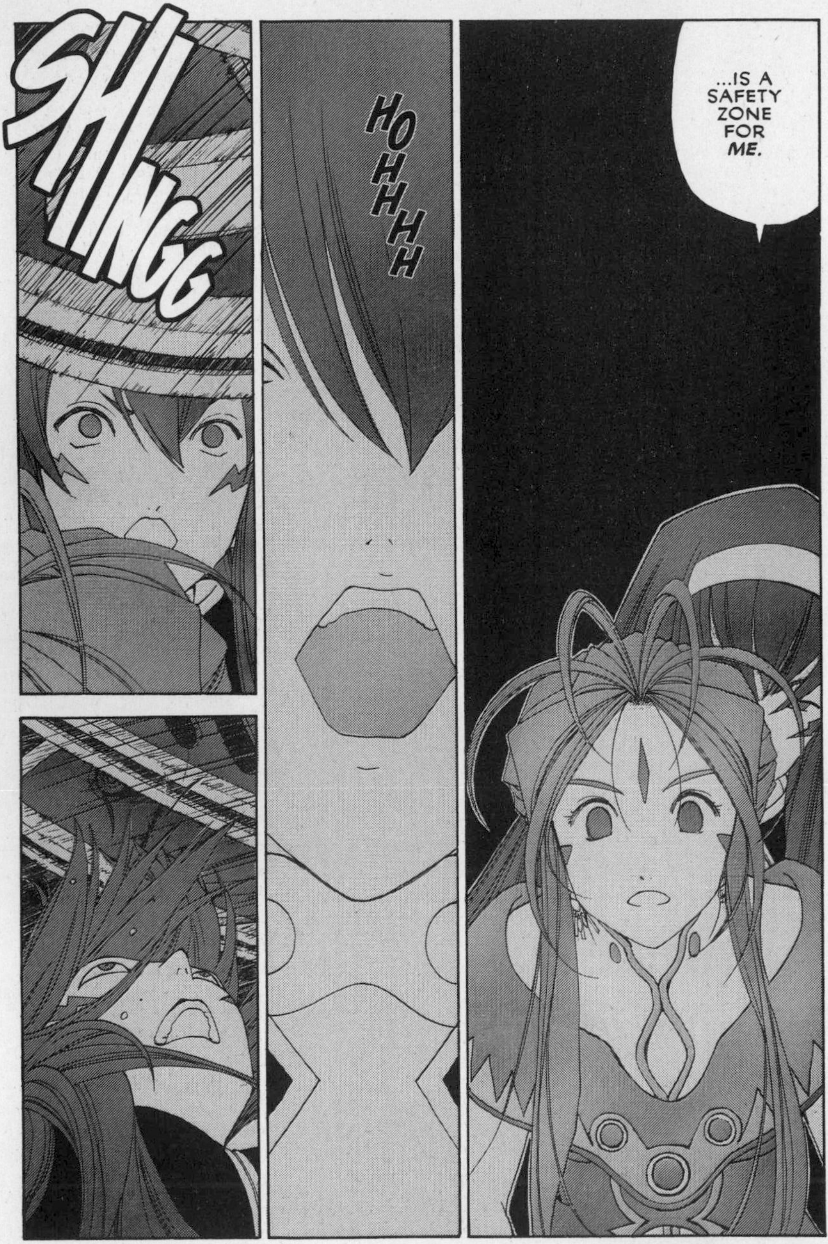
...IS A SAFETY ZONE FOR *ME.*
HOHHHH
SHINGG

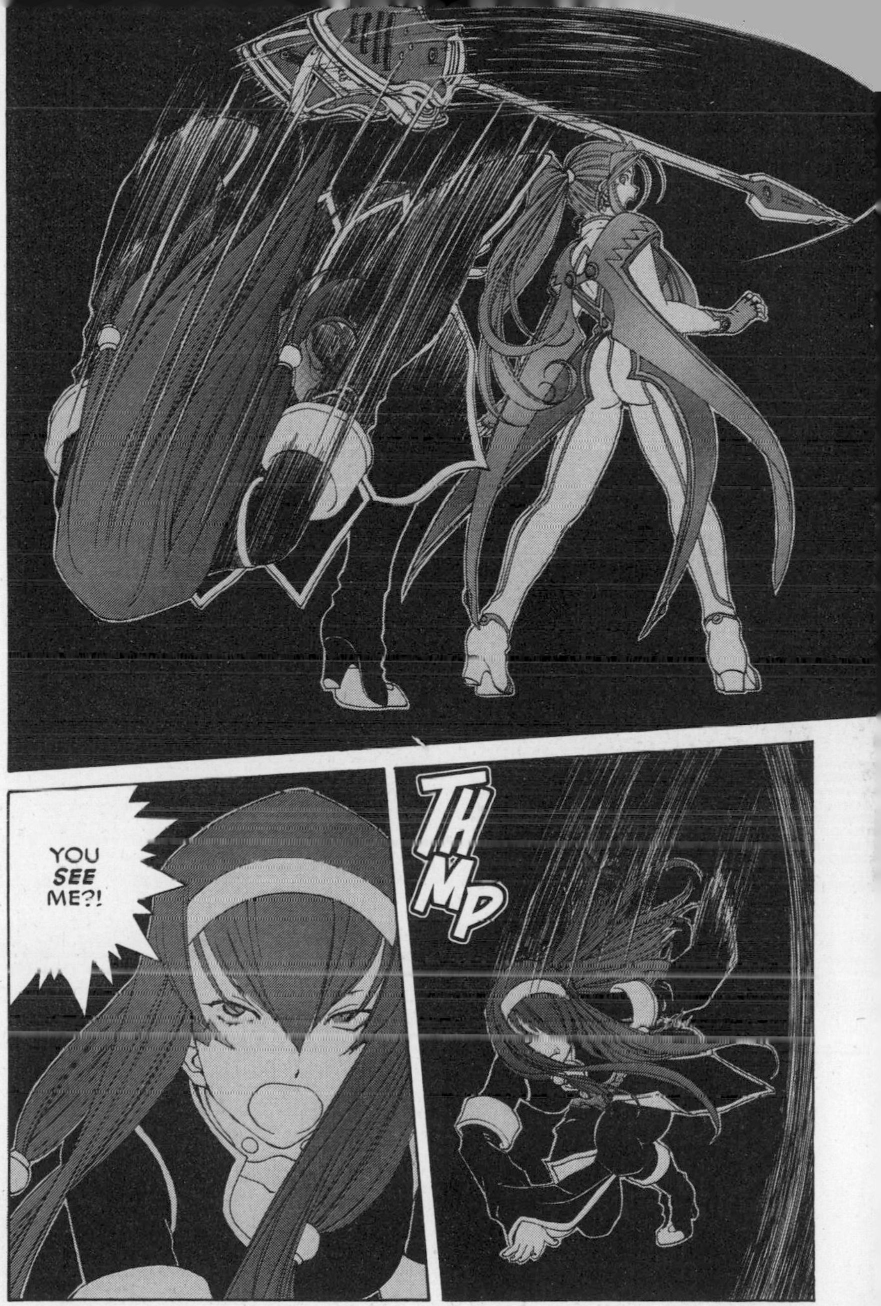
THMP
YOU SEE ME?!

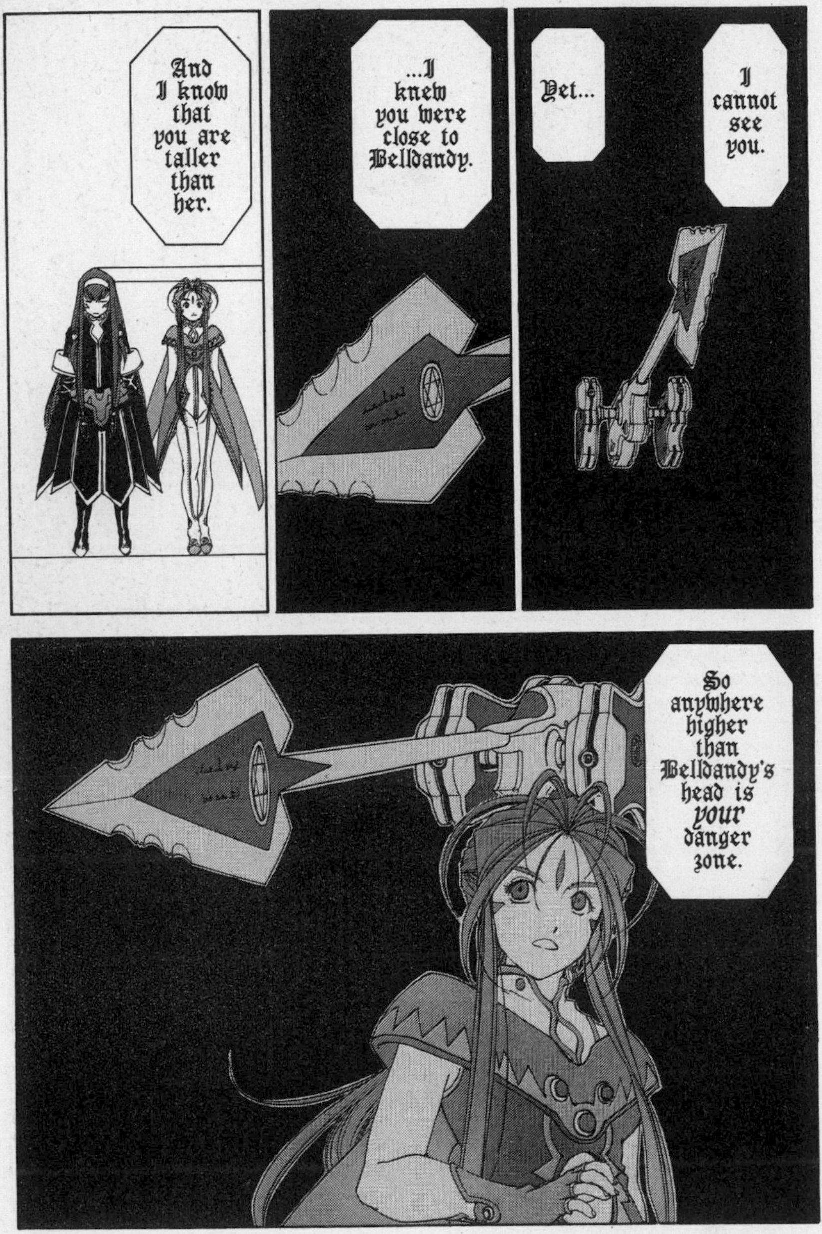
I cannot see you.
Yet...
...I knew you were close to Belldandy.
And I know that you are taller than her.
So anywhere higher than Belldandy's head is *your* danger zone.

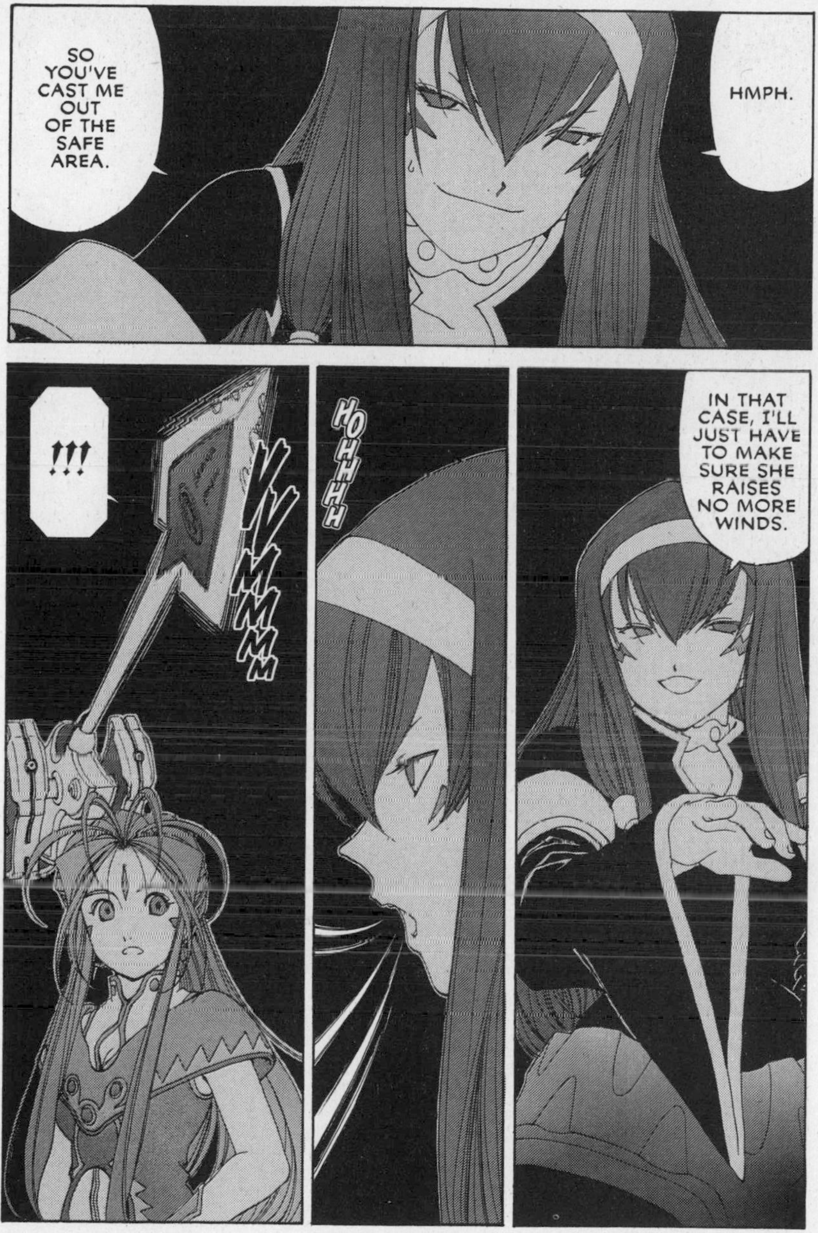
HMPH.
SO YOU'VE CAST ME OUT OF THE SAFE AREA.
IN THAT CASE, I'LL JUST HAVE TO MAKE SURE SHE RAISES NO MORE WINDS.
HOHHHH
VVMMMMM
!!!

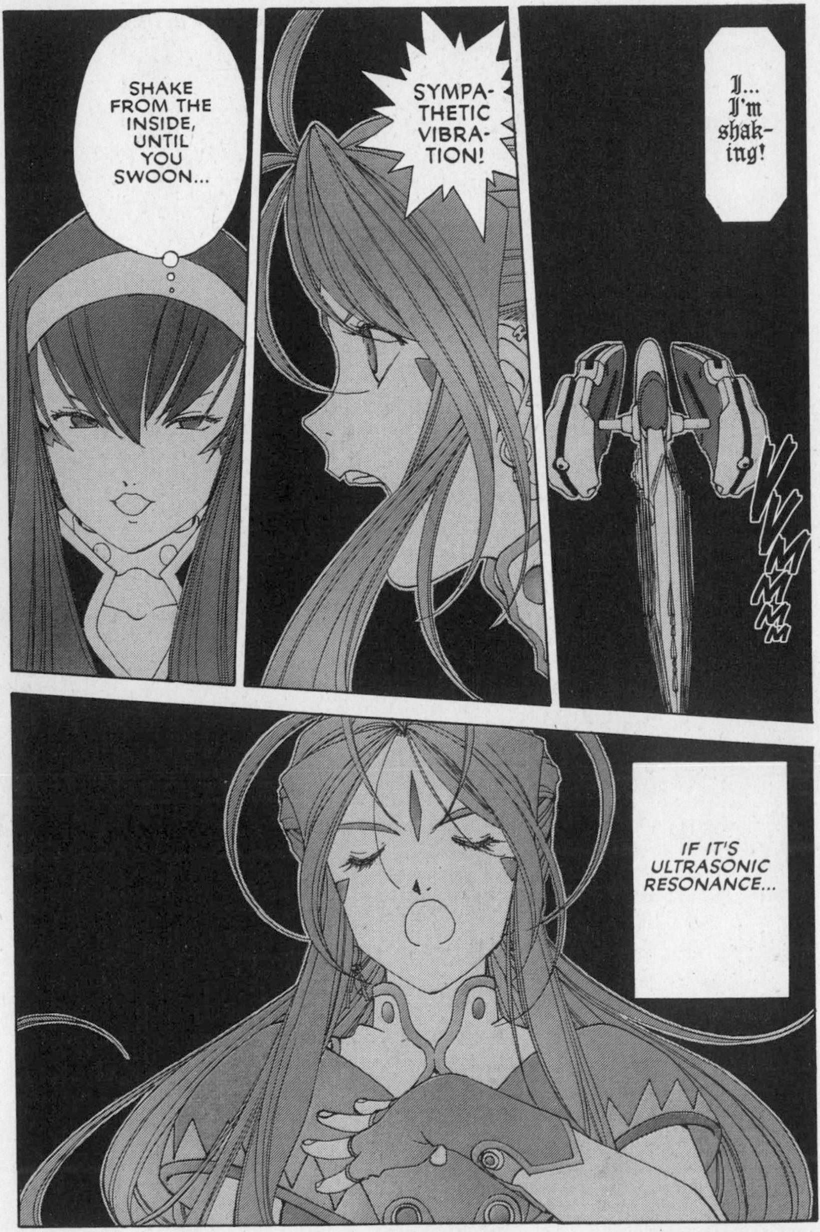
I... I'm shaking!
VVMMMM
SYMPATHETIC VIBRATION!
SHAKE FROM THE INSIDE, UNTIL YOU SWOON...
IF IT'S ULTRASONIC RESONANCE...

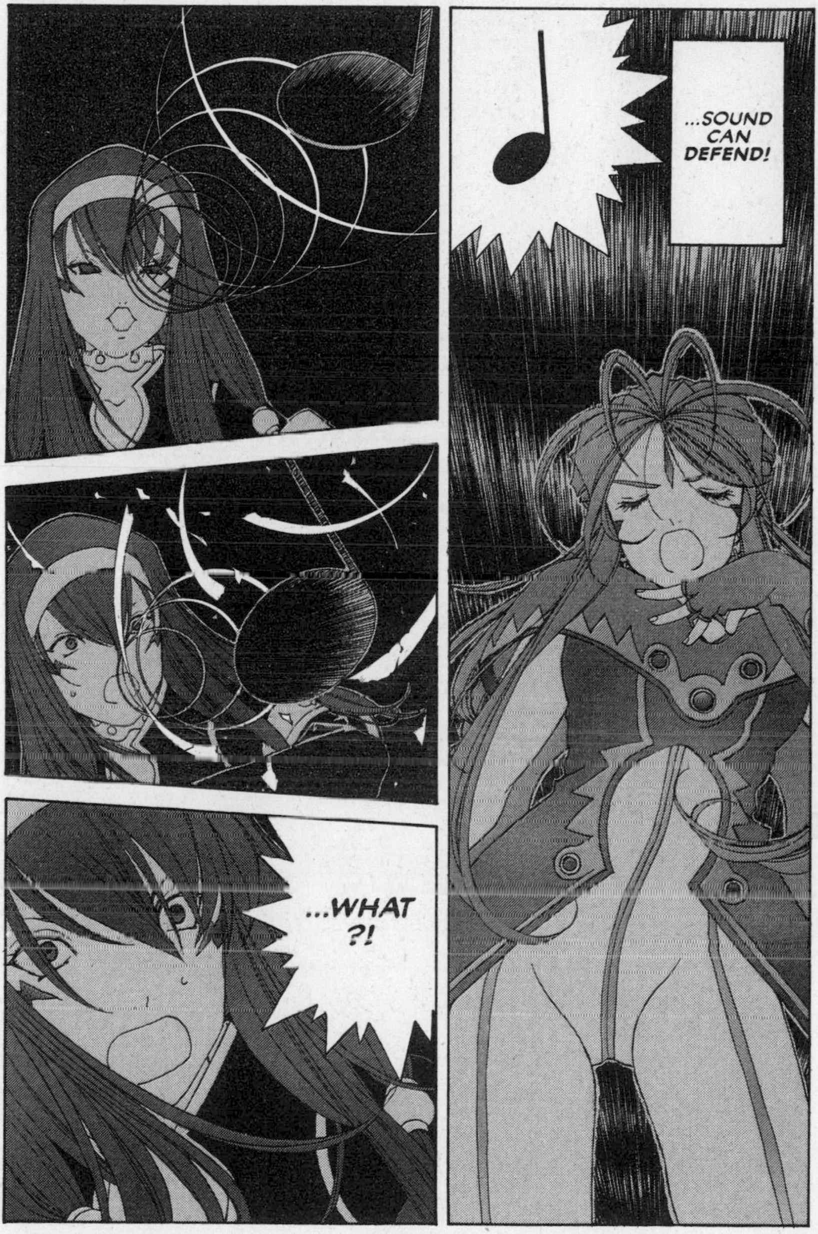
...SOUND CAN DEFEND!
...WHAT ?!

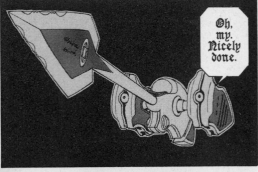

Oh, my. Nicely done.
WHAT'S GOING ON?!
She's attacking via ultrasonic resonance.
?
...I thought you were an engineering student.
...If you can make something vibrate at a frequency close to its natural resonance frequency....
...you can *amplify* the oscillations.
AH!

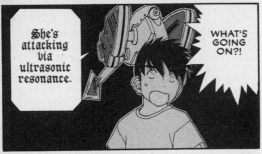

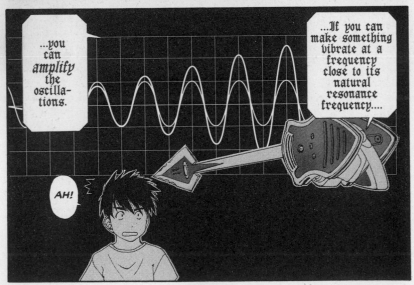

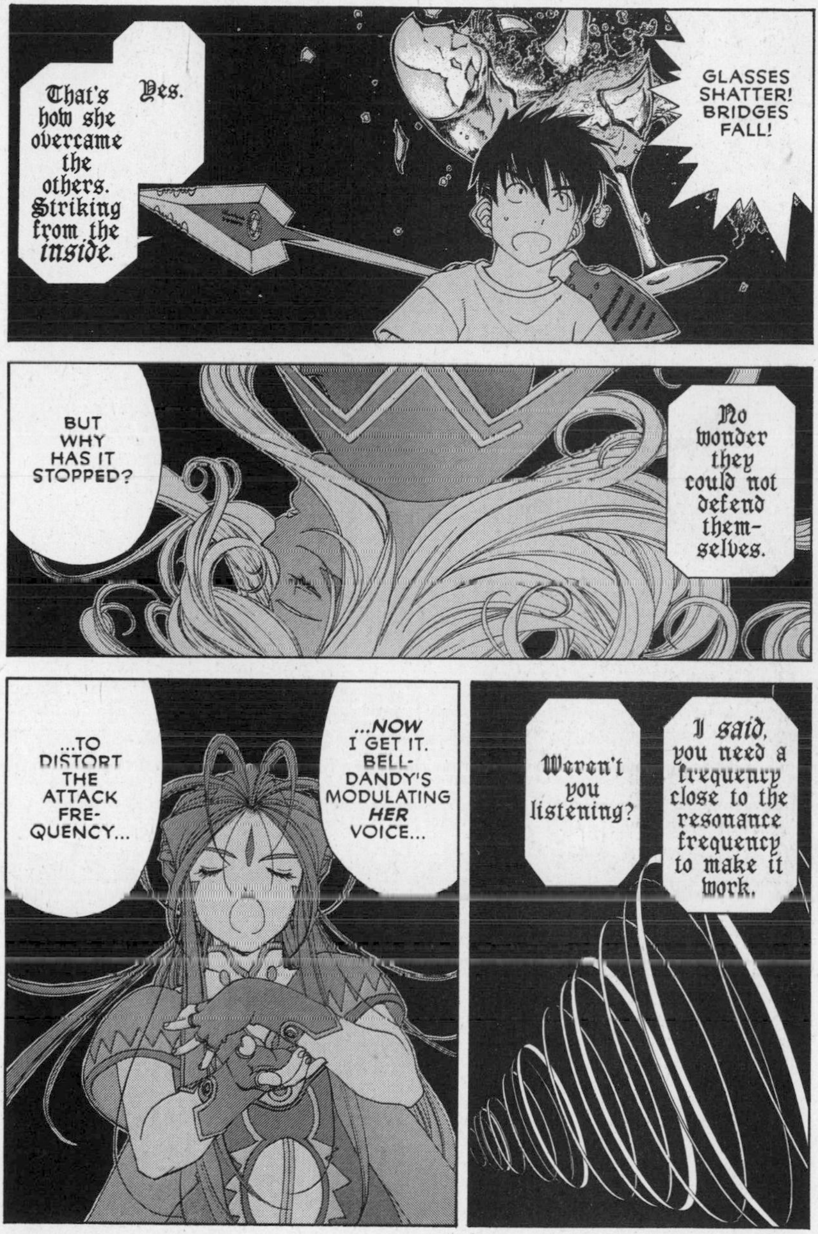
GLASSES SHATTER! BRIDGES FALL!
Yes.
That's how she overcame the others. Striking from the inside.
No wonder they could not defend them-selves.
BUT WHY HAS IT STOPPED?
I said, you need a frequency close to the resonance frequency to make it work.
Weren't you listening?
...NOW I GET IT. BELL-DANDY'S MODULATING HER VOICE...
...TO DISTORT THE ATTACK FRE-QUENCY...

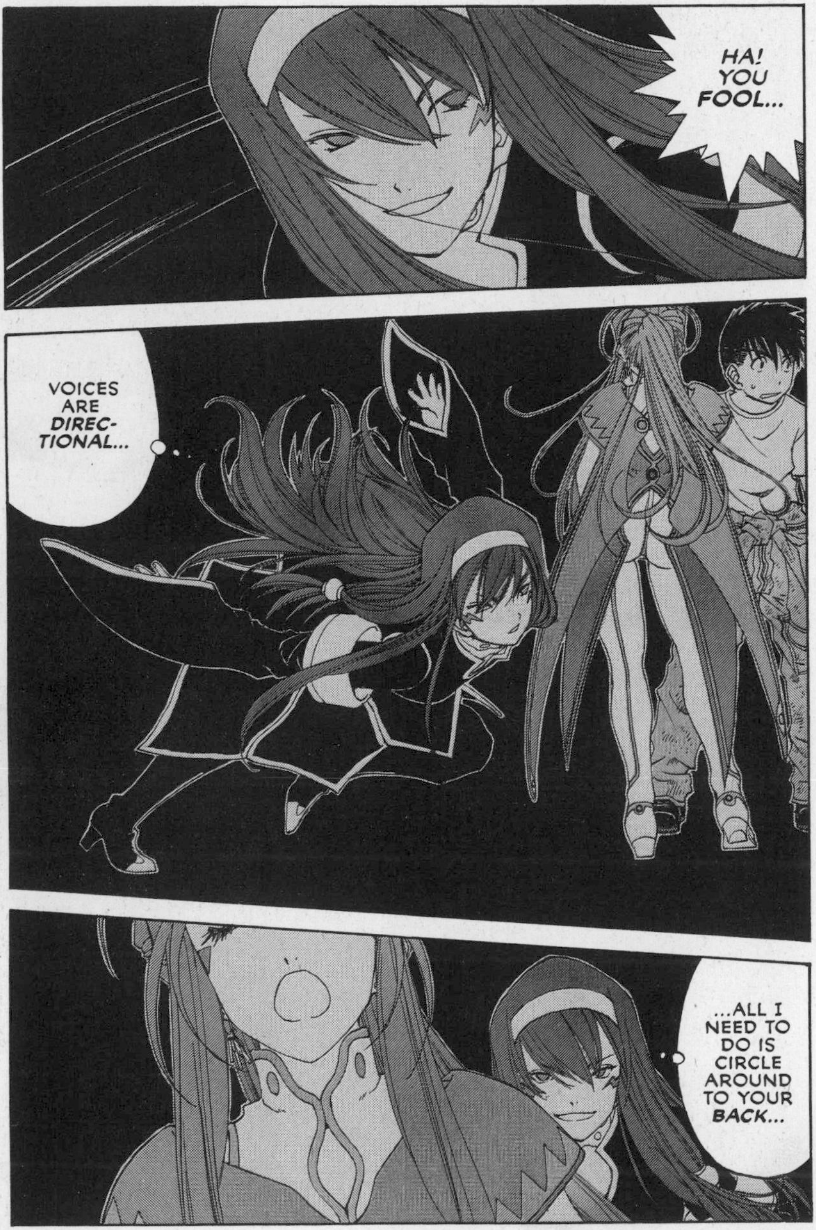
HA! YOU FOOL...
VOICES ARE DIRECTIONAL...
...ALL I NEED TO DO IS CIRCLE AROUND TO YOUR BACK...

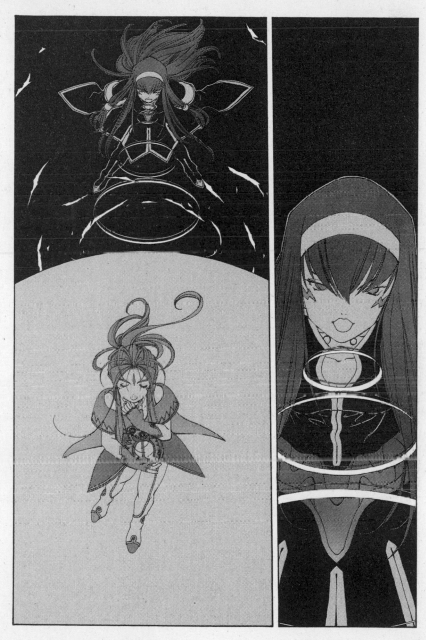

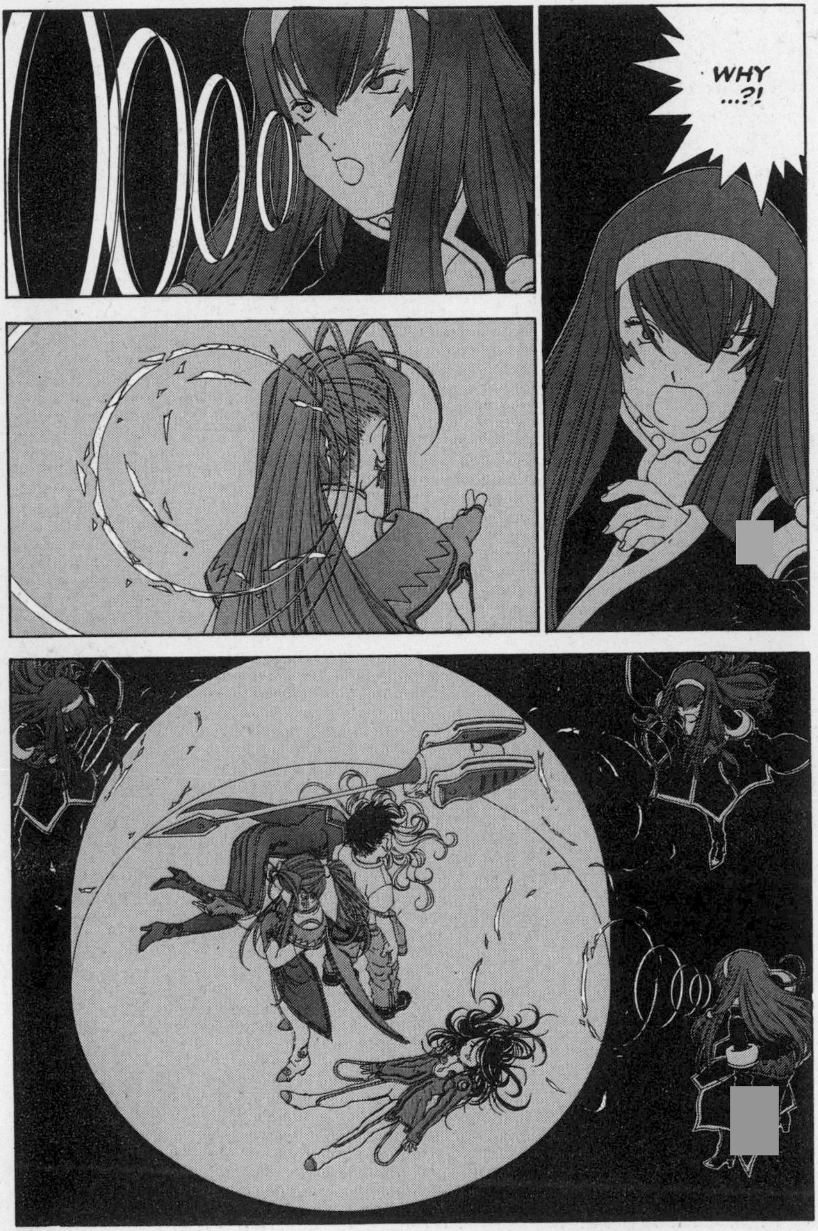
WHY ...?!

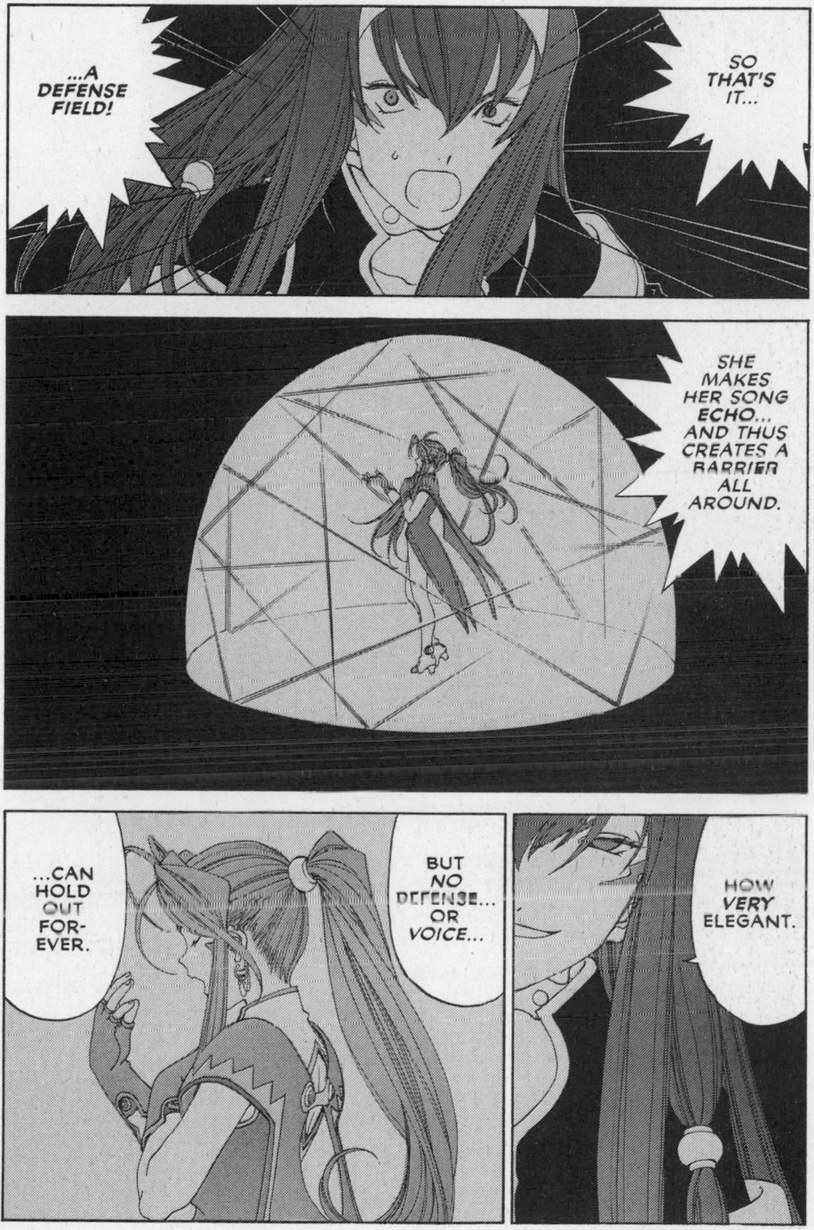
SO THAT'S IT...
...A DEFENSE FIELD!
SHE MAKES HER SONG ECHO... AND THUS CREATES A BARRIER ALL AROUND.
HOW *VERY* ELEGANT.
BUT *NO* DEFENSE... OR *VOICE*...
...CAN HOLD OUT FOR-EVER.

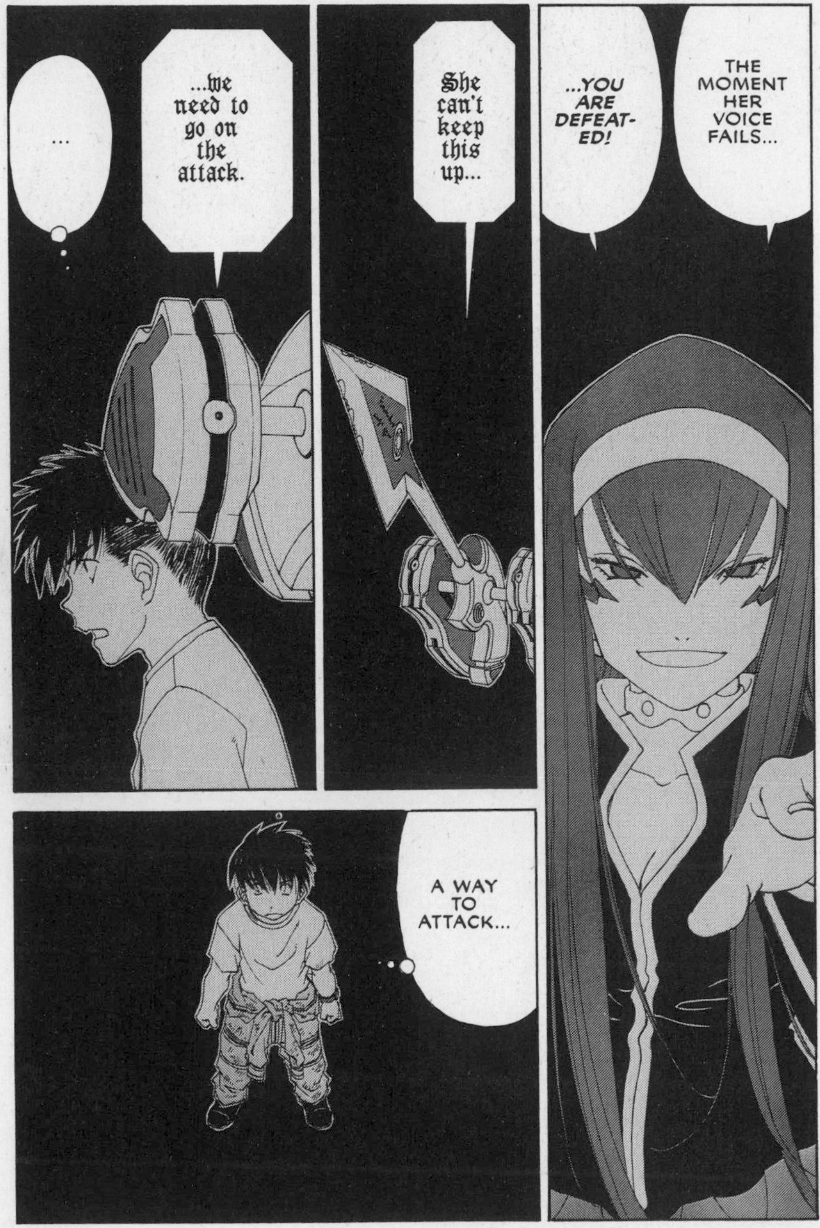
THE MOMENT HER VOICE FAILS...
...YOU ARE DEFEAT-ED!
She can't keep this up...
...we need to go on the attack.
...
A WAY TO ATTACK...

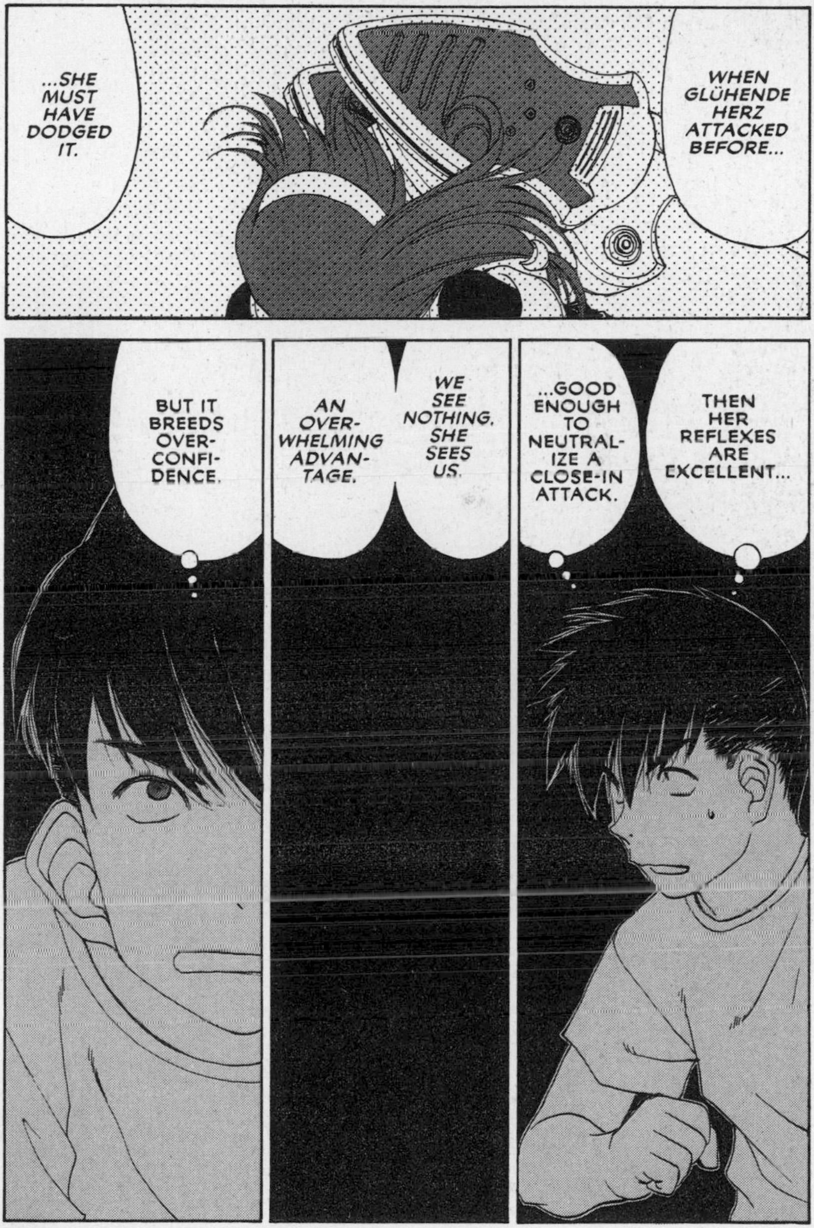
WHEN GLÜHENDE HERZ ATTACKED BEFORE...
...SHE MUST HAVE DODGED IT.
THEN HER REFLEXES ARE EXCELLENT...
...GOOD ENOUGH TO NEUTRAL-IZE A CLOSE-IN ATTACK.
WE SEE NOTHING. SHE SEES US.
AN OVER-WHELMING ADVAN-TAGE.
BUT IT BREEDS OVER-CONFI-DENCE.

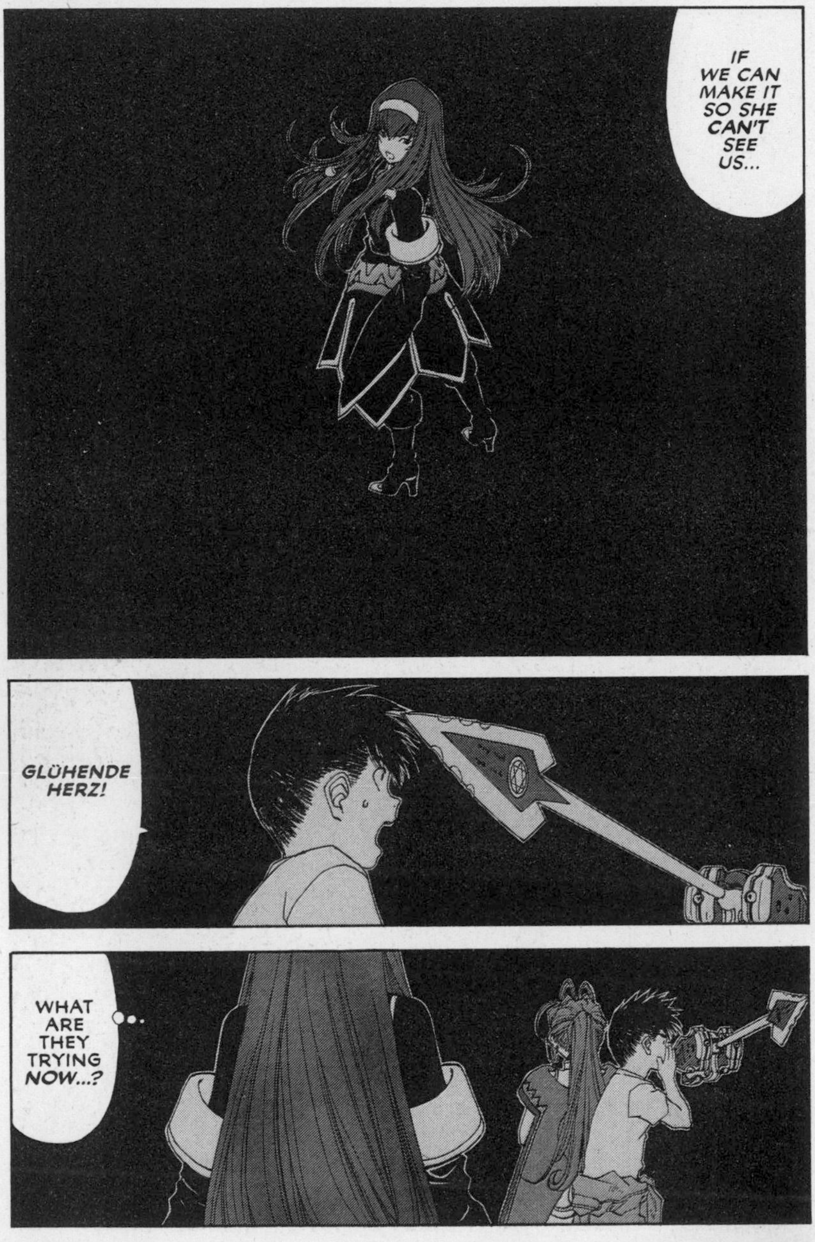
IF WE CAN MAKE IT SO SHE CAN'T SEE US...
GLÜHENDE HERZ!
WHAT ARE THEY TRYING NOW...?

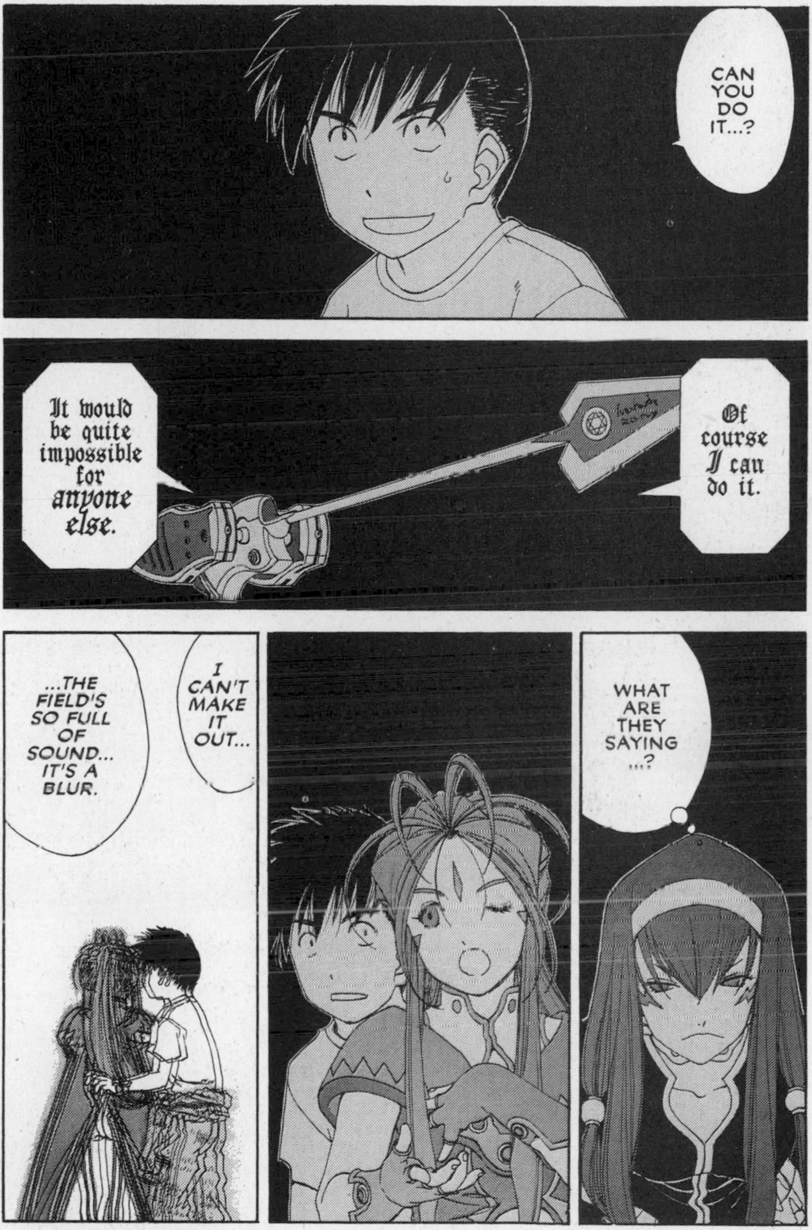
CAN YOU DO IT...?
Of course I can do it.
It would be quite impossible for anyone else.
WHAT ARE THEY SAYING ...?
I CAN'T MAKE IT OUT...
...THE FIELD'S SO FULL OF SOUND... IT'S A BLUR.

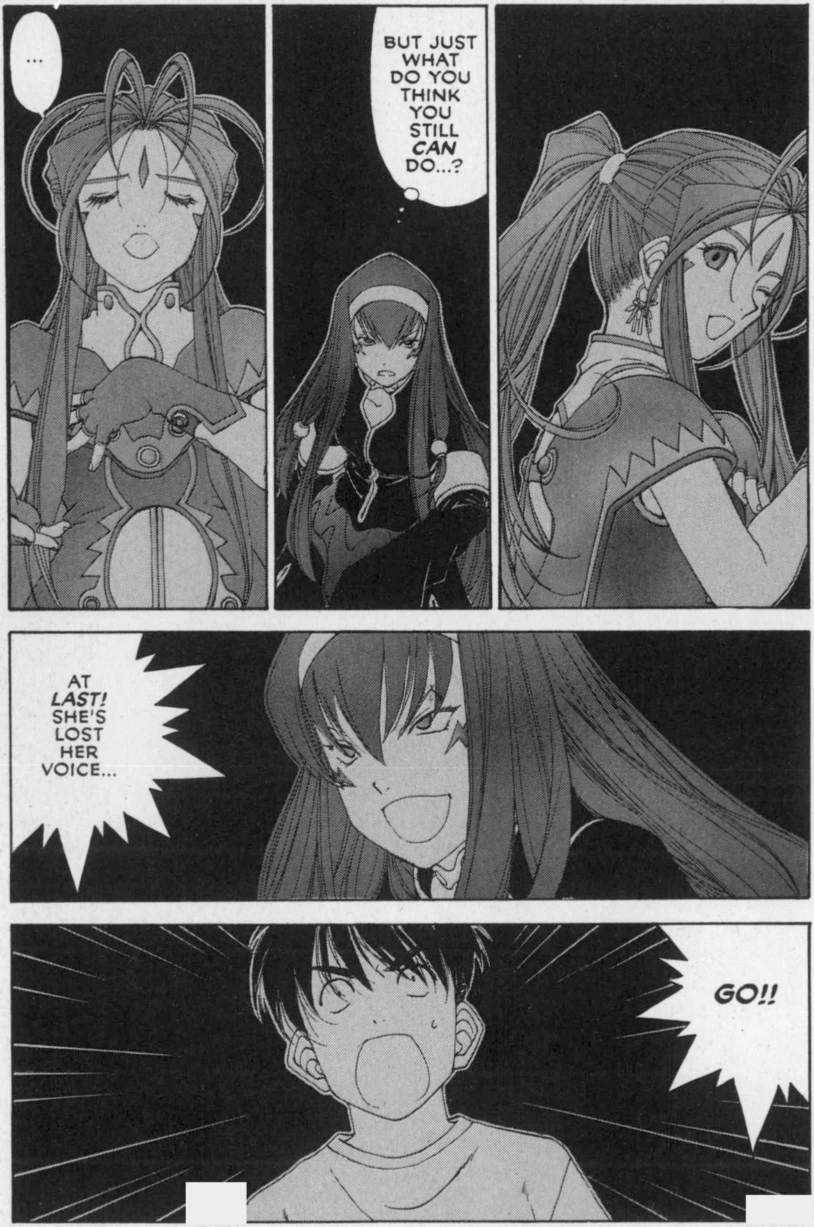
BUT JUST WHAT DO YOU THINK YOU STILL *CAN* DO...?
...
AT *LAST!* SHE'S LOST HER VOICE...
GO!!

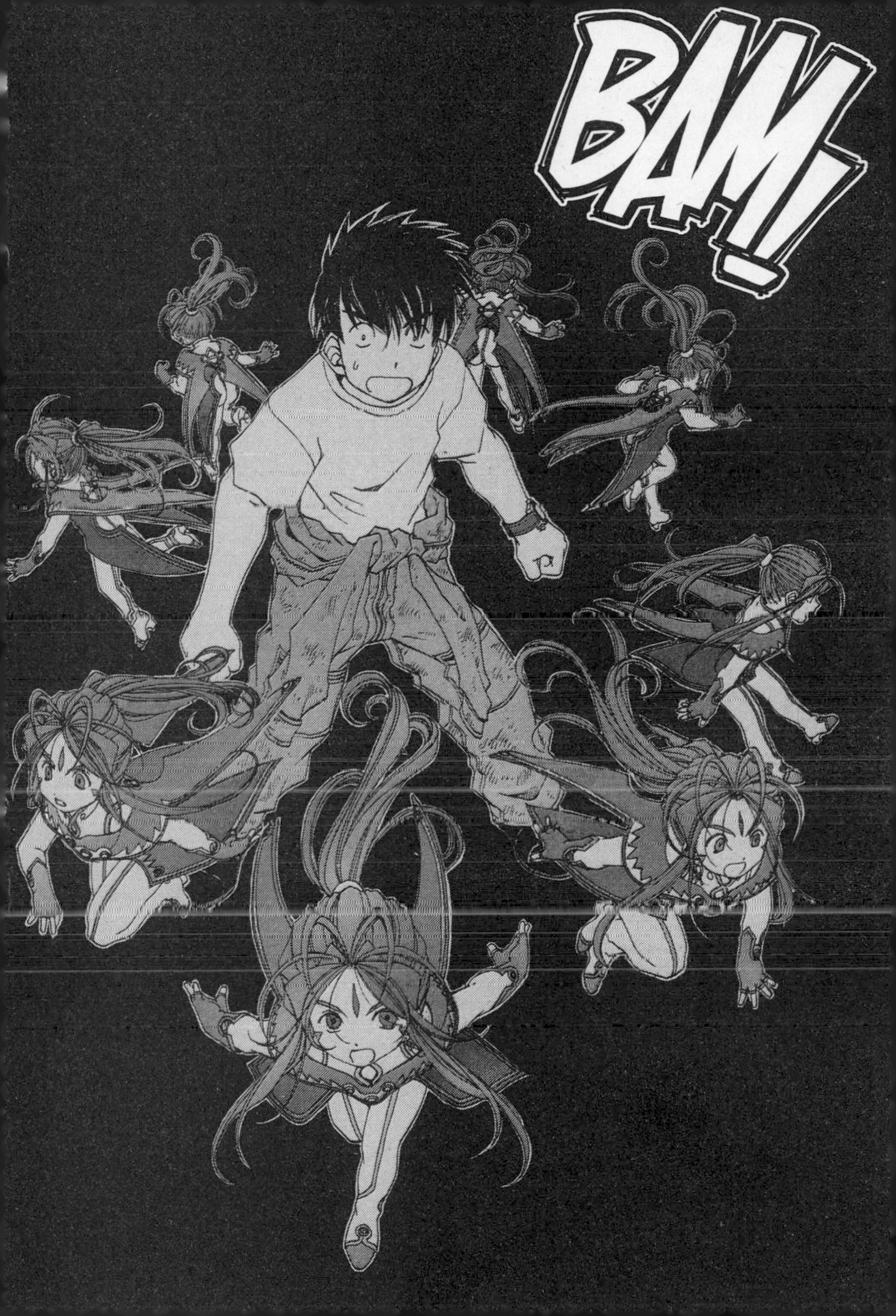
BAM!!

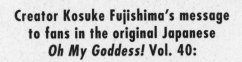

Creator Kosuke Fujishima's message to fans in the original Japanese *Oh My Goddess!* Vol. 40:

I wish to offer my deepest thanks to all my readers who have stayed the course with me this long, long time, all forty volumes' worth.

No matter how much I may hunger to do Oh My Goddess!, I could not move the tale along one chapter, or even one page, if you were not there to read it for me.

In other words, the person who has really upheld and supported this long, long story is you, my reader.

And now, even now, we are still only partway along the journey. If you find yourself musing about what will finally become of Keiichi, Belldandy, and all the gang, then please keep picking up Afternoon magazine or these Oh My Goddess! graphic novels.

If you find a story inside that warms your heart, then nothing can make me, your artist and author, happier than that.

Kosuke
Fujishima

EDITOR
Carl Gustav Horn

DESIGNER
Kat Larson

PUBLISHER
Mike Richardson

English-language version
produced by Dark Horse Comics

OH MY GODDESS! Vol. 40

Published by Dark Horse Manga
A division of Dark Horse Comics, Inc.
10956 SE Main Street
Milwaukie, OR 97222
DarkHorse.com

To find a comics shop in your area,
call the Comic Shop Locator Service
toll-free at 1-888-266-4226

First edition: December 2011
ISBN 978-1-59582-870-5

1 3 5 7 9 10 8 6 4 2

Printed at Lake Book Manufacturing, Inc.,
Melrose Park, IL, USA

letters to the
ENCHANTRESS

10956 SE Main Street, Milwaukie, Oregon 97222
OMG@DarkHorse.com • DarkHorse.com

NOTE: Full addresses and e-mail addresses will not be printed, unless you ask! All fan artwork, letters, and e-mails submitted become the property of Dark Horse Comics.

Well, here we are at *Oh My Goddess!* Volume 40 (just in case you somehow missed that info on the front cover, back, and spine ^_^). It's not difficult to think of manga that have reached this many volumes—*One Piece* and *Naruto* come to mind. But while they are among Japan's top-selling manga, the fact that those stories come out in weekly magazines in Japan shows they got to more than forty volumes in a much shorter time than *Oh My Goddess!*

It's a different kind of achievement for a manga that comes out in a monthly magazine, such as *Oh My Goddess!*, to reach forty volumes, because that means it had to hold on to people's attention for much longer. In the case of *Oh My Goddess!*, it was twenty-one years and one month; *OMG!* chapter 1 ran in the November 1988 issue of *Afternoon* magazine, whereas the last chapter in this volume, chapter 254, ran in the December 2009 issue of *Afternoon*.

In fact, I can't think of another manga that has had such a long run in a single Japanese monthly magazine as *Oh My Goddess!* has (some long-running manga bounce around different magazines to keep going, and even go to different publishers). As I noted back in vol. 1's Enchantress, Ronald Reagan was still president when *OMG!* began, and in America, Japan was still viewed the way China is today—as the country that rivaled and would perhaps surpass the United States economically and in global influence. It's a sad turnaround to see US politicians today talk about how we have to *avoid* stagnating economically like Japan, when twenty years ago they all thought Japan was going to eat our lunch (really—if you had a nice bento, would you want to eat an American's Lunchables?)

But through good times and bad, *Oh My Goddess!* has endured. Vol. 40 is a landmark, but it's certainly not the end of the series! Vol. 43 of *Oh My Goddess!* just came out in Japan this September, and Dark Horse will continue to release future volumes. By the way, perhaps you're wondering why there's such a difference in page count between different volumes of *OMG!* This is something you'll especially notice in the recent unflopped reissues of older volumes such as vols. 16 and 17, which are literally twice the size of vol. 40.

Well, in the immortal words of the Dirty Pair, it's not our fault. ^_^ The number of *Oh My Goddess!* manga chapters in each of the English volumes is based directly on how many there were in the original Japanese volumes.

I say the chapters are the same, because obviously such things as Letters to the Enchantress are unique to the English edition. Japanese fans do write letters to *OMG!* (as you know, we've been translating those old letters since vol. 34), but they appeared in *Afternoon* magazine, rather than in the Japanese graphic novels. Don't forget *your* letters have been appearing recently in our reissues of older volumes, the most recent of which was vol. 19. The last of those reissued volumes, of course, will be vol. 20 in February 2012, but at that point we will continue to feature your letters in vols. 41, 42, etc. Don't stop writing in! ^_^

So the difference in page counts is fundamentally due to differences in the original Japanese volumes. But don't worry; this isn't a permanent downgrade, like those sneaky smaller packages you get in the supermarket these days—vol. 41 will be back up to seven chapters. Why vol. 40 is so short I don't quite know, but there may have been a desire to get it out for the 2009 end-of-year holidays in Japan.

We'll return once again to the feature we've run in recent newer volumes of *Oh My Goddess!*—Kosuke Fujishima's remarks to readers from the early days of the story. As ever, these are translated as they appeared in the Japanese volumes of *OMG!*, in this case the original version of vol. 40, of course. Previous volumes of the commentary had text alone, but starting with vol. 40, the commentary also began to feature panels from the manga to better illustrate the discussion, so we are featuring the corresponding English-language panels in our version as well.

The Japanese editor started off this volume's comments by offering double congratulations to Fujishima-sensei, pointing out that the end of 2009 marks not only the fortieth volume of *Oh My Goddess!*, but its twenty-first anniversary as well. But let's rewind back twenty years to December 1991. The month began with U2's *Achtung Baby* the number-one album in the United States; the month would end with the dissolution of the Soviet Union, marking the end of the Cold War that had dominated world politics in the second half of the twentieth century.

This peaceful resolution to a struggle many believed could only conclude in apocalypse was oddly mirrored by chapter 39, the end of the "Lord of Terror" story arc in *Oh My Goddess!* (which included a reference to the US-Soviet conflict, the only one ever to occur in the series). Having exorcised the Lord of Terror from Keiichi's body just before he could destroy the universe, Belldandy now sits with him atop a pile of rubble. The Yggdrasil System has gone down in the aftermath, meaning the old reasons for Bell being with Keiichi have been suspended. He's afraid she'll go home now, but she turns toward him and explains there are reasons for her to stay beyond their contract:

"Even guessing it would turn out this way, I'm still moved anew. Mr. Fujishima's art can make a grown man cry," said a reader signing as "Yutanbo," age twenty-two, from Hokkaido. Hosaka, a sixteen-year-old reader from Shizuoka, had a similar reaction, having been unable to wait until they traveled home to read the outcome: "The moment I saw the last page, my eyes filled

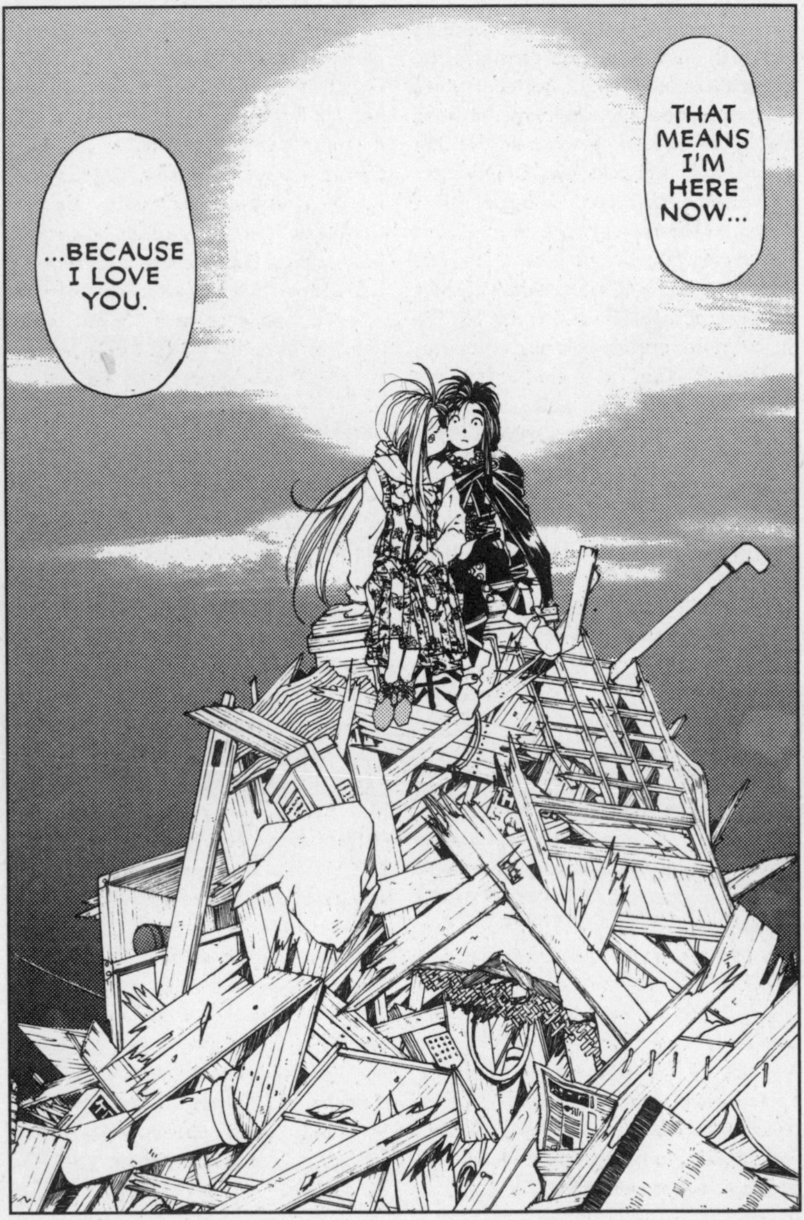
THAT MEANS I'M HERE NOW...
...BECAUSE I LOVE YOU.

with tears just standing there in the corner store. Ah! Love is so sweet . . ." Fujishima replied, "I always feel a little goofy and embarrassed when I draw scenes like this, but it seems a lot of people liked it. What a relief! Still, that mountain of rubbish was brutal on my assistant. I really should stop doing that to him (he says, for the umpteenth time . . .)."

In the January 1992 issue of Afternoon, Fujishima advised readers to not just read Afternoon magazine, but to make it part of their regular exercise routine, pointing out that raising and lowering it thirty times will help build up one's arm muscles (as noted in vol. 39, a single issue of Afternoon can be a thousand pages long). He then made the somewhat cryptic remark, "My Harley arrived at last! It was a long time coming, but wow! It's just too cool! It's so cool that I'm afraid to park it on the street in case something happens to it. Instead, I've just been walking around, boasting about how it's the best bike in the world." The remark is "cryptic," of course, because just that last spring, in the May 1991 issue (see vol. 37, p. 151), Fujishima said, "On a recent windy day, I stepped outside to find my DR250 tipped over and lying on top of my Harley," which would seem to indicate he already had one. Was this a second Harley, or perhaps a replacement for the first, which might explain what he said about being afraid to park it on the street?

Naturally, the January 1992 issue of Afternoon featured reader response to the December 1991 issue, which happened to contain the Skuld vs. Megumi battle royale in Oh My Goddess! chapter 40, "Robot Battle" (This is one of the English-language editor's favorite stories—he loves stories

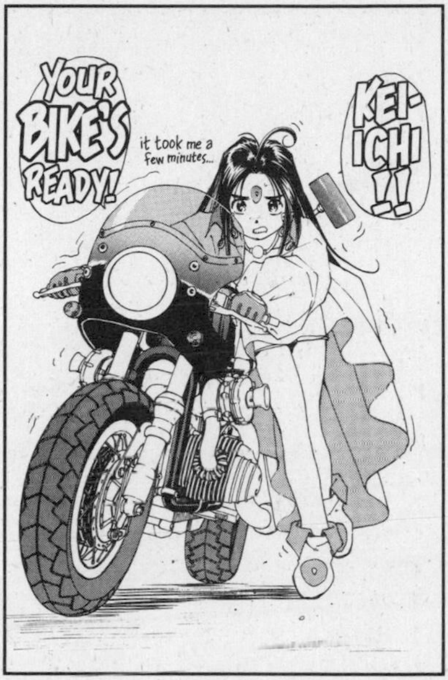
KEI-ICHI!!
it took me a few minutes...
YOUR BIKE'S READY!

about college campuses gone crazed, which is why one of his favorite manga of recent years is Masayuki Ishikawa's Moyasimon. Although, to paraphrase Fujishima-sensei, all the banners in that chapter were brutal on the letterer . . .). Reader Ken Ishikawa (which, for once, sounds like a real name), age sixteen, from Kanagawa Prefecture, wrote in to say, "Little Skuld is really cute. She seems so childish. Just how old is she anyway?" Fujishima said he estimated her age to be "1,000,013" (at this point in the original Japanese there is a note, "uso!" meaning "no way!" or "you're kidding!"), "but as far as the goddesses' ages go, I've made her pretty young." Is this just Fujishima's way of saying she's existed for a very long time in years, but her maturity in human terms is about that of a thirteen-year-old?

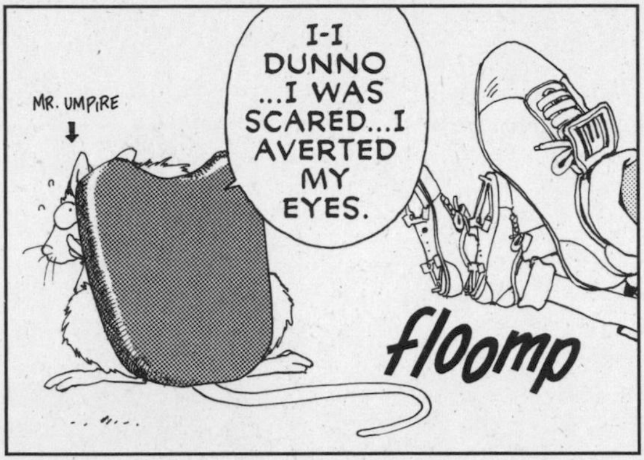
I-I DUNNO ...I WAS SCARED...I AVERTED MY EYES.
floomp
MR. UMPIRE

The December 1991 issue of Afternoon *also contained the Adventures of Mini-Urd story "Stormwrack: A Tale of Baseball," but it seemed reader sympathy lay not with the goddesses, but with Ratty, who had to deal with them as umpire. "That rat ref was too much!" wrote seventeen-year-old Yankee Hayato of Saitama Prefecture. "I'm looking forward to more." Fujishima claimed that Ratty was rumored to be an umpire for the major leagues, known for his "demon umpiring" and "super spinning umpiring." Fujishima's Japanese editor, known only as "Y-da," cut in at this point to say that while the names of these techniques sound awesome, "what about the content? I am deeply concerned."*

In the February 1992 issue of Afternoon*, before getting into reader remarks, Fujishima noted that he had recently bought* Flyover*, a collection of Shigeo Koike's illustrations of aircraft. "Quite aside from the beauty of the airplanes themselves, the exquisite contrast of sky, sea, and clouds in his work shines forth. Airplanes really are a joy. When I'm old and gray, I'd like to try doing illustrations like this as a hobby."*

The English-language editor notes that Shigeo Koike is one of those Japanese artists who developed an international fan base even before the manga era, ^_^ based on the paintings Fujishima referred to—they were done as box art for Hasegawa's line of model airplane kits, sold around the world since the 1970s. In fact, Koike has a better English-language site than most manga artists do, at ShigeoKoike.com. Fujishima came from a generation that liked to build model kits of planes, battleships, and so forth (as noted in vol. 38). There is an impression that the

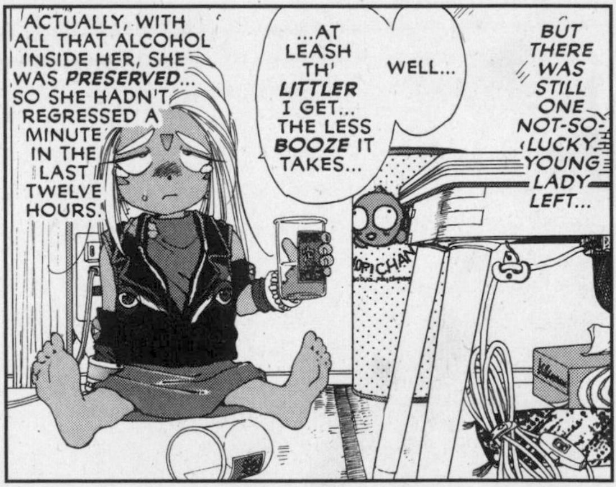
BUT THERE WAS STILL ONE NOT-SO-LUCKY YOUNG LADY LEFT...
WELL...
...AT LEASH TH' *LITTLER* I GET... THE LESS *BOOZE* IT TAKES...
ACTUALLY, WITH ALL THAT ALCOHOL INSIDE HER, SHE WAS *PRESERVED*... SO SHE HADN'T REGRESSED A MINUTE IN THE LAST TWELVE HOURS.

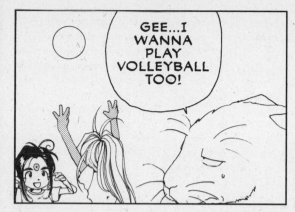

GEE...I WANNA PLAY VOLLEYBALL TOO!

younger generation of fans in Japan don't really do this anymore, although Genshiken suggested that building Gunpla (Gundam plastic model kits) is still considered something you need to do at least a little to keep your otaku cred.

The two-part story that began with chapter 41 ("The Trials of Morisato") saw the continuing effects of the Yggdrasil System being down for repairs—in this case, the goddesses had to rely on their alternate energy systems instead of getting their power from Heaven, and their emblem programs (those things on their foreheads—just in case you forgot what they were ^_^), responsible for managing their essential functions, went out of sync.

The emblem-program malfunction didn't affect Belldandy, because of her status as the goddess of the present—but Skuld, being the goddess of the future, began to grow physically older in appearance, while Urd, goddess of the past, appeared to regress in age. She was seen at the end of the chapter ruefully clutching some of her alternate energy source (booze) while the narrator reflected that she was

a "not-so-lucky" young lady. This was a play on hakko, which means both "unlucky" and "fermented." But reader Burua, a seventeen-year-old student from Yamanashi Prefecture, reflected that if Urd were to use her ability to subdivide herself into mini-Urds, she could also be hakko, meaning "eight girls." "Killer pun!" said Fujishima in response. "I wish I'd thought of that. Right. Next time I'll have Urd change into a bird, so she can also be a kakko [cuckoo] girl. Hmm. Maybe I should have quit while I was ahead."

Another reader response in the February 1992 issue of Afternoon, from an eighteen-year-old Yamaguchi Prefecture student going by the name of Suimugetsu: "'Stormwrack: A Tale of Baseball' might as well have been 'wrecked up' for Ratty," making a play on fu-un, meaning "stormy, ominous weather," and fu-un, meaning "bad luck, misfortune." "What's up with all these puns?!" shrieked Fujishima on the letters page. "Okay, if that's the way you want it, my next series will be a tale of fighting volleyball! [The mini-Urd strip excerpted above indeed involved a tail—ed.] Try and stop me!!! Looks like editor Y-da's stress can only worsen." Editor Y-da cut in again to say this was true, that the stress was taking a toll on his heart, and that he too should have quit while he was ahead (it is worth noting that "iya da" is an expression of alarm in Japanese, and usually quite a high-pitched one).

Fujishima then switched gears, as it were, to say, "Recently America's really been annoying me with all its harping about 'Buy American cars, buy American cars!' Really, who the heck do they think is going to buy an American car that's a copy of a Japanese car? Some of those pickup trucks and classics from the sixties and seventies would fly, though. I wish they'd think for a moment about why Harleys do so well over here." Of course, American motorcycles don't have the problem American automobiles do of needing to be built in a right-hand-drive version for Japanese roads, but Fujishima's argument was that if Japanese people were to buy American vehicles, they would want something with classic American looks, rather than the more Japanese-style cars the US was making in the early nineties to compete directly with Japan—he was possibly referring to vehicles like the Plymouth Laser and the Eagle Talon, both of which were made as joint ventures between Chrysler and Mitsubishi.

The English-language editor recalls that trade friction with Japan used to be a big political issue in America; it's not so much that the situation got solved (we still have a big trade deficit with Japan, just as we did in 1992) but that it's not really seen as a problem in the US anymore, possibly because globalization and free trade have become stronger philosophies. In the 1980s, Japanese cars were so popular in the US (because they were perceived as cheaper, better built, and more fuel efficient) that American consumers couldn't even buy all they wanted; to keep good relations with the US government (which, naturally, wanted to protect the US auto industry), Japan agreed to "voluntarily" restrict the total number of cars they would sell in the US each year. Imagine if a few years back, the US comics industry had the clout in Congress to demand limits on manga. ^_^

The US auto industry has gone through a lot of hard times, but today it can make vehicles on the cutting edge (such as the Chevrolet Volt), and to see how much things have changed, when Toyota was being accused of mechanical defects not long ago, it was American politicians (namely, the governors of four states with Toyota plants) who wrote to Congress in the Japanese automaker's defense, saying that the federal government's investigation of Toyota was a conflict of interest because of its financial stake in the US auto industry!

Well, we've just about run out of gas on this installment of Enchantress, but don't forget in two months we'll see you again with vol. 20, the last of the unflopped reissues of Oh My Goddess!, and then two months after that, it's vol. 41, and onward from there—as far as Kosuke Fujishima wants to go! Just as the creator did on page 113, Dark Horse would like to thank all of the readers of this edition for taking us this far. Oh My Goddess! isn't the longest-running manga series in the English language just because we like it—it's because you like it, and have supported it since 1994, through its days as a comic book, flopped graphic novel, and unflopped tankobon. Thank you.

—CGH

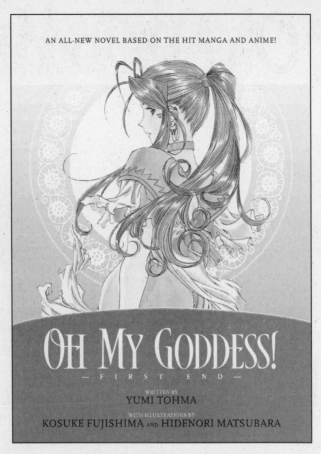

AN ALL-NEW NOVEL BASED ON THE HIT MANGA AND ANIME!

OH MY GODDESS!

—FIRST END—

WRITTEN BY
YUMI TOHMA

WITH ILLUSTRATIONS BY
KOSUKE FUJISHIMA AND HIDENORI MATSUBARA

Keiichi Morisato was a typical college student—a failure with women, he was struggling to get through his classes and in general living a pretty nondescript life. That is, until he dialed a wrong number and accidentally summoned the goddess Belldandy. Not believing Belldandy was a goddess and that she could grant his every wish, Keiichi wished for her to stay with him forever. As they say, be careful what you wish for! Now bound to Earth and at Keiichi's side for life, the lives of this goddess and human will never be the same again!

ISBN 978-1-59582-137-9 | $14.95

DARK HORSE BOOKS

darkhorse.com

AVAILABLE AT YOUR LOCAL COMICS SHOP OR BOOKSTORE
To find a comics shop in your area, call 1.888.266.4226. For more information or to order direct: •On the web: darkhorse.com •E-mail: mailorder@darkhorse.com •Phone: 1.800.862.0052 Mon.–Fri. 9 AM to 5 PM Pacific Time.

BRIDE of the WATER GOD

When Soah's impoverished, desperate village decides to sacrifice her to the Water God Habaek to end a long drought, they believe that drowning one beautiful girl will save their entire community and bring much-needed rain. Not only is Soah surprised to be *rescued* by the Water God instead of killed; she never imagined she'd be a welcomed guest in Habaek's magical kingdom, where an exciting new life awaits her! Most surprising, however, is the Water God himself, and how very different he is from the monster Soah imagined . . .

Created by Mi-Kyung Yun, who received the "Best New Artist" award in 2004 from the esteemed *Dokja-manhwa-daesang* organization, *Bride of the Water God* was the top-selling *shoujo* manhwa in Korea in 2006!

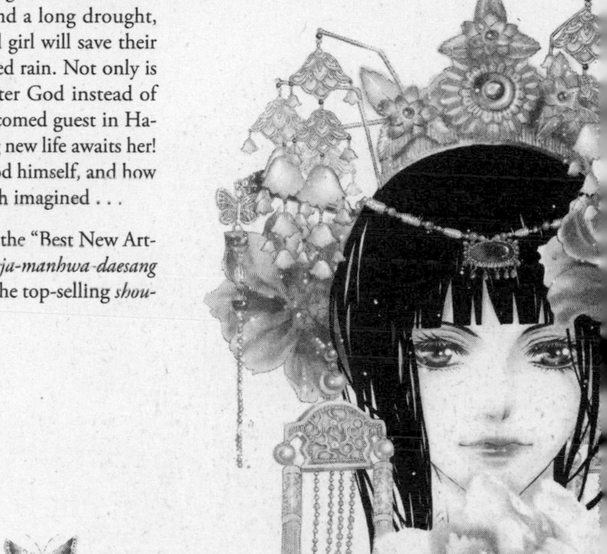

Volume 1
ISBN 978-1-59307-849-2

Volume 2
ISBN 978-1-59307-883-6

Volume 3
ISBN 978-1-59582-305-2

Volume 4
ISBN 978-1-59582-378-6

Volume 5
ISBN 978-1-59582-445-5

Volume 6
ISBN 978-1-59582-605-3

Volume 7
ISBN 978-1-59582-668-8

Volume 8
ISBN 978-1-59582-687-9

Volume 9
ISBN 978-1-59582-688-6

$9.99 each

Previews for BRIDE OF THE WATER GOD and other DARK HORSE MANHWA titles can be found at darkhorse.com!

AVAILABLE AT YOUR LOCAL COMICS SHOP OR BOOKSTORE! TO FIND A COMICS SHOP IN YOUR AREA, CALL 1-888-266-4226.

For more information or to order direct visit darkhorse.com or call 1-800-862-0052 Mon.–Fri. 9 AM to 5 PM Pacific Time. *Prices and availability subject to change without notice.

NEON GENESIS EVANGELION

Dark Horse Manga is proud to present two new original series based on the wildly popular *Neon Genesis Evangelion* manga and anime! Continuing the rich story lines and complex characters, these new visions of *Neon Genesis Evangelion* provide extra dimensions for understanding one of the greatest series ever made!

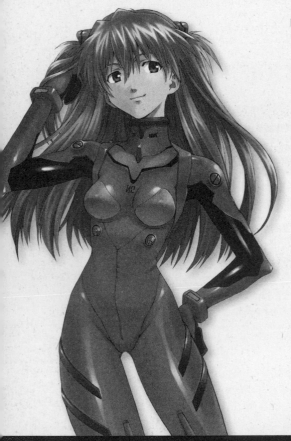

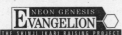

NEON GENESIS EVANGELION — THE SHINJI IKARI RAISING PROJECT

**STORY AND ART
BY OSAMU TAKAHASHI**

VOLUME 1
ISBN 978-1-59582-321-2 | $9.99

VOLUME 2
ISBN 978-1-59582-377-9 | $9.99

VOLUME 3
ISBN 978-1-59582-447-9 | $9.99

VOLUME 4
ISBN 978-1-59582-454-7 | $9.99

VOLUME 5
ISBN 978-1-59582-520-9 | $9.99

VOLUME 6
ISBN 978-1-59582-580-3 | $9.99

VOLUME 7
ISBN 978-1-59582-595-7 | $9.99

VOLUME 8
ISBN 978-1-59582-694-7 | $9.99

VOLUME 9
ISBN 978-1-59582-800-2 | $9.99

NEON GENESIS EVANGELION — Campus Apocalypse

**STORY AND ART
BY MINGMING**

VOLUME 1
ISBN 978-1-59582-530-8 | $10.99

VOLUME 2
ISBN 978-1-59582-661-9 | $10.99

VOLUME 3
ISBN 978-1-59582-680-0 | $10.99

VOLUME 4
ISBN 978-1-59582-689-3 | $10.99

**Each volume of *Neon Genesis Evangelion* features bonus color pages,
your *Evangelion* fan art and letters, and special reader giveaways!**

AVAILABLE AT YOUR LOCAL COMICS SHOP OR BOOKSTORE
To find a comics shop in your area, call 1-888-266-4226 • For more information or to order direct: • On the web: darkhorse.com
E-mail: mailorder@darkhorse.com • Phone: 1-800-862-0052 Mon.–Fri. 9 AM to 5 PM Pacific Time.

DARK HORSE MANGA®
DarkHorse.com

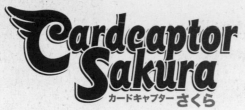

Story and Art by
CLAMP

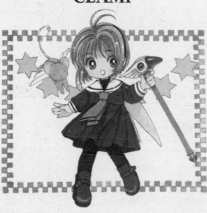

Fourth grader Sakura Kinomoto has found a strange book in her father's library—a book made by the wizard Clow to store dangerous spirits sealed within a set of magical cards. But when Sakura opens it up, there is nothing left inside but Kero-chan, the book's cute little guardian beast...who informs Sakura that since the Clow cards seem to have escaped while he was asleep, it's now her job to capture them!

With remastered image files straight from CLAMP, Dark Horse is proud to present *Cardcaptor Sakura* in omnibus form! Each book collects three volumes of the original twelve-volume series, and features thirty bonus color pages!

OMNIBUS BOOK ONE
ISBN 978-1-59582-522-3 $19.99

OMNIBUS BOOK TWO
ISBN 978-1-59582-591-9 $19.99

AVAILABLE AT YOUR LOCAL COMICS SHOP OR BOOKSTORE!
To find a comics shop in your area, call 1-888-266-4226
For more information or to order direct: • On the web: DarkHorse.com
E-mail: mailorder@darkhorse.com • Phone: 1-800-862-0052 Mon.–Fri. 9 AM to 5 PM Pacific Time

DARK
HORSE
MANGA
DarkHorse.com

CLAMP

Chobits
ちょびっツ

BOOK 1

In near-future Japan, the hottest style for your personal computer, or "persocom," has the appearance of an attractive android! Hideki, a poor student trying to get into a Tokyo university, has neither money nor a girlfriend—then finds a persocom seemingly discarded in an alley. Hideki takes the cute, amnesiac robot home and names her "Chi."

But who is this strange new persocom in his life? Instead of having a digital assistant, Hideki finds himself having to teach Chi how to get along in the everyday world, even while he and his friends try to solve the mystery of her origins. Is she one of the urban-legendary *Chobits*—persocoms built to have the riskiest functions of all: real emotions and free will?

A crossover hit for both female and male readers, CLAMP's best-selling manga ever in America is finally available in omnibus form! Containing sixteen bonus color pages, *Chobits* Volume 1 begins an engaging, touching, exciting story.

ISBN 978-1-59582-451-6

$24.99

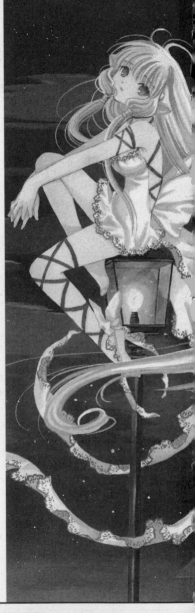

DARK HORSE MANGA
DarkHorse.com

AVAILABLE AT YOUR LOCAL COMICS SHOP OR BOOKSTORE
To find a comics shop in your area, call 1.888.266.4226. For more information or to order direct: • On the web: DarkHorse.com • E-mail: mailorder@darkhorse.com • Phone: 1.800.862.0052 Mon.–Fri. 9 AM to 5 PM Pacific Time.

CHOBITS™ 2010 CLAMP. Publication rights for this English edition arranged through Pyrotechnist, Ltd. All rights reserved. Dark Horse Manga™ is a trademark of Dark Horse Comics, Inc. All rights reserved. (BL 7093)

STOP! This is the back of the book!

This manga collection is translated into English, but arranged in right-to-left reading format to maintain the artwork's visual orientation as originally drawn and published in Japan. If you've never read comics this way before, take a look at the diagram below to give yourself an idea of how to go about it. Basically, you'll be starting in the upper right-hand corner, and will read each word balloon and panel moving right to left. It may take a little getting used to, but you should get the hang of it very quickly. Have fun! If this is the millionth manga you've read this way, never mind. ^_^

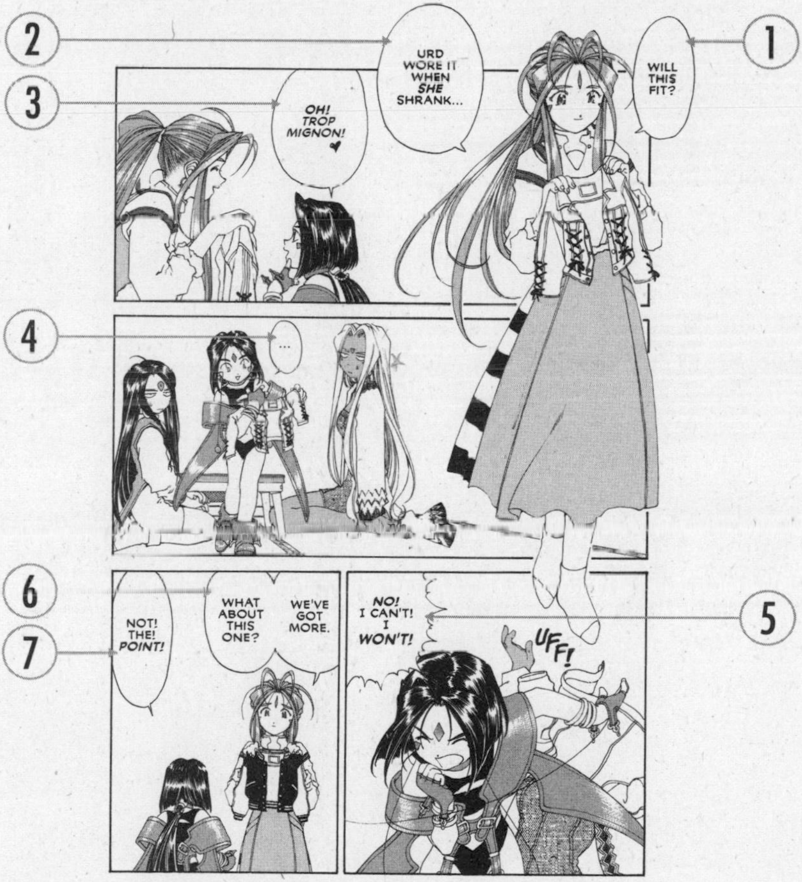
1
WILL THIS FIT?
2
URD WORE IT WHEN SHE SHRANK...
3
OH! TROP MIGNON!
4
...
5
NO! I CAN'T! I WON'T!
UFF!
6
WE'VE GOT MORE.
WHAT ABOUT THIS ONE?
7
NOT! THE! POINT!